A Research Agenda for Women and Entrepreneurship

**Elgar Research Agendas** outline the future of research in a given area. Leading scholars are given the space to explore their subject in provocative ways, and map out the potential directions of travel. They are relevant but also visionary.

Forward-looking and innovative, Elgar Research Agendas are an essential resource for PhD students, scholars and anybody who wants to be at the forefront of research.

Titles in the series include:

# A Research Agenda for Women and Entrepreneurship

## Identity Through Aspirations, Behaviors and Confidence

*Edited by*

PATRICIA G. GREENE

Paul T. Babson Chair in Entrepreneurial Studies, Babson College, USA

CANDIDA G. BRUSH

Franklin W. Olin Distinguished Chair of Entrepreneurship and Vice Provost of Global Entrepreneurial Leadership, Babson College, USA

Elgar Research Agendas

Edward Elgar
PUBLISHING

Cheltenham, UK • Northampton, MA, USA

Published by
Edward Elgar Publishing Limited
The Lypiatts
15 Lansdown Road
Cheltenham
Glos GL50 2JA
UK

Edward Elgar Publishing, Inc.
William Pratt House
9 Dewey Court
Northampton
Massachusetts 01060
USA

A catalogue record for this book
is available from the British Library

Library of Congress Control Number: 2017950449

This book is available electronically in the **Elgar**online
Business subject collection
DOI 10.4337/9781785365379

ISBN 978 1 78536 536 2 (cased)
ISBN 978 1 78536 537 9 (eBook)

Typeset by Servis Filmsetting Ltd, Stockport, Cheshire
Printed and bound by CPI Group (UK) Ltd, Croydon, CR0 4YY

*This book is dedicated to Fyllis Berg-Elton. Her professional approach, attention to detail, superb coordination and commitment to this project developed and polished this book into its final form. We are most grateful Fyllis was our partner in this effort.*

# Contents

# Contributors

**Thomas H. Allison** is Assistant Professor of Entrepreneurship in the Carson College of Business at Washington State University, USA. He received his PhD from the University of Oklahoma, USA. His research centers on entrepreneurial finance; novel forms of entrepreneurial resource acquisition, including crowdfunding; and the effects of narrative and rhetoric on investment decisions.

**Malin Brännback**, DSc, BSc (Pharm) is Dean and Professor of International Business at Åbo Akademi University, Finland, where she received her doctorate in management science in 1996. She also holds a BSc in pharmacy. She was Visiting Professor in Entrepreneurship at Stockholm University 2012–2014. She has published widely on entrepreneurship, biotechnology business and knowledge management. She has co-authored with Alan Carsrud several books: *Understanding the Entrepreneurial Mind: Opening the Black Box* (2009), *Revisiting the Entrepreneurial Mind: Inside the Black Box* (2017), *Understanding Family Businesses* (2012) and *Handbook of Research Methods and Applications in Entrepreneurship and Small Business* (2014). She is on the review board of the *Journal of Small Business Management.* Her current research interests are in entrepreneurial intentionality, entrepreneurial cognition, entrepreneurial growth and performance in technology entrepreneurship and family business.

**Candida G. Brush** is the Vice Provost of Global Entrepreneurial Leadership and a Full Professor at Babson College, USA, and holder of the Franklin W. Olin Distinguished Chair of Entrepreneurship. She is well known for her pioneering research in women's entrepreneurship. She is a Visiting Adjunct Professor to the Nord University, Bodø Graduate School in Bodø, Norway. Professor Brush is a founding member of the Diana Project International and holds an honorary doctorate from Jönköping University, Sweden for her contributions to entrepreneurship research. Her research investigates nascent entrepreneurial ventures, women's entrepreneurship and financing of growth-oriented ventures. She is an active angel investor and serves on the boards of several companies.

**Alan L. Carsrud**, PhD, EcD (HC), is Visiting Research Professor at Åbo Akademi School of Business and Economics of Åbo Akademi University in Finland. He was previously the Loretta Rogers Chaired Professor of Entrepreneurship at Ryerson University in Toronto, Canada. He has published more than a dozen books in entrepreneurship and family business and more than 200 articles on entrepreneurship, family business, social and clinical psychology.

**Eliana Crosina** is a doctoral candidate in the Management and Organization Department at Boston College, USA. She holds a BSc in business administration and an MBA from Babson College, USA as well as an MSc in organization studies from Boston College. Her current research explores how individuals go about crafting their work identities when they do not have an established organization to rely upon. She tackles these issues through largely qualitative methods in two main research streams: (1) exploring identity and organizing among nascent entrepreneurs; (2) examining novel processes of identity work.

**Cristina Cruz** (PhD, University Carlos III, Madrid, Spain) is Entrepreneurship Department Head and Professor of Entrepreneurship and Family Business at IE Business School/IE University, Madrid, Spain. Her research interests are focused at the interaction between family business and entrepreneurship, with a special focus on understanding how enterprising families create value across generations. She is also an expert on corporate governance issues in family firms.

**Julio O. De Castro** (PhD, University of South Carolina, USA) is Professor of Entrepreneurship and Chair of the PhD program at IE Business School/IE University, Madrid, Spain. His research deals with firm strategy and entrepreneurship. Currently his research uses an entrepreneurial perspective to examine informal businesses, product piracy, knowledge management, legitimacy, and drivers of entrepreneurial activity by those at the base of the pyramid.

**Catherine Elliott** is a Professor at the University of Ottawa's Telfer School of Management, Canada, where she teaches organizational behavior and human resources management. She is co-author of *Feminine Capital: Unlocking the Power of Women Entrepreneurs* (Stanford University Press, 2015, with B. Orser) and co-chair of the Women Entrepreneurs Ontario Collective (2016). Her research interests focus on gender influences in entrepreneurship, including entrepreneurial identity and self-efficacy as well as mentoring for entrepreneurial learning and women's career advancement. As an experienced human resources professional, educator, and management consultant, she has worked for more than 20 years with clients to solve management issues related to human capital and performance management.

**Patricia G. Greene** is the Paul T. Babson Chair in Entrepreneurial Studies at Babson College, USA where she formerly served first as Dean of the Undergraduate School and later as Provost. Greene's most recent assignment at Babson was to serve as the academic director for the Goldman Sachs *10,000 Small Businesses* and *10,000 Women* programs. Dr Greene is a founding member of the Diana Project, a research group dedicated to studying women business owners and their businesses. She is a former federal appointee to the national advisory board for the SBA's Small Business Development Centers. She loves to talk about entrepreneurship, sharing her soapboxes on changing the way the world does business with anyone who will listen. Her latest entrepreneurial endeavor is as a co-owner of Artworks, a specialty store in Gettysburg, PA, USA.

**Richard T. Harrison** is Professor of Entrepreneurship and Innovation and Co-Director of the Centre for Strategic Leadership at the University of Edinburgh Business School, UK. He was previously Dean of Queen's University Management School, UK and Founding Director of the Leadership Institute. His current research interests fall into a number of broad themes that can be linked by a unifying interest in the nature of the entrepreneurial and business growth process – in social and corporate as well as new venture contexts – as it is reflected in business development (particularly in the financing of innovation and growth), and in the implications of research and theorizing for practice and public policy. Professor Harrison is a world-leading authority on business angel and early stage venture finance and has advised governments, development agencies and business groups internationally on risk capital and venture finance issues. He also researches entrepreneurial learning and leadership processes, studies the role of entrepreneurship and innovation in emerging economies (notably China and sub-Saharan Africa), examines the nature of peace entrepreneurship in conflict societies (Northern Ireland, Rwanda, Kosovo), analyzes the process of business model innovation, and investigates the generation, protection and exploitation of intellectual capital, including studies of academic entrepreneurship and technology transfer. He is author of more than 125 papers and book chapters and has published books on crowdfunding, business angel investing, innovation and economic development, regional policy, entrepreneurial learning and entrepreneurial leadership.

**Diana Hechavarria** is an Assistant Professor of Entrepreneurship in the Muma College of Business at the University of South Florida, USA. She investigates the various dynamics confronted by founders during the start-up process. Her research interests tend to focus on how various social processes and institutional factors influence individuals differentially when aiming to establish a new firm. Her research has been published in journals such as *Entrepreneurship Theory and Practice, Small Business Economics, International Journal of Gender and Entrepreneurship, Journal of Business and Entrepreneurship, International Journal of Entrepreneurial Behavior and Research, International Journal of Entrepreneurship and Innovation* and *International Entrepreneurship and Management Journal.* Diana has a PhD in business administration from the University of Cincinnati, (Cincinnati, OH, USA), an MA in liberal studies from Florida International University (Miami, FL, USA), and a BA in sociology from the University of Florida (Gainesville, FL, USA).

**Rachida Justo** is an Associate Professor Entrepreneurship at IE Business School, Spain. Her research, which focuses on social entrepreneurship and women entrepreneurs, has been published in top-tier international journals such as the *Journal of Business Venturing* and *Small Business Economics,* where she has been recently appointed as an Editorial Board member. She has also received several awards such as the 'Best Women's Entrepreneurship Paper Award' from the Entrepreneurship division of the Academy of Management, and the 'Outstanding Award for Best Doctoral Dissertation' from the Universidad Autónoma de Madrid, Spain.

**Katherina Kuschel**, PhD in social psychology from Universitat Autònoma de Barcelona, Spain, is Visiting Scholar at Lazaridis School of Business and Economics, at Wilfrid Laurier University, Canada, and at Universidad Tecnológica Metropolitana, Chile. She was also Assistant Professor of Management at Universidad del Desarrollo in Santiago de Chile. Her area of specialization and research is entrepreneurship, focused on work–life balance and leadership of women entrepreneurs in the technology industry. Dr. Kuschel has worked at universities in Canada, Germany and Chile, concentrating in the study of the challenges that women start-up founders and innovators face. She is consolidating a global network of scholars researching work–family issues among men and women entrepreneurs.

**Juan-Pablo Labra** is a civil industrial engineer from Catholic University of Chile, and has an MBA from Adolfo Ibáñez University, Chile. He lives in Santiago, Chile, where he teaches at the Engineering School of the Universidad Nacional Andrés Bello. His research interests are entrepreneurship and start-ups, business models, design thinking and business storytelling.

**Claire M. Leitch** (DPhil) holds the Chair in Entrepreneurial Leadership at Lancaster University Management School, UK, and is Head of the Department of Leadership and Management. Her research interests concentrate on the development, enhancement and growth of individuals and organizations in an entrepreneurial context with a particular focus on leadership, leadership development and learning. Current work takes a critical approach and draws on ideas of gender and power to examine the interrelationships between the micro- and macro-level influences impacting agents. She has published in a number of leading international journals and is the editor of the *International Small Business Journal*.

**Magdalena Markowska** is Assistant Professor at Jönköping International Business School (JIBS), Jönköping, Sweden. She is a recipient of a Postdoctoral Transition Grant, where as part of the grant she explores the processes of entrepreneurial identification among creative workers. She is also working on a project sponsored by the Swedish Knowledge Foundation looking at the phenomenon of 'mumpreneurship', the motivation for and the implications of becoming a mumpreneur for the woman's career, the business she creates as well as more broadly the society. Her research interests involve entrepreneurial identity and entrepreneurial careers as well as issues of contextualizing entrepreneurship.

**Shahrokh Nikou** is a Docent of Business Administration, especially in information systems, at Åbo Akademi University, Finland. Currently, he is a senior lecturer/researcher at Åbo Akademi University. He has also studied at the Delft University of Technology, Delft, The Netherlands and at the Royal Institute of Technology in Stockholm, Sweden. He received his PhD (Econ) from Åbo Akademi University in 2012. He is a member of several journal editorial boards and a member of the program committee in several IEEEs and international conferences. His current research interest includes entrepreneurial intent, consumer purchasing and digital economy and entrepreneurship. He has published more than 40 articles in journals and conference proceedings.

**Pyayt P. Oo** is an Assistant Professor in the Department of Entrepreneurship, Central Michigan University. His research centers on entrepreneurial emotions, entrepreneurial entry strategies, and their influences on investment decisions in crowdfunding and other novel means of resource acquisitions.

**Barbara Orser** is a Full/Deloitte Professor in the Management of Growth Enterprises at the Telfer School of Management, University of Ottawa, Canada. Co-author of *Feminine Capital: Unlocking the Power of Women Entrepreneurs* (Stanford University Press, 2015 with C. Elliott), two small business finance books, and the primary investigator of more than 100 academic and trade studies, Barbara Orser's current research interests focus on gender and enterprise growth, financial literacy, federal procurement and women's entrepreneurship policy research. She is the Founder and Chair of the Canadian Taskforce for Women's Enterprise Growth (2011) and Co-Chair of the Women Entrepreneurs Ontario Collective (2016). Dr. Orser is the recipient of several awards that recognize her support for women's enterprise, including the Women's Executive Network '100 Most Powerful Women in Canada' and the International Alliance of Women 'World of Difference 100 Award'.

**Arvin Sahaym** is Associate Professor of Strategy and Entrepreneurship in the Carson College of Business at Washington State University, USA. His research is motivated by the real-world phenomena at the interface of strategy, innovation and entrepreneurship. He draws upon the theories of organization to understand these phenomena and contributes to both the theory and the practice of management. His research has been published in a number of journals including *Organization Science, Strategic Management Journal, Journal of Business Venturing, MIS Quarterly, Journal of Business Research* and *International Business Review.*

**Smita Srivastava** is a doctoral student majoring in entrepreneurship in the Carson College of Business at Washington State University, USA. Her research interests include entrepreneurial resource acquisition and entrepreneurial alertness.

**Smita K. Trivedi**, PhD is Assistant Professor of Business and Society/Sustainable Business in the Management Department at the College of Business of San Francisco State University. Professor Trivedi received her undergraduate degree from Duke University, USA, in public policy, her master's degree in administration, planning and social policy from Harvard University, USA, and her PhD in strategic management and public policy from the George Washington University School of Business, USA. Her research is focused on business and poverty alleviation. Her publications have been in the areas of business ethics education, business and peace, and her dissertation focused on Indian women entrepreneurs in the context of poverty.

# 1 Introduction: the ABCs of women's entrepreneurial identity – aspirations, behaviors and confidence

*Patricia G. Greene and Candida G. Brush*

> *I am not one and simple, but complex and many.* (Virginia Woolf, 1992: *The Waves*)

Who am I? This existential question has been central to philosophical pondering since the actual beginning of philosophy. It is largely a question of personal meaning, and one to which early philosophers brought different ideas. Descartes built on Plato, purporting that the soul is the answer to personal identity. Later, John Locke disagreed, maintaining that continuity is the primary issue. His approach was that one starts with a *tabula rasa* and is subsequently shaped by experience, sensations, reflections, and so on. More recently, research regarding identity has focused on the social aspects, 'Who am I?' in reference to something else: groups (Tajfel, 1978; Tafjel and Turner, 1979) or roles (Stryker, 1980; Stryker and Serpe, 2012).

Our goal for this book is to use a concept of identity to explore ideas related to entrepreneurial identity for women and their businesses. We believe this is important for two reasons. First, the concept of an entrepreneur has historically been that of a male, and in essence the role and identity are masculine in image and expected behavior (Bird and Brush, 2002). Second, the bulk of current research on entrepreneurship generally, and on the topic of identity and individual aspects of entrepreneurs, focuses predominantly on male samples. Some estimate that only 10 percent of all research in entrepreneurship includes or studies women (Jennings and Brush, 2013). This suggests that both practically and theoretically there is reason to examine entrepreneurial identity for women and their businesses.

However, given the very broad nature and long history of investigation of identity, we overlay another set of entrepreneurial concepts to provide insight into women's entrepreneurship. We focus this volume (and associated articles) on three concepts – aspirations, behaviors and confidence – each related to identity in that they provide insights into our understanding of women entrepreneurs, their ventures and experiences. We consider aspirations to explore what women want to create or achieve, behaviors to look at how they create and grow businesses, and confidence to relate to the 'why', considered as their trust in themselves and their degree of self-assurance. Together, these concepts shape and enhance a woman's

1

identity in the entrepreneurial process. We are joined in this endeavor by a set of authors who are also curious about identity and women's entrepreneurship, and the relationship to aspirations, behaviors and/or confidence.

The pathway for our exploratory journey is to first quite briefly review the notion of identity in general, what it is and how it is constructed, and then consider the linkages between identity, aspirations, behavior and confidence. We then move to entrepreneurial identity and its particular construction, and finally we explore women's entrepreneurial identity. This chapter then provides an overview of each of the chapters in this volume regarding women's entrepreneurial identity and aspirations, behaviors and confidence. We conclude with thoughts on what we have learned through this process, and suggestions for future research.

## The question of identity

Identity as a topic of inquiry is found in many social science disciplines, with conceptual differences readily evident both across and within these disciplines (Stryker and Burke, 2000). However, the main approaches include personal identity, social identity theory (SIT) (Tajfel, 1982) and identity theory (Stryker and Serpe, 2012).

### Personal identity

Personal identity generally includes an individual's attributes and traits, values, beliefs and bodily attributes, and in some considerations, also their interests and competencies (Ashforth and Mael, 1989). While it would seem that the personal at this level would be the starting point for an identity, it can also be considered as more of an end, or integrative mechanism, coalescing aspects of group memberships and/or roles (Markus and Nurius, 1986). Personal identity is also described as under-researched and, we propose more specifically, under-theorized in entrepreneurship. When thinking of the relationship to the field of entrepreneurship in which attributes and traits were an early point of fascination, we have seen the field largely move beyond these two concepts to other types of questions.

### Social identity theory

On the other hand, social identity theory (SIT) is a fairly well-researched concept that looks at 'the group in the individual' (Hogg and Abrams, 1988: 3). As such, SIT is a social-psychological perspective which focuses on social categories. These categories are defined by categorization schemas which are determined through what are seen as the 'prototypical characteristics' of the group (Ashford and Mael, 1989; Turner, 1985). The groups may be based on demographic characteristics such as race, gender or age. They may also be based on affiliations such as political parties or religious denominations, and may be perceived positively or negatively in relation to another group (Tajfel, 1982; Hogg et al., 1995).

The purpose of the group classification is primarily to cognitively segment and thus provide order to one's social environment, thereby providing a means of adopting a self-definition while also providing a systematic means of defining others (Ashforth and Mael, 1989). Personal attributes are often more consistent, while social identities can be more dynamic as people move in and out of different groups; for example, move into a different age bracket or stage of life, or change political party. How social identities are perceived can also be dynamic, changing positively or negatively in relation or reaction to any particular group (Hogg et al., 1995; Brush and Gale, 2014).

## Identity theory

Role-based identities (mother, architect, entrepreneur, and so on) are at the core of identity theory (Hogg et al., 1995; Stryker, 1987; Brush and Gale, 2014), a focus which perhaps more readily accounts for changes in identities (for example, bachelor to husband, or manager to entrepreneur) as individuals change personal identity characteristics (such as competencies) and also make decisions about relationships, behaviors, occupations, and so on. Given that we all hold many roles, and therefore we all belong to a number of groups, each of us has multiple, and potentially overlapping, identities, related to those roles we enact (Meister et al., 2014; Burke and Reitzes, 1991). This approach again presents identities as cognitive schemas, built from comparisons with expectations, specifically the perception of expectations held for each role (Stryker and Burke, 2000). People generally try to enact their roles in modes and behaviors deemed socially appropriate for specific roles, while valuing different roles in potentially different ways and for situationally different contexts (Adler and Adler, 1987; Schneider et al., 1971; Brush and Gale, 2014).

In the management and business literature, work-related identity is an important element of a personal or social identity. Merton (1957) defines roles as social positions that carry expectations for behaviors and obligations to other actors, ideally to positively affect both the individual and the organization (Brown, 1979; Hall et al., 1970; Ashforth and Mael, 1989). At the same time, within organizational behavior, social identity can be derived from that organization as well as sub-organizational levels, with an outcome, of course, of multiple identities (see Ashforth and Mael, 1989). Not only does the individual derive a social identity from the organization, but also the work role that a person holds can guide their action (McCall and Simmons, 1978). At the same time, while a work role will guide action, the role identity becomes individualized by the role occupant's interpretation of that role (Ibarra, 1999).

## Identity construction and durability

Because our interest in identity is prompted by questions of how individuals become entrepreneurs, or entrepreneurial, this begs the question of how identity is created or constructed, and how durable it is over time. Identity construction takes place through a complex interplay of cognitive, affective and social interactions that are contextualized (Marková, 1987); identity motives, pressures that move us toward certain identity states and away from others, help to guide identity construction (Breakwell, 1988). The motives themselves may vary through time or situation and may include things such as affinities for self-esteem, continuity, distinctiveness, as well as belonging or a sense of meaningfulness (Vignoles et al., 2006). Identity might be considered both as category-based and role-based (for example, a woman entrepreneur or an African-American student). However, one identity might be more salient in different situations, such as a classroom, a social group meeting or other context (Ashforth et al., 2000) such as a professional environment. While identity construction might start with personal aspects and group membership, the identity outcome is also largely dependent on the prioritization of those identity inputs, or the saliency of each individual part, which is considered to be both muta- ble and dynamic in reaction to social environments (Meister et al., 2014).

One way to look at saliency is through an individual's level of commitment to the identity. 'Commitment shapes identity salience shapes role choice behavior' (Mead, in Stryker and Burke, 2000, p. 286). In other words, commitment to a particular role identity is high if people perceive that many of their important social relationships are predicated on occupancy of that role (Stryker and Stratham, 1985). The more strongly a person is committed to an identity, the greater the level of identity sali- ence (Stryker, 1980), measured by what it costs to lose important relationships to others if that identity were closed (Stryker and Burke, 2000).

Overall, ongoing 'identity work', indeed 'conscious identity work', will include not only forming, but also maintaining upkeep through repairs and revisions (Svengingsson and Alvesson, 2003: 1165). The development of narrative has been presented as a tool for identity construction (Ibarra and Barbulescu, 2010). The approach views identity as 'the internalized and evolving story that results from a person's selective appropriate of past, present, and future' (McAdams, 1999: 486, in Ibarra and Barbulescu, 2010: 135). As such, narratives are the means of captur- ing self-schemas and meanings associated with individuals as they interact with others.

## Entrepreneurial identity

In one of the earliest specific works on entrepreneurial identity, Stanworth and Curran (1976) explicitly drew forth the difference between their analysis of entre- preneurial roles as related to self-definition and the ubiquitous earlier perspective of an indelible personality type in place before the undertaking of any entrepre- neurial roles. Instead, Stanworth and Curran acknowledge the contribution of social aspects in building the identity, and posit three latent social identities as role components: artisan, classical entrepreneur and the manager. Since then a variety of different types of entrepreneurial identities and typologies have been proposed in the entrepreneurship literature (Woo et al., 1991; Westhead and Wright, 1998; Vesalainen and Pihkala, 2000; Fauchart and Gruber, 2011), along with a variety of definitions for the overarching entrepreneurial identity (for a summary see Crosina, Chapter 5 in this volume).

This body of research has grown significantly and has evolved from the idea of typologies and the investigation of stereotypes to a deeper, and also broader, study of entrepreneurial identity, including the contribution of discourse and narrative as a methodology (Fletcher, 2007; Foss, 2004; Johansson, 2004; Warren, 2004; Downing, 2005; Berglund, 2008; Down and Warren, 2008; Phillips et al., 2013), passion (Cardon et al., 2009; Chen et al., 2009; Murnieks et al., 2014) and persistence (Hoang and Gimeno, 2010), industry (Vesala et al., 2007; Lindgren and Packendorff, 2008; Jain et al., 2009), family business (Shepherd and Haynie, 2009; Watson, 2009), type of company (Miller et al., 2011) and geographic region and/or culture (Erogul and McCrohan, 2008; Farmer and Kung-Mcintyre, 2008; Kikooma, 2011; Gill and Larson, 2014). Two more recent compelling paths have included the pursuit of understanding any potential differences related to identities within a defined arena of social entrepreneurship (Light, 2005; Jones et al., 2008), and the role of entrepreneurship education in shaping entrepreneurial identities (Edwards and Muir, 2012; Vanevenhoven and Liguori, 2013; Hytti and Heinonen, 2013; Donnellon et al., 2014).

In looking across the existing research in entrepreneurial identity, we see that there are connections to organizational identity in three ways: distinctiveness, or what is meant by a specifically entrepreneurial identity; centrality, which we connect with salience; and endurance, which we connect with construction and/or durability (Kreiner et al., 2015).

The idea that entrepreneurs are somehow distinct and different represents a central theme in the entrepreneurship literature (e.g., Baker and Nelson, 2005), and to identify oneself as an entrepreneur provides individuals with the opportunity to satisfy their need for distinctiveness, while recognizing a potential imbalance with a need for belonging (Shepherd and Haynie, 2009; Tajfel and Turner, 1986; Turner, 1985). In much of the work related to identity, this is generally ascribed to be through membership in an organization, one which provides an identity that is intended to have positive effects for both the individual and the organization (Brown, 1969; Hall et al., 1970; Lee, 1971, in Ashforth and Mael, 1989: 20). We posit that the business organization itself is of interest in a quite different way to those acting as entrepreneurs, especially those in the process of creating an organization.

Not only may the organization not yet exist, but also other groups potentially contributing to the work identity, such as 'work group, department, union, lunch group, age cohort, fast-track group, and so on' (Ashforth and Mael, 1989: 22), also either do not exist or at best are emerging. Further, the entrepreneur is often in the process of creating the new organization, and therefore simultaneously creating a role identity as the entrepreneur, and the organizational identity, which is often manifested in the culture of the emerging venture (Gartner and Brush, 2007). More specifically, the entrepreneurs rely on their tacit knowledge, experience and social contacts to build the systems, boundaries and overall identity of the emerging organization. In this process the entrepreneur may actually try on different identities, as the organizational and entrepreneurial identities are shaped simultaneously.

Distinctiveness must be considered not only in differentiating between an entrepreneurial identity and another work identity, but also within types or approaches to entrepreneurship. For instance, an entrepreneur opening a food truck business may theoretically hold a different entrepreneurial identity than one pursuing venture capital for a technology venture. These differences may be predicated on a number of bases, including motivation and previous experience, role models, funding needs and sources, team structure, common obstacles, networks, and definitions of successful outcomes.

The issue of centrality is also critical, raising the question of the saliency of the entrepreneurial identity in the personal identity hierarchy. This question will be particularly relevant as we later move into the question of women's entrepreneurial identity (Kreiner et al., 2015). Recognizing that there is not an entrepreneurial identity (Stanworth and Curran, 1976), we are intrigued by the situation of the entrepreneurial identity as one of the multiple and overlapping identities that make up any person, as well as the effect of social interactions in that process (Meister et al., 2014). Like Meister et al. (2014), we are especially intrigued by the saliency question, including the movement from affirmation or self-acceptance to validation (the need for others to recognize that identity).

And finally, we consider the construction, adoption and endurance of an entrepreneurial identity, looked at from a diachronic perspective of how the identity changes over time. Some will adopt the identity of entrepreneur from the moment they have a concept, while some may not consider themselves entrepreneurs until others suggest that they are becoming entrepreneurs, and they therefore may then adopt the identity. But how durable is the identity? In other words, when does a person gain an entrepreneurial identity, how does it last, and how or when might a person stop identifying as an entrepreneur? While the category of nascent entrepreneur has been established (Shaver et al., 2001), the question of when one might no longer be 'an entrepreneur' remains.

Drawing from the career development literature, as an individual engages in activities to start and launch a venture, their identity is somewhat malleable and impressionable. But as they gain experience that solidifies their self-concept as an entrepreneur, their identity develops and the narrative becomes more focused and clarified (Carlsen, 2006; Hall, 2002). Again, much of this depends on the self-identification of the roles that must be filled depending on the perception of being entrepreneurial.

## Identity and aspirations, behavior and confidence

### Identity and aspirations

Our use of aspirations follows Farmer et al.'s (2011: 245) description as 'longings, aims, or ambitions', while we posit that 'aspiration' is actually an underdefined and under-researched concept throughout entrepreneurship. Two exceptions exist: the aspiration to start a business, which can be seen as the assumption of the identity of an entrepreneur (Farmer et al., 2011); and aspirations for a high-growth venture (Cassar, 2007). What is needed is a more articulated approach to investigating and/ or describing what an individual really wants to accomplish through their entre- preneurial behaviors. Currently, specificity about the overall value desired to be created through the behaviors generally remains largely amorphous.

The question of aspirations is one that is also too often missed in economic devel- opment programs. Policy approaches generally adopt 'three stylized facts' (Hessels et al., 2008):

1.  The entrepreneur (as business owner) enhances economic growth (Carree and Thurik, 2003).
2.  '[H]i-growth firms contribute more to economic growth than small, new firms' (Hessels et al., 2008).
3.  There is currently little research on growth aspirations within the diversity of entrepreneurs.

We also question the assumption from an economic development perspective that business growth is always good and desirable.

In fact, the use of the term 'aspiration' itself is in question. While the term 'aspira- tion' is occasionally used interchangeably with 'goal', 'growth ambitions' (Krueger and Carsrud, 1993) or 'objective', as a cognitive measure it can also be seen as having possible ties to entrepreneurial motivation, achievement motivation, as well as Ajzen's (1991) theory of planned behavior (Krueger and Carsrud, 1993). Simply put, aspirations relate to what you want to accomplish; motivations put forth why you want to accomplish something. We also differentiate between aspirations (what you want to happen) and expectations (what you think is going to happen) (Manolova et al., 2012; Hessels et al., 2008).

The stage of business creation and development does play a role in the relation- ship between identity and entrepreneurial aspirations. At the nascent stage, the desired entrepreneurial identity (possible self) serving as the foundation for the work identity can be seen to guide both thoughts and behaviors (Cross and Markus, 1994; Markus and Nurius, 1986; Farmer et al., 2011). The identity aspired to as an entrepreneur would depend on the individuals' perspectives on the definition and required roles of an entrepreneur. One way to consider this is to look at the relationship between business accomplishments and entrepreneurial self-image (Verheul et al., 2005). (These authors also added a consideration of gender which

**Table 1.1**    Typology of entrepreneurial identities

| Name/type | Entrepreneurial activity |
| --- | --- |
| Starter | Enters an independent business by creating a new one |
| Acquirer | Enters an independent business by acquiring an ongoing concern |
| Runner | Manages a small to medium-sized business beyond start-up |
| Take-off artist | Steers a company into a high-growth trajectory |
| Turnaround artist | Saves a failing company |
| Innovator | Makes something new happen that is not a company |
| Champion | Supports an innovator |
| Intrepreneur | Takes initiative for business unit creation inside an established business |
| Industry captain | Runs a big business |
| Mumpreneur | A woman running a business and caring for children simultaneously, balancing work and life |
| Social entrepreneur | An entrepreneur with innovative solutions to society's most pressing problems |

*Source:*    Adapted from K.H. Vesper, in Verheul et al. (2005), Neck et al. (2009), Nel et al. (2010).

will be reviewed in the next section of this chapter.) We added to these authors' use of Vesper's (1999) entrepreneurial typology to include additional potential entrepreneurial identities which may impact aspirations, and vice versa. Table 1.1 summarizes a typology of entrepreneurial identities.

One helpful exception is seen in the work of Kolvereid (1992), where he recognizes that 'most firms are born small and stay small' and finds only a weak relationship between motives to start the business and growth aspirations. Patterns in his findings suggest that 'entrepreneurs with no growth aspirations have a tendency to be driven by independence and opportunism, entrepreneurs with revenue growth aspirations by welfare and tax considerations, and entrepreneurs with both revenue and employment growth aspirations by their achievement motive'. However, he declares these findings to be weak, concluding that overall aspirations are not found to be significantly affected by 'experience, sex, location, or firm size by employee'. Other work finds that nascent entrepreneurs will be motivated to grow if they believe that the efforts expended will lead to the outcome they seek (Douglas and Shepherd, 2000; Krueger and Carsrud, 1993). Growth is a choice, even though it is often a measure of firm success (Delmar et al., 2003).

## Identity and behavior

Identity is at the root of drivers of behavior (Stryker and Burke, 2000). The personal search for identity can then be considered as a 'family of existential motives' including searches for such fundamental things such as 'meaning, connectedness, empowerment, and even immortality' (e.g., Denhardt, 1987; Fox, 1980; Katz and

Kahn, 1978; all in Ashforth and Mael, 1989: 22). They define situations by providing an increased sensitivity and receptiveness for behavior cues, therefore providing guidance on how to act (Stryker and Burke, 2000). They can be motivational and aspirational as to their desired identity for the future; identity can serve to support, or debilitate feelings of authenticity, especially in times of transition (Ibarra and Barbulescu, 2010).

Mead (1934, in Stryker and Burke, 2000) situates the study of identity as creating a framework to analyze sociological and social psychological issues, providing a conceptual pathway from identity to behavior. Later, Burke and Reitzes (1981) concluded that the link between identity and behavior was a sense of shared meanings, with Stryker and Burke (2000) eventually proposing an identity theory model: (1) recognizing the identity standard as a 'set of culturally prescribed meanings which are held by the individual to define the role identity in a particular situation' (ibid.: 287), in other words, what is expected, or what should be; (2) taking the perception of meanings in a situation and matching them to the meanings in the identity standard for that situation; (3) acknowledging the mechanisms that provide the comparison between the standard and the perception of the existing; and then (4) concluding with the differences that prompt behaviors to address the differences between the two (Stryker and Burke, 2000).

One of the challenges in holding multiple identities is to recognize that different situations contextually activate different behaviors, as different identities are invoked in different situations (Stryker and Burke, 2000). Which identity takes precedence in determining behavior? Backing up from there, each of us has an internal salience hierarchy which determines which identity takes precedence, as well as precedence in which situation. A particular situation may cause a specific identity to be evoked (Stryker and Burke, 2000).

And then there is the question of identity symmetry, essentially the difference between the actual and the perceived identity. Meister et al. (2014) report that there is actually little research on any positive effects of identity symmetry. However, as lack of that perceived validity can potentially lead to a lack of confidence, including self-questioning, and uncertainty regarding behaviors (Meister et al., 2014), lack of symmetry (internal and external identity alignment) may exacerbate relationship issues, particularly at work.

## Identity and confidence

Within the field of entrepreneurship, confidence (self-assurance stemming from one's trust in one's own abilities) is most often investigated as self-efficacy, 'the conviction that one can successfully execute the behavior required to produce the outcomes' (Bandura, 1977: 193). In Bandura's early specification of this concept, self-efficacy expectations mediate between the person and the behavior, while outcome expectations act between behavior and outcomes (expectation that a specific behavior will lead to certain outcomes) (Bandura, 1977, 1982). As such, self-efficacy has the potential to affect both the start and the persistence of a particular behavior (Bandura, 1977).

Over the course of Bandura's work in this area he suggests several relevant components to the theory. First, the dimensions of self-efficacy include magnitude (simple to difficult), generality (circumscribed to more general), and strength (weak to strong) (Bandura, 1977), emphasizing that an assessment of these dimensions must match the precision of the measurement of the efficacy. Second, the four major sources of efficacy information, or the ways one obtains information about one's own capability, are performance accomplishments, vicarious experience, verbal persuasion and emotional arousal (Bandura, 1977). Third, enhanced self-efficacy may be transferable to substantially different activities; however, the most predictable transfers are to more similar activities (Bandura, 1977; Bandura et al., 1969). And finally, one of Bandura's more recent yet less-discussed works includes the consideration of an agentic perspective: 'To be an agent is to influence intentionally one's functioning and life circumstances' (Bandura, 2006: 164).

Self-efficacy primarily entered the field of entrepreneurship through career preference, conceptually interpreted as an interest in becoming an entrepreneur (Scherer et al., 1989; Krueger and Carsrud, 1993; Krueger and Brazeal, 1994), and evolving into consideration of other types of entrepreneurial behaviors (Boyd and Vozikis, 1994; Krueger and Dickson, 1994). The first empirical study of entrepreneurial self-efficacy (Chen et al., 1998) has been followed by a variety of others to further distinguish the task domains (DeNoble et al., 1999; Kickul and D'Intino, 2005; McGee et al., 2009). And a variety of methodological approaches have been used to study self-efficacy differences in numerous areas, with examples including behaviors (Cassar and Friedman, 2009; Smith and Woodworth, 2012; Tumasian and Braun, 2012), country and/or culture (Jung et al., 2001; Urban, 2006; Naktiyok et al., 2010), entrepreneurial education (Peterman and Kennedy, 2003; Karlsson and Moberg, 2013; Piperopoulos and Dimov, 2015) and family business (Carr and Sequeira, 2007; DeNoble et al., 2007). Gender, of course, has also been an important part of self-efficacy studies, and this will be included in the next section of this chapter.

## Women's entrepreneurial identity (why it is different for women)

'A central premise of SIT is that people identify with groups that contribute to a positive sense of self, such as high-status or high-power groups (Ellemers, 1993; Haslam et al., 2000)' (Justo et al., Chapter 3 in this volume). The perception of entrepreneurs as traditionally men, independent and risk-takers is mostly a myth, which is perpetuated by the media, our teaching cases, classroom materials, and in general conversation (Bird and Brush, 2002). This role stereotype may fit some entrepreneurs, but not all. Traditional entrepreneurs are thought of in the ideal as those who brilliantly conceive of a new technology innovation, capture a giant market, take a company public and make millions of dollars. These entrepreneurs are financially motivated, take big risks, have networks that are male-dominated, and start businesses in traditional product and market sectors, hoping to generate jobs and personal wealth (Kirzner, 1973; Schumpeter, 1935; Delmar et al., 2003; Aldrich et al., 1989; Fairlie and Robb, 2009; Shane and Venkataraman, 2000).

These stereotypes of entrepreneurs being male refer to the traits and behaviors that are culturally deemed appropriate for men and women, and whether these relate to the individual's role or occupation (Heilman, 2001; Meuhlenhard and Peterson, 2011). For example, jobs can become stereotyped as masculine or feminine (Heilman, 1983), and therefore success in these gendered occupations is then believed to require correspondingly stereotypical characteristics (Heilman, 1997). Stereotypical characteristics are quite common as they pertain to dichotomous, visible behaviors typically labelled as 'masculine' and 'feminine' (Gupta and Turban, 2012).

Because of stereotypical beliefs about entrepreneurs as being male/masculine, women entrepreneurs may face competing social identities. Theory suggests that when an individual faces a competing social identity, they will use cultural associations of status-worthiness and competence as cues for self-definition. Thus, given positive associations with masculine entrepreneurial attributes and negative, or at best neutral associations with feminine entrepreneurial attributes (Ahl, 2006; Bruni et al., 2004), entrepreneurs more often identify with masculine characteristics. 'Because of this, and due to the higher status attached to masculine entrepreneurial values, we expect women entrepreneurs to report masculine values, that is, ones that are similar to those of their male counterparts' (Justo et al., Chapter 3 in this volume).

The same is true for aspirations. The very practice of pursuing high-growth entrepreneurship – with its aggressive funding goals and interest in pursuing venture capital funding – has been consistently considered a masculine behavior (Gupta et al., 2009; Gupta and Turban, 2012). Gupta et al. (2009) found that most entrepreneurs, and in particular those who created high-performing, high-growth ventures, are perceived as more stereotypically masculine than feminine.

On the one hand, several scholars have highlighted the importance of women's non-monetary expectations from the business as a key to understand gender differences in business ownership patterns (e.g., MacNabb et al., 1993; Buttner and Moore, 1997; Fenwick and Hutton, 2000; Walker and Brown, 2004). Others, however, have found little gender-based variance in values and attitudes toward success (e.g., Catley and Hamilton, 1998; Kalleberg and Leicht, 1991; Shane et al., 1991). Either way, the general social expectation that entrepreneurs should hold high aspirations for growth may create internal identity conflict for women entrepreneurs who may wish to grow more steadily, slowly, or not at all. In fact, one study of nascent entrepreneurs finds that growth aspirations for men were motivated only by financial success, while women were motivated by status or role, financial success and self-realization (Manolova et al., 2012).

The general masculinization of the social role of entrepreneurs also influences expectations for behavior. In most Western societies, masculine behaviors are commonly associated with assertiveness and dominance, while feminine behaviors are connected with warmth and emotional expressiveness (Eagly, 1987). Achieving success as an entrepreneur has also been traditionally associated with masculinity (Bird and Brush, 2002; Collins and Moore, 1964; Hisrich and Brush, 1984; Gupta et al., 2009; Gupta and Turban, 2012; Schein, 1975), as successful entrepreneurs have been described as bold, aggressive risk-takers; behaviors that are typically associated with masculinity (Baughn et al., 2006; Gupta and Turban, 2012). Conversely, femininity has not been associated with 'successful' entrepreneurs (Bird and Brush, 2002; Ridgeway, 2001; Rudman and Glick, 2001). Entrepreneurs who exhibit more femininity may not be considered to have the level of competency required for business growth and success (Bird et al., 2012; Cejka and Eagly, 1999). By behaving in a feminine manner, entrepreneurs are likely to perpetuate the perception of societal myths regarding the incompatibility between femininity and venture success.

Not only do masculine stereotypes and identity influence aspirations and behaviors, but these also have an impact on confidence. To be an entrepreneur, one has to believe one has the necessary skills and capabilities to pursue a particular career generally, or to be an entrepreneur (Bandura, 1989; Chen et al., 1998). More specifically, individuals with high entrepreneurial self-efficacy have higher entrepreneurial intentions (Chen et al., 1998; Krueger et al., 2000). Career literature shows that, not surprisingly, women have lower self-efficacy in careers perceived as 'non-traditional', and that societal expectations for women in a particular career shape their self-confidence (Eddleston et al., 2006). As a consequence, women entrepreneurs may have less self-efficacy in performing entrepreneurial tasks such as creating and growing a business, or more specifically, in building a team, seeking resources or interacting with stakeholders (Mueller and Dato-On, 2008).

The next section presents an overview of the chapters in this volume in Part I: Aspirations, Part II: Behaviors and Part III: Confidence.

## Part I: Women entrepreneurs, identity and aspirations

The chapters in Part I explore the relationship between women's entrepreneurial identity and aspirations. Identity theory posits that an individual's personal identity is linked to motivations, goals and aspirations. In other words, how a person self-identifies, and sees themselves, can motivate them to aspire to a different or new identity.

Chapter 2, 'Developing entrepreneurial identity among start-ups' female founders in high-tech: policy implications from the Chilean case', studies the intersection of various categories of identity by focusing on a particular industry: women entrepreneurs in technology. As such, the authors Katherina Kuschel and Juan-Pablo Labra touch on issues related to personal, social and work identities. Building on a relatively thin thread in the entrepreneurship literature, the authors use a social identity framework to investigate identity construction, focusing first on identifying and examining elements that contribute to women building an entrepreneurial identity, and subsequently sharing conclusions on the constraints and obstacles faced during this process. This is a qualitative study, based upon the ubiquitous Berglund (2008) approach in search of theory development. One of the notable questions addressed in this chapter concerns a woman's degree of agency to contribute to the construction of her entrepreneurial identity, particularly within specific social contexts, in this case from an industry perspective, the entrepreneurial ecosystem supporting technological ventures, and geographically: Latin America (largely Chile).

In Chapter 3, 'Perception of success of men and women entrepreneurs: a social identity approach', Rachida Justo, Cristina Cruz and Julio De Castro build from a post-structural feminist view to apply social identity theory (SIT) to explore their contention that for women entrepreneurs, parenthood (especially the presence of dependent children) is a powerful driver of change in an entrepreneur's perceptions of success. The authors' proposition is that the effects of parenthood are stronger for women than for men. One aspect of aspirations that demands more research is the relationship of aspirations to existing measures of entrepreneurial success. This chapter makes four main contributions to the entrepreneurship literature. First, it more firmly connects SIT inside the field of entrepreneurship. Second, it looks at the effect of the work–family interface on shifts in perceptions and values. Third, it expands the measures of entrepreneurial success to include non-monetary measures of success. And fourth, it further disentangles within-gender differences regarding business aspirations in order to better understand the heterogeneity amongst women entrepreneurs.

'Aspirations of women entrepreneurs in poverty: the livelihood entrepreneur', by Smita Trivedi, is Chapter 4. This, our final chapter related to identity and aspirations, presents the consideration of aspirations as quite relative, and unleashes it from any stereotypical assumptions regarding an innate connection between aspirations and opportunity-based entrepreneurship. Trivedi grounds her work in her interest in poverty alleviation to propose a new definition, 'livelihood entrepreneurship'. As such, Trivedi places this concept on a continuum between the concepts of social entrepreneurship and traditional entrepreneurship, recognizing that 'An entrepreneur must first meet her family's basic needs before she can dream about expanding or helping others'. In this chapter, poverty is presented as a multidimensional construct presenting itself as part of economic uncertainty. Further, Trivedi places the concept of community-based enterprise (CBE) as a pathway to sustainable local development (Peredo and Chrisman, 2006), while recognizing the need for a more individual level of analysis and therefore proposing 'livelihood entrepreneurs'.

## Part II: Women, entrepreneurial identity and behavior

The chapters in Part II connect and explore the relationship between women's social identity and behaviors. It is posited that identity, especially gender identity, influences behaviors. More specifically:

> Social identity theory (SIT) is utilized to examine when entrepreneurs are more likely to act consistently with their gender-stereotypic role and when they are more likely to adopt attitudes more congruent with traditional entrepreneurial archetypes. The central assumption underlying social identity theory (Tajfel, 1974, 1978) is that while there are elements of self-identity that are derived from individual traits and interpersonal relationships (personal identity), there are many social settings in which people do not act as independent individuals. (Justo et al., Chapter 3 in this volume)

Part II begins with Chapter 5 by Eliana Crosina, 'On becoming an entrepreneur: unpacking entrepreneurial identity'. Following a brief review of literature on identity and then, more specifically, identity among women entrepreneurs, Crosina compares entrepreneurial identity among professionals and entrepreneurs, then highlights what might be unique or different for women. She notes that the current literature overlooks how entrepreneurial identity forms and evolves. However, there is little consensus on what constitutes entrepreneurial identity, other than it is flexible and requires active 'work'. The chapter offers a framework for entrepreneurial identity construction and includes gender as a key aspect. She argues that for women entrepreneurs, there is a need to gain legitimacy, and to be flexible or 'juggle' their identities based on their multiple roles. The chapter concludes with suggested research directions.

The next chapter in Part II, Chapter 6 by Catherine Elliott and Barbara Orser, 'Feminist entrepreneurial identity: reproducing gender through founder decision-making', examines how feminist entrepreneurial identity is expressed through founder decision-making. The authors examine how feminist entrepreneurial identity is expressed through entrepreneurial actions. Beginning with a review of literature that covers adult learning theory, they point out that being female may conflict with one's entrepreneurial self-image. To examine their research question, 15 self-identified 'feminist entrepreneurs' were recruited through Canadian Women's Enterprise Centers. They were interviewed in semi-structured phone calls, where verbatim transcripts were analyzed using an interpretive inductive methodology. Results showed that their feminist entrepreneurial identity was articulated through their acquisition of human and financial resources, strategic compromises, market positioning, governance structures, and relationships. The results yield insight into the gendered nature of venture creation, and in particular, entrepreneurial identity. The investigation yields a conceptual model and future research directions.

The final chapter in Part II, Chapter 7 by Richard Harrison and Claire Leitch, 'Identity and identity work in constructing the woman entrepreneur', examines the organizational context and how the identity construction processes take place.

Taking a feminist perspective, they ask what is the nature of the identity work undertaken by women in the process of identity formation, identity activation and resultant behavior in an entrepreneurial context. The authors use an ethnographic case study of a female entrepreneur involved in the start-up and growth of her family business. Data collection took place over 18 months and utilized a combination of observation, conversations, interviews and documentary materials. Three overarching themes about identity and identity construction emerged, as well as two others related to gender. The three overarching themes were identity representation, identity construction as an unconscious process, and the influence of life history. For women in particular, the issue of attaining and gaining credibility and issue of invisibility for women in family business were important findings.

## Part III: Women, entrepreneurial identity and confidence

Part III explores the relationship between confidence (self-assurance stemming from trust in one's own abilities), most often studied as self-efficacy, and how this influences the start and persistence of entrepreneurial behaviors (Bandura, 1977). The general masculinization of the social role of the entrepreneur, and characterizations of abilities, influence expectations for behavior.

First is Chapter 8 by Malin Brännback, Shahrokh Nikou, Alan Carsrud and Diana Hechavarria, entitled 'Context, cognition and female entrepreneurial intentions: it is all about perceived behavioral control'. The authors explore the concept of perceived behavioral control, which is a person's subjective belief about their capacity to carry out a task. This subjective belief over the behavior, not the outcome, is significantly influenced by the context of the entrepreneurial activity and the self-efficacy of the individual. For their study, the authors explore family business background and compare male and female entrepreneurs. The study of 2282 students, representing universities in eight countries, includes previously used reliable measures. Their results show that family business does not influence the subjective belief as to whether women think they will become entrepreneurs, but it does influence whether they think they will succeed in doing so. They find that perceived behavioral control and self-efficacy are distinct concepts, and that their impact is gendered.

The second chapter, Chapter 9 by Magdalena Markowska, 'Motherhood as a springboard for women's entrepreneurial action', examines one form of entrepreneurial identity, 'mumpreneurs', and considers the relationship between becoming entrepreneurial and motherhood. Following Bandura's social learning theory, the author posits that mastery experiences, such as giving birth and raising a child, will have a positive effect on a woman's confidence in general and on entrepreneurial self-efficacy in particular. Specifically, she explores whether or not skills and abilities in child-raising are similar and transferable to entrepreneurial experience. For example, she argues that the budgeting, multi-tasking, persuasive and negotiation skills required for being a mother are similar to those required to be an entrepreneur.

This theoretical chapter offers a unique perspective – motherhood as a resource – which is somewhat contradictory to previous literature which considered mother-hood as a cost, or a disadvantage for women starting and growing businesses (Allen et al., 2007).

The third chapter in Part III is Chapter 10, 'Kickstart or jumpstart? Understanding women entrepreneurs' crowdfunding performance', by Smita Srivastava, Pyayt Oo, Arvin Sahaym and Thomas Allison. The authors examine factors that influence women entrepreneurs' seeking funds from crowdfunding lenders through online platforms. They explore the relationship between social identity, passion, self-efficacy and prior business knowledge as this relates to crowdfunding performance. Using data from Kickstarter, a large crowdfunding site, they selected a random sample of female-led projects from three categories – gaming, technology and product design – and analyzed the videos created by these entrepreneurs. Their analysis of 197 projects shows that women entrepreneurs with high self-efficacy will engender more support from potential backers through their strong self-belief. Passion reflects preparedness and commitment, which also influences backers to believe in the entrepreneur's idea.

## Conclusion

We began with a general discussion of the elements of identity, self-concept, social identity and role identity, and how entrepreneurs construct or adopt their entrepreneurial identity during organizational emergence or move into a new organization. We considered how entrepreneurial identity may be distinctive, central or salient, or enduring depending on the context. We argued that entrepreneurial identity is inherently tied to three other key concepts: aspirations, behaviors and confidence. From this general background, we discussed how entrepreneurial identity is different for women, largely because of the historical male participation and association with masculine characteristics and behaviors. Further, the fact that an estimated 90 percent of all research on entrepreneurship focuses on men suggests that much of what we know about entrepreneurial identity is based on studies of men. Given this foundation, we proposed that the linkages between entrepreneurial identity, and aspirations, behaviors and confidence, will shed light on why women will create and grow businesses, how they will grow businesses, and why women are self-assured in creating and growing their businesses.

Our call for papers set forth this premise and the authors included in this volume provide new insights into women's entrepreneurship. But at the same time, new research questions are raised. The chapters examining entrepreneurial identity and aspirations point out that women face contradictions depending on the expectations or norms in an industry, and therefore they may adopt provisional identities (Kuschel and Labra, Chapter 2). In addition, parenthood is experienced differently, which in turn influences personal values as these relate to entrepreneurship (Justo, Cruz and De Castro, Chapter 3). Further, we learned that socio-economic context, or a drive for livelihood, also influences identity construction (Trivedi, Chapter 4). Together, these suggest future research questions:

- What is the nature of provisional identities – how are they conceived? Are they shaped to become enduring identities?
- What are the contextual factors that influence provisional identities?
- How does parenthood influence the construction of entrepreneurial identity?

The chapters exploring linkages between entrepreneurial identities and behavior show that women entrepreneurs are motivated to gain legitimacy (Crosina, Chapter 5) and credibility (Harrison and Leitch, Chapter 7). Further, the masculine image of the entrepreneur influences identity construction and representation (Harrison and Leitch, Chapter 7). On the other hand, Elliott and Orser (Chapter 6) suggest that a feminist entrepreneurial identity is manifested by the behaviors of an entrepreneur in acquiring resources and market positioning. These also suggest future research questions:

- Is there a relationship between legitimating or credibility-building behaviors and endurance of entrepreneurial identity over time?
- Is there also a relationship between identity validation (the need for others to recognize the identity) and the degree to which the entrepreneur self-identifies with this role?
- Do women adopting a feminist entrepreneurial identity benefit in resource acquisition behaviors?

Finally, Part III of this book examines the relationship between entrepreneurial identity and confidence. Resource acquisition, in the form of crowdfunding, was significantly related to success in crowdfunding (Srivastava, Oo, Sahaym and Allison, Chapter 10). Brännback, Nikou, Carsrud and Hechavarria (Chapter 8) find gender differences in perceived behavioral control, and confidence in ability to complete tasks associated with entrepreneurship. Markowska (Chapter 9) argues that tasks or behaviors associated with entrepreneurial activity are similar to those gained in child-rearing and motherhood, and should be considered as a resource. Questions for future consideration related to these findings are:

- Is there a difference between male and female entrepreneurs and their entrepreneurial self-efficacy in the venture creation process based on experience in parenting or child-rearing tasks?
- How is perceived behavioral control and self-efficacy similar and different for entrepreneurs in other contexts (for instance, high-technology? Consumer products?)
- What are the educational and training interventions that would support the development of higher levels of entrepreneurial self-efficacy?

While we believe that this volume answers some questions, others raised, like those above, merit continued research, especially recognizing that the question of identity overlap at the individual and organizational levels potentially is more salient for business owners than for those who work for organizations owned by others. Continued investigation into entrepreneurial identity will provide us with the knowledge to guide entrepreneurship education, policy recommendations and the practice of entrepreneurship.

## References

Adler, P.A. and P. Adler (1987), *Membership Roles in Field Research*, Thousand Oaks, CA: SAGE Publications.

Ahl, H. (2006), 'Why research on women entrepreneurs needs new directions', *Entrepreneurship Theory and Practice*, 30(5), 595–621.

Ajzen, I. (1991), 'The theory of planned behavior', *Organizational Behavior and Human Decision Processes*, 50(2), 179–211.

Aldrich, H.E., P.R. Reese and P. Dubini (1989), 'Women on the verge of a breakthrough? Networking among entrepreneurs in the United States and Italy', *Entrepreneurship and Regional Development*, 1, 339–356.

Allen, E., A. Elam, N. Langowitz and M. Dean (2007), 'Report on Women and Entrepreneurship', *Global Entrepreneurship Monitor*, Wellesley, MA: Babson College.

Ashforth, B.E., G.E. Kreiner and M. Fugate (2000), 'All in a day's work: boundaries and micro role transitions', *Academy of Management Review*, 25(3), 472–491.

Ashforth, B.E. and F. Mael (1989), 'Social identity theory and the organization', *Academy of Management Review*, 4(1), 20–39.

Baker, T. and R.E. Nelson (2005), 'Creating something from nothing: resource construction through entrepreneurial bricolage', *Administrative Science Quarterly*, 50(3), 329–366.

Bandura, A. (1977), 'Self-efficacy: toward a unifying theory of behavioral change', *Psychological Review*, 84(2), 191.

Bandura, A. (1982), 'Self-efficacy mechanism in human agency', *American Psychologist*, 37(2), 122–147.

Bandura, A. (1989), 'Regulation of cognitive processes through perceived self-efficacy', *Developmental Psychology*, 25(5), 729.

Bandura, A. (2006), 'Toward a psychology of human agency', *Perspectives on Psychological Science*, 1(2), 164–180.

Bandura, A., E.B. Blanchard and B. Ritter (1969), 'Relative efficacy of desensitization and modeling approaches for inducing behavioral, affective, and attitudinal changes', *Journal of Personality and Social Psychology*, 13(3), 173.

Baughn, C.C., B.L. Chua and K.E. Neupert (2006), 'The normative context for women's participation in entrepreneurship: a multi-country study', *Entrepreneurship Theory and Practice*, 30, 687–708.

Berglund, K. (2008), 'Discursive diversity in fashioning entrepreneurial identity', Chapter 11 in Chris Steyaert and Daniel Hjorth (eds), *Entrepreneurship As Social Change: A Third New Movements in Entrepreneurship Book*, Cheltenham, UK and Northampton, MA, USA: Edward Elgar Publishing, pp. 231–250.

Bird, B. and C. Brush (2002), 'A gendered perspective on organizational creation', *Entrepreneurship Theory and Practice*, 26(3), 41–65.

Bird, B., L. Schjoedt and J.R. Baum (2012), 'Editor's introduction. Entrepreneurs' behavior: elucidation and measurement', *Entrepreneurship Theory and Practice*, 36(5), 889–913.

Boyd, N.G. and G.S. Vozikis (1994), 'The influence of self-efficacy on the development of entrepreneurial intentions and action', *Entrepreneurship Theory and Practice*, 18, 63–63.

Breakwell, G.M. (1988), 'Strategies adopted when identity is threatened', *Revue Internationale de Psychologie Sociale*, 1, 189–203

Brown, M.E. (1979), 'Identification and some conditions of organizational involvement', *Administrative Science Quarterly*, 14, 346–355.

Bruni, A., S. Gherardi and B. Poggio (2004), 'Doing gender, doing entrepreneurship: an ethnographic account of intertwined practices', *Gender, Work and Organization*, 11(4), 406–429.

Brush, C.G. and M. Gale (2014), 'Becoming entrepreneurial: constructing an entrepreneurial identity in an elective entrepreneurship course', in V. Crittenden, K. Esper, N. Karst and R. Slegers (eds), *Evolving Entrepreneurial Education: Innovation in the Babson Classroom*, Bingley, UK: Emerald Publishing, pp. 305–322.

Burke, P.J. and D.C. Reitzes (1991), 'An identity theory approach to commitment', *Social Psychology Quarterly*, 54, 239–251.

Buttner, H. and D. Moore (1997), 'Women's organizational exodus to entrepreneurship: self-reported motivations and correlates with success', *Journal of Small Business Management*, 35(1), 34–46.

Cardon, M.S., J. Wincent, J. Singh and M. Drnovsek (2009), 'The nature and experience of entrepreneurial passion', *Academy of Management Review*, 34(3), 511–532.

Carlsen, A. (2006), 'Organizational becoming as dialogic imagination of practice: the case of the indomitable Gauls', *Organization Science*, 17(1), 132–149.

Carr, J.C. and J.M. Sequeira (2007), 'Prior family business exposure as intergenerational influence and entrepreneurial intent: a theory of planned behavior approach', *Journal of Business Research*, 60(10), 1090–1098.

Carree, M.A. and A.R. Thurik (2003), 'The impact of entrepreneurship on economic growth', in D.B. Audretsch and Z.J. Acs (eds), *Handbook of Entrepreneurship Research*, Boston, MA, USA and Dordrecht, the Netherlands: Kluwer Academic Publishers, pp. 437–471.

Cassar, G. (2007), 'Money, money, money: a longitudinal investigation of entrepreneurial career reasons for growth preferences and achieved growth', *Entrepreneurship and Regional Development*, 19(1), 80–107.

Cassar, G. and H. Friedman (2009), 'Does self-efficacy affect entrepreneurial investment?', *Strategic Entrepreneurship Journal*, 3(3), 241–260.

Catley, S. and R.T. Hamilton (1998), 'Small business development and gender of owner', *Journal of Management Development*, 71(1), 75–82.

Cejka, M.A. and A.H. Eagly (1999), 'Gender-stereotypic images of occupations correspond to the sex segregation of employment', *Personality and Social Psychology Bulletin*, 25(4), 413–423.

Chen, C.C., P.G. Greene and A. Crick (1998), 'Does entrepreneurial self-efficacy distinguish entrepreneurs from managers?', *Journal of Business Venturing*, 13(4), 295–316.

Chen, X.P., X. Yao and S. Kotha (2009), 'Entrepreneur passion and preparedness in business plan presentations: a persuasion analysis of venture capitalists' funding decisions', *Academy of Management Journal*, 52(1), 199–214.

Collins, O.F. and D.G. Moore (1964), *The Enterprising Man*, East Lansing, MI: Michigan State University Press.

Cross, S.E. and H.R. Markus (1994), 'Self-schemas, possible selves, and competent performance', *Journal of Educational Psychology*, 86(3), 423.

Delmar, F., P. Davidsson and W. Gartner (2003), 'Arriving at the high-growth firm', *Journal of Business Venturing*, 18(2), 189–216.

Denhardt, R.B. (1987), 'Images of death and slavery in organizational life', *Journal of Management*, 13, 529–541.

De Noble, A.F., D. Jung and B. Ehrlich (1999), 'Entrepreneurial self-efficacy: the development of a measure and its relationship to entrepreneurial intentions and actions', *Entrepreneurship Theory and Practice*, 18(4), 63–77.

DeNoble, A., S. Ehrlich and G. Singh (2007), 'Toward the development of a family business self-efficacy scale: a resource-based perspective', *Family Business Review*, 20(2), 127–140.

Donnellon, A., S. Ollila and K.W. Middleton (2014), 'Constructing entrepreneurial identity in entrepreneurship education', *International Journal of Management Education*, 12(3), 490–499.

Douglas, E.J. and D.A. Shepherd (2000), 'Entrepreneurship as a utility maximizing response', *Journal of Business Venturing*, 15(3), 231–251.

Down, S. and L. Warren (2008), 'Constructing narratives of enterprise: clichés and entrepreneurial self-identity', *International Journal of Entrepreneurial Behavior and Research*, 14(1), 4–23.

Downing, S. (2005), 'The social construction of entrepreneurship: narrative and dramatic processes in the coproduction of organizations and identities', *Entrepreneurship Theory and Practice*, 29(2), 185–204.

Eagly, A.H. (1987), *Sex Differences in Social Behavior: A Social-Role Interpretation*, Hillsdale, NJ: Erlbaum.

Eddleston, K.A., J.F. Viega and G.N. Powell (2006), 'Explaining sex differences in managerial career satisfiers preferences', *Journal of Applied Psychology*, 91(2), 437–456.

Edwards, L.-J. and E.J. Muir (2012), 'Evaluating enterprise education: why do it?', *Education + Training*, 54(4), 278–290.

Ellemers, N. (1993), 'The influence of socio-structural variables on identity management strategies', *European Review of Social Psychology*, 4(1), 27–57.

Erogul, M.S. and D. McCrohan (2008), 'Preliminary investigation of Emirati women entrepreneurs in the UAE', *African Journal of Business Management*, 2(10), 177.

Fairlie, R.W. and A.M. Robb (2009), 'Gender differences in business performance: evidence from the characteristics of business owners survey', *Small Business Economics*, 33, 375–395.

Farmer, S.M. and K. Kung-Mcintyre (2008), 'Entrepreneur role prototypes and role identity in the US, China, and Taiwan', *Academy of Management Proceedings*, 2008(1), 1–6.

Farmer, S.M., X. Yao and K. Kung-Mcintyre (2011), 'The behavioral impact of entrepreneur identity aspiration and prior entrepreneurial experience', *Entrepreneurship Theory and Practice*, 35(2), 245–273.

Fauchart, E. and M. Gruber (2011), 'Darwinians, communitarians, and missionaries: the role of founder identity in entrepreneurship', *Academy of Management Journal*, 54(5), 935–957.

Fenwick, T. and S. Hutton (2000), 'Women crafting new work: the learning of women entrepreneurs', paper presented at the Adult Education Conference, Vancouver.

Fletcher, D. (2007), '"Toy Story": the narrative world of entrepreneurship and the creation of interpretive communities', *Journal of Business Venturing*, 22(5), 649–672.

Foss, L. (2004), '"Going against the grain . . .", construction of entrepreneurial identity through narratives', in D. Hjorth and C. Steyaert (eds), *Narrative and Discursive Approaches in Entrepreneurship*, Cheltenham, UK and Northampton, MA, USA: Edward Elgar Publishing, pp. 80–104.

Fox, A. (1980), 'The meaning of work', in G. Esland and G. Salaman (eds), *The Politics of Work and Occupations*, Toronto: University of Toronto Press, pp. 139–191.

Gartner, W.B. and C.G. Brush (2007), 'Entrepreneurship as organizing: emergence, newness and transformation', in M. Minitt (ed.), *Entrepreneurship*, Santa Barbara, CA: Praeger Publishing, pp. 1–20.

Gill, R. and G.S. Larson (2014), 'Making the ideal (local) entrepreneur: place and the regional development of high-tech entrepreneurial identity', *Human Relations*, 67(5), 519–542.

Gupta, V.K. and D. Turban (2012), 'Evaluation of new business ideas: do gender stereotypes play a role?', *Journal of Managerial Issues*, 24(2), 140–156.

Gupta, V.K., D. Turban, S.A. Wasti and A. Sikdar (2009), 'The role of gender stereotypes in perceptions of entrepreneurs and intentions to become an entrepreneur', *Entrepreneurship Theory and Practice*, 33(2), 397–417.

Hall, D.T. 2002. *Careers In and Out of Organizations*. Los Angeles, CA: SAGE Publications.

Hall, D.T., B. Schneider and H.T. Nygren (1970), 'Personal factors in organizational identification', *Administrative Science Quarterly*, 176–190.

Haslam, S.A., C. Powell and J. Turner (2000), 'Social identity, self-categorization, and work motivation:

rethinking the contribution of the group to positive and sustainable organisational outcomes', *Applied Psychology*, 49(3), 319–339.

Heilman, M.E. (1983), 'Sex bias in work settings: the lack of fit model', *Research in Organizational Behavior*, 5, 269–298.

Heilman, M.E. (1997), 'Sex discrimination and the affirmative action remedy: the role of sex stereotypes', *Journal of Business Ethics*, 16(9), 877–889.

Heilman, M.E. (2001), 'Description and prescription: how gender stereotypes prevent women's nascent up the organizational ladder', *Journal of Social Issues*, 51(4), 657–674.

Hessels, J., M. Van Gelderen and R. Thurik (2008), 'Entrepreneurial aspirations motivations, and their drivers', *Small Business Economics*, 31(3), 323–339.

Hisrich, R. and C. Brush (1984), 'The woman entrepreneur: management skills and business problems', *Journal of Small Business Management*, 22(1), 30–37.

Hoang, H. and J. Gimeno (2010), 'Becoming a founder: how founder role identity affects entrepreneurial transitions and persistence in founding', *Journal of Business Venturing*, 25(1), 41–53.

Hogg, M.A. and D. Abrams (1988), *Social Identification: A Social Psychology of Intergroup Relations and Group Processes*, London: Routledge.

Hogg, M.A., D.J. Terry and K.M. White (1995), 'A tale of two theories: a critical comparison of identity theory with social identity theory', *Social Psychology Quarterly*, 58(4), 255–269.

Hytti, U. and J. Heinonen (2013), 'Heroic and humane entrepreneurs: identity work in entrepreneurship education', *Education + Training*, 55(8/9), 886–898.

Ibarra, H. (1999), 'Provisional selves: experimenting with image and identity in professional adaptation', *Administrative Science Quarterly*, 44(4), 764–791.

Ibarra, H. and R. Barbulescu (2010), 'Identity as narrative: prevalence, effectiveness, and consequences of narrative identity work in macro work role transitions', *Academy of Management Review*, 35(1), 135–154.

Jain, S., G. George and M. Maltarich (2009), 'Academics or entrepreneurs? Investigating role identity modification of university scientists involved in commercialization activity', *Research Policy*, 38(6), 922–935.

Jennings, J.E. and C.G. Brush (2013), 'Research on women entrepreneurs: challenges to (and from) the broader entrepreneurship literature?', *Academy of Management Annals*, 7(1), 663–715.

Johansson, A.W. (2004), 'Narrating the entrepreneur', *International Small Business Journal*, 22(3), 273–293.

Jones, R., J. Latham and M. Betta (2008), 'Narrative construction of the social entrepreneurial identity', *International Journal of Entrepreneurial Behavior and Research*, 14(5), 330–345.

Jung, D.I., S.B. Ehrlich, A.F. De Noble and K.B. Baik (2001), 'Entrepreneurial self-efficacy and its relationship to entrepreneurial action: a comparative study between the US and Korea', *Management International*, 6(1), 41.

Kalleberg, A.L. and K.T. Leicht (1991), 'Gender and organizational performance: determinants of small business survival and success', *Academy of Management Journal*, 34(1), 136–161.

Karlsson, T. and K. Moberg (2013), 'Improving perceived entrepreneurial abilities through education: exploratory testing of an entrepreneurial self efficacy scale in a pre-post setting', *International Journal of Management Education*, 11(1), 1–11.

Katz, D. and R.L. Kahn (1978), *The Social Psychology of Organization*, 2nd edn, New York: Wiley.

Kickul, J. and R.S. D'Intino (2005), 'Measure for measure: modeling entrepreneurial self-efficacy onto instrumental tasks within the new venture creation process', *New England Journal of Entrepreneurship*, 8(2), 6.

Kikooma, J.F. (2011), 'Negotiating enterprising identities: African woman entrepreneur stories of challenge, perseverance and triumph', *China–USA Business Review*, 10(7), 573–586.

Kirzner, I.M. (1973), *Competition and Entrepreneurship*, Chicago, IL: University of Chicago Press

Kolvereid, L. (1992), 'Growth aspirations among Norwegian entrepreneurs', *Journal of Business Venturing*, 7(3), 209–222.

Kreiner, G.E., E. Hollensbe, M.L. Sheep, B.R. Smith and N. Kataria (2015), 'Elasticity and the dialectic tensions of organizational identity: how can we hold together while we are pulling apart?', *Academy of Management Journal*, 58(4), 981–1011.
Krueger, N.F. and D.V. Brazeal (1994), 'Entrepreneurial potential and potential entrepreneurs', *Entrepreneurship Theory and Practice*, 18, 91–91.
Krueger, Norris F. and Alan L. Carsrud (1993), 'Entrepreneurs intentions, applying the theory of planned behavior', *Entrepreneurship and Regional Development*, 5(4), 315–330.
Krueger, N. and P.R. Dickson (1994), 'How believing in ourselves increases risk taking: perceived self-efficacy and opportunity recognition', *Decision Sciences*, 25(3), 385–400.
Krueger, N.F., M.D., Reilly and A.L. Carsrud (2000), 'Competing models of entrepreneurial intentions', *Journal of Business Venturing*, 15(5), 411–432
Lee, S.M. (1971), 'An empirical analysis of organizational identification', *Academy of Management Journal*, 14, 213–226.
Light, P.C. (2005), 'Searching for social entrepreneurs: who they might be, where they might be found, what they do', draft presented at the Conference of the Association for Research on Nonprofit and Voluntary Organizations, November.
Lindgren, M. and J. Packendorff (2008), 'Woman, teacher, entrepreneur: on identity construction in female entrepreneurs of Swedish independent schools', in I. Aaltio, P. Kyro and E. Sundin (eds), *Women Entrepreneurship and Social Capital*, Copenhagen: Copenhagen Business School Press, pp. 193–223.
Manolova, T., C. Brush, L. Edelman and K. Shaver (2012), 'One size does not fit all: entrepreneurial expectancies and growth intentions of US women and men nascent entrepreneurs', *Entrepreneurship Theory and Practice*, 24(1–2), 7–27.
Marková, H.R. (1987), 'In the interaction of opposites in psychological processes', *Journal for the Theory of Social Behavior*, 17, 279–299.
Markus, H. and P. Nurius (1986), 'Possible selves', *American Psychologist*, 41(9), 954.
McAdams, D.P. (1999), 'Personal narratives and the life story', in L. Pervin and O. John (eds), *Handbook of Personality: Theory and Research*, 2nd edn, New York: Guilford Press, pp. 478–500.
McCall, G.J. and J.L. Simmons (1978), *Identities and Interactions: An Examination of Human Associations in Everyday Life*, rev. edn, New York: Free Press
McGee, J.E., M. Peterson, S.L. Mueller and J.M. Sequeira (2009), 'Entrepreneurial self-efficacy: refining the measure', *Entrepreneurship Theory and Practice*, 33(4), 965–988.
MacNabb, A., J. McCoy, P. Weinreich and M. Northover (1993), 'Using identity structure analysis (ISA) to investigate female entrepreneurship', *Entrepreneurship and Regional Development*, 5(4), 301–313.
Mead, G.H. (1934), *Mind, Self and Society*, Chicago, IL: University of Chicago Press.
Meister, A., K.A. Jehn and S.M.B. Thatcher (2014), 'Feeling misidentified: the consequences of internal identity asymmetries for individuals at work', *Academy of Management Review*, 39(4), 488–512.
Merton, R.K. (1957), 'The role-set: problems in sociological theory', *British Journal of Sociology*, 8(2), 106–120.
Miller, D., L. Breton-Miller and R.H. Lester (2011), 'Family and lone founder ownership and strategic behaviour: social context, identity, and institutional logics', *Journal of Management Studies*, 48(1), 1–25.
Muehlenhard, C.L. and Z.D. Peterson (2011), 'Distinguishing between sex and gender: history, current conceptualization and implications', *Sex Roles*, 64(11), 791–803.
Mueller, S. and M.C. Dato-On (2008), 'Gender-role orientation as a determinant of entrepreneurial self-efficacy', *Journal of Developmental Entrepreneurship*, 13(1), 3–20.
Murnieks, C.Y., E. Mosakowski and M.S. Cardon (2014), 'Pathways of passion identity centrality, passion, and behavior among entrepreneurs', *Journal of Management*, 40(6), 1583–1606.
Naktiyok, A., C.N. Karabey and A.C. Gulluce (2010), 'Entrepreneurial self-efficacy and entrepreneur-

ial intention: the Turkish case', *International Entrepreneurship and Management Journal*, 6(4), 419–435.

Neck, H., C. Brush and E. Allen (2009), 'The landscape of social entrepreneurship', *Business Horizons*, 52, 13–19.

Nel, P., A. Martiz and O. Thongprovati (2010), 'Motherhood and entrepreneurship: the mumpreneur phenomenon', *International Journal of Organizational Innovation*, 3(1), 6–34.

Peredo, A.M. and J.J. Chrisman (2006), 'Toward a theory of community-based enterprise', *Academy of management Review*, 31(2), 309–328.

Peterman, N.E. and J. Kennedy (2003), 'Enterprise education: influencing students' perceptions of entrepreneurship', *Entrepreneurship Theory and Practice*, 28(2), 129–144.

Phillips, N., P. Tracey and N. Karra (2013), 'Building entrepreneurial tie portfolios through strategic homophily: the role of narrative identity work in venture creation and early growth', *Journal of Business Venturing*, 28(1), 134–150.

Piperopoulos, P. and D. Dimov (2015), 'Burst bubbles or build steam? Entrepreneurship education, entrepreneurial self-efficacy, and entrepreneurial intentions', *Journal of Small Business Management*, 53(4), 970–985.

Ridgeway, C. (2001), 'Gender, status, and leadership', *Journal of Social Issues*, 57(4), 637–655.

Rudman, L. and P. Glick (2001), 'Prescriptive gender stereotypes and backlash toward agentic women', *Journal of Social Issues*, 57(4), 743–762.

Schein, V.E. (1975), 'Relationships between sex role stereotypes and requisite management characteristics among female managers', *Journal of Applied Psychology*, 60(3), 340–344.

Scherer, R.F., J.S. Adams, S. Carley and F.A. Wiebe (1989), 'Role model performance effects on development of entrepreneurial career preference', *Entrepreneurship Theory and Practice*, 13, 53–81.

Schneider, B., D.T. Hall and H.T. Nygren (1971), 'Self image and job characteristics as correlates of changing organizational identification', *Human Relations*, 24(5), 397–416.

Schumpeter, J. (1935), *The Theory of Economic Development*, New York: Oxford University Press.

Shane, S., L. Kolvereid and P. Westhead (1991), 'An exploratory examination of the reasons leading to new firm formation across country and gender', *Journal of Business Venturing*, Special International Issue, 6(6), 431–446.

Shane, S. and S. Venkataraman (2000), 'The promise of entrepreneurship as a field of research', *Academy of Management Review*, 25(1), 217–236.

Shaver, K.G., N.M. Carter, W.B. Gartner and P.D. Reynolds (2001), 'Who is a nascent entrepreneur? Decision rules for identifying and selecting entrepreneurs in the Panel Study of Entrepreneurial Dynamics (PSED)', Technical Paper, Jönköping International School of Business, Jönköping.

Shepherd, D. and J.M. Haynie (2009), 'Birds of a feather don't always flock together: identity management in entrepreneurship', *Journal of Business Venturing*, 24, 316–337.

Smith, I.H. and W.P. Woodworth (2012), 'Developing social entrepreneurs and social innovators: a social identity and self-efficacy approach', *Academy of Management Learning and Education*, 11(3), 390–407.

Stanworth, M.J.K. and J. Curran (1976), 'Growth and the small firm – an alternative view', *Journal of Management Studies*, 13(2), 95–110.

Stryker, S. (1980), *Symbolic Interactionism: A Social Structural Version*, Menlo Park, CA: Benjamin/Cummings Publishing Company.

Stryker, S. (1987), 'Identity theory: developments and extensions', in Krysia Yardley and Terry Honess (eds), *Self and Identity: Psychosocial Perspectives*, London: Wiley, pp. 89–104.

Stryker, S. and P.J. Burke (2000), 'The past, present, and future of an identity theory', *Social Psychology Quarterly*, 63, 284–297.

Stryker, S. and R.T. Serpe (2012), 'Commitment, identity salience, and role behavior: theory and research example', in W. Ickes and E.S. Knowles (eds), *Personality, Roles, and Social Behavior*, New York: Springer, pp. 199–218.

Stryker, S. and A. Stratham (1985), 'Symbolic interaction and role theory', in I.G. Lindzey and E. Aronson (eds), *Handbook of Social Psychology*, New York: Random House, pp. 311–378.

Sveningsson, S. and M. Alvesson (2003), 'Managing managerial identities: organizational fragmentation, discourse and identity struggle', *Human Relations*, 56(10), 1163–1193.

Tajfel, H. (1974), 'Social identity and intergroup behaviour', *Information (International Social Science Council)*, 13(2), 65–93.

Tajfel, H.E. (1978), *Differentiation between Social Groups: Studies in the Social Psychology of Intergroup Relations*, London: Academic Press.

Tajfel, H. (1982), 'Social psychology of intergroup relations', *Annual Review of Psychology*, 33(1), 1–39.

Tajfel, H. and J.C. Turner (1979), 'An integrative theory of intergroup conflict' *Social Psychology of Intergroup Relations*, 33(47), 74.

Tajfel, H. and J.C. Turner (1986), 'The social identity theory of intergroup behavior', in W.G. Austin and S. Worchel (eds), *Psychology of Intergroup Relations*, 2nd edn, Chicago, IL: Nelson-Hall, pp. 7–24.

Tumasian, A. and R. Braun (2012), 'In the eye of the beholder: how regulatory focus and self-efficacy interact in influencing opportunity recognition', *Journal of Business Venturing*, 27(6), 622–636.

Turner, J.C. (1985), 'Social categorization and the self-concept: a social cognitive theory of group behavior', in E.J. Lawler (ed.), *Advances in Group Processes*, Vol. 2, Greenwich, CT: JAI Press, pp. 77–122.

Urban, B. (2006), 'Entrepreneurship in the rainbow nation: effect of cultural values and ESE on intentions', *Journal of Developmental Entrepreneurship*, 11(3), 171–186.

Vanevenhoven, J. and E. Liguori (2013), 'The impact of entrepreneurship education: introducing the entrepreneurship education project', *Journal of Small Business Management*, 51(3), 315–328.

Verheul, I., L. Uhlaner and R. Thurik (2005), 'Business accomplishments, gender and entrepreneurial self-image', *Journal of Business Venturing*, 20(4), 483–518.

Vesala, K., J. Peura and G. McElwee (2007), 'The split entrepreneurial identity of the farmer', *Journal of Small Business and Enterprise Development*, 14(1), 48–63.

Vesalainen, J. and T. Pihkala (2000), 'Entrepreneurial identity, intentions and the effect of the push-factor', *International Journal of Entrepreneurship*, 4, 105.

Vesper, K.H. (1999), 'Unfinished business (entrepreneurship) of the 20th century', paper presented at USASBE conference, San Diego, CA, January.

Vignoles, V.L., C. Regalia, C. Manzi, J. Golledge and E. Scabini (2006), 'Beyond self-esteem: influence of multiple motives on identity construction', *Journal of Personality and Social Psychology*, 90(2), 308.

Walker, E. and A. Brown (2004), 'What success factors are important to small business owners?', *International Small Business Journal*, 22(6), 577–594.

Warren, L. (2004), 'Negotiating entrepreneurial identity: communities of practice and changing discourses', *International Journal of Entrepreneurship and Innovation*, 5(1), 25–35.

Watson, T.J. (2009), 'Entrepreneurial action, identity work and the use of multiple discursive resources the case of a rapidly changing family business', *International Small Business Journal*, 27(3), 251–274.

Westhead, P. and M. Wright (1998), 'Novice, portfolio, and serial founders: are they different?', *Journal of Business Venturing*, 13(3), 173–204.

Woo, C.Y., A.C. Cooper and W.C. Dunkelberg (1991), 'The development and interpretation of entrepreneurial typologies', *Journal of Business Venturing*, 6(2), 93–114.

Woolf, V. (1992), *The Waves*. In *Collected Novels of Virginia Woolf*, London: Palgrave Macmillan, pp. 335–508.

# PART I

Aspirations

# 2 Developing entrepreneurial identity among start-ups' female founders in high-tech: policy implications from the Chilean case

*Katherina Kuschel and Juan-Pablo Labra*

## Entrepreneurial identity and female founders

The science, technology, engineering and mathematics (STEM) sector is driving economic growth (Csorny, 2013). Although female participation in the technology industry is growing (Institute for Women's Policy Research, 2016), the process is still slow and female founders represent an underexplored sample in the current literature of technology entrepreneurship and other social fields. Some studies on female founders focus on founders' career advancement and identity (Dy, Marlow, and Martin, 2017; Marlow and McAdam, 2015), and some report their participation rate (Berger and Kuckertz, 2016) and barriers they face while raising risk capital (Gatewood, Brush, Carter, Greene, and Hart, 2009) or scaling their businesses (Kenney and Patton, 2015; Kuschel et al., 2017).

### Entrepreneurial identity

Social identity is a component of the personal identity associated with the membership in social cohorts (Alvesson and Due Billing, 2009; Ashforth, 2001). 'Entrepreneur' may be a category or social identity. A review of the literature on entrepreneurial identity conducted by Ollila and Williams-Middleton (2012) reported that many of the articles reviewed present identity as a fixed state of existence, resulting in categorizations of entrepreneurial identities (e.g., Vesalainen and Pihkala, 2000). These categories include entrepreneurial identity as it relates to ethnicity, gender, career path and family framework, rather than as a method or process of construction and growth. A small portion of the literature reviewed discusses themes such as narrative and storytelling as a means towards shaping an entrepreneurial identity (Jones et al., 2008). Of this selection, some authors also propose entrepreneurial identity as being constructed in a situation (Down and Warren, 2008; Hytti, 2003; Johansson, 2004) and through socialization (Falck et al., 2012; Rigg and O'Dwyer, 2012).

## Entrepreneurial identity among women

Nadin (2007) studied female entrepreneurs in the care-giving sector and found that they often silenced their entrepreneurial identity and embraced their female identity, explained in terms of their desire for legitimacy and integrity. This study also displays the diversity of positioning and the potential contradictions (for example, between 'boss' and 'friend'). In other words, their sense of self is shaped by the social context, but these women also have agency to enact gendered practices and to contribute to the construction of their identity. Similarly, a study on the narratives of women in family business show how they challenge forces of patriarchy or paternalism by using an alternative discourse (Hamilton, 2006). A qualitative study on Spanish women entrepreneurs explained how women perceived the dissonance between the two discourses of being a woman and an entrepreneur, and how they engaged in practices of doing and redoing gender (Díaz-García and Welter, 2011).

Morris et al. (2006) pointed out the relevance of identity studies on female entrepreneurs. They found that modest- and high-growth entrepreneurs differ in how they view themselves, their families, their ventures and the larger environment. Their results suggest that growth is a deliberate choice and that women know the costs and benefits of growth and make cautious trade-off decisions.

To our knowledge, the question of how entrepreneurial identity is constructed among different industries has not been significantly explored in the literature, nor have the peculiarities of the identity construction of female founders in the technology industry and in countries outside the United States (US). This chapter aims to address the call for discussing two issues that have been not fully recognized within the entrepreneurship research agenda (Ahl, 2006; Bruni et al., 2005; Díaz-García and Welter, 2011): first, the use of masculine constructs that position women as the 'others' who need to adapt to existing systems and structures; and second, the vast heterogeneity of women's entrepreneurship.

## Female founders in the technology industry

The technology sector is, by a wide margin, a male-dominated industry. This fact has been well reported. According to estimations of Coleman and Robb (2009), 5–6 percent of high-technology entrepreneurs are women, and normally 3–5 percent of incubated or accelerated projects are led by women. A recent review of the literature revealed that there is very limited research on technology businesses run by women, and even less conducted in Latin American countries (Kuschel and Lepeley, 2016a). The same authors have analyzed the performance of women in high-technology industries and observed that, although the proportion of women in entrepreneurship generally compared with men has increased considerably, the proportion of women in the high-tech industry – an opportunity-driven type of entrepreneurship – is still very low. This evidence uncovers the need to increase efforts to bring women into high-tech participation. Furthermore, women in high-tech start-ups and entrepreneurship positions can be used as a proxy to assess the effects of women leadership (that is, women investors, executive women in tech companies, women leading networks). At the same time, this solution can also deal with the need to increase the proportion of women leaders in global and fast-growing industries by providing role models and access to meaningful education (Lepeley et al., 2016).

Although the identity construction of female founders in Latin America can be a prolific line of research and contribute to entrepreneurial education, the lack of knowledge in the literature is a limit to developing efforts to increase the total number of female entrepreneurs participating in economic activity (Cohoon et al., 2010).

In Chile in 2010, the government created the Start-Up Chile program. It is a public acceleration endeavor intended to expand the entrepreneurial ecosystem and promote a pro-entrepreneurship culture by 'importing entrepreneurs' (Leatherbee and Eesley, 2014). Today Chile is considered one of the main innovation hubs in Latin America and around the world, often referred to as 'Chilecon Valley' (*The Economist*, 2012; *Washington Post*, 2014).

The aim of this chapter is to identify and examine the elements that contribute to building identity among female entrepreneurs in the technology industry. Results will show the constraints and obstacles female entrepreneurs face when attempting to build their entrepreneurial identity and we expect that these may help policy-makers to design and implement new reforms that facilitate female participation in entrepreneurship. Higher women's entrepreneurship rate will serve as an important component of economic development supporting high growth among women entrepreneurs.

## Methodology

Specifically, this study is based on start-ups that participated in the Start-Up Chile acceleration program (SUP), a public grant of US$33,000 per project. The grant is 'equity-free', meaning that the government is not taking business participation. Normally, three batches of 80 start-ups have been selected each year since 2010. A start-up is a temporary organization designed to search for a repeatable and scalable business model (Blank, 2010). We have used data from the Start-Up Chile program because of its viability and ease of access and also because it may serve as a proxy of the total population of female founders in tech.

### Sample design

Our dataset consisted of 11 participants: (1) eight interviews conducted with female founders in technology who are participating or have participated in the Start-Up Chile acceleration program (therefore, from different 'batches', generations, or cohorts); (2) two interviews with female founders whose start-up was not accelerated; and (3) one venture capital investor (Table 2.1). By this procedure, we

**Table 2.1**   Sample characteristics

| Participant ID | Country | Industry | Age | Co-founders + employees | SUP Chile cohort |
|---|---|---|---|---|---|
| CM | Argentina | Fashion e-commerce | 32 | 4 + 6 | 11 |
| DG | Chile | E-commerce | 31 | 3 + 43 | 9 |
| LF | USA | Energy | 31 | 1 + 1 | 1 |
| PC | Chile | Education | 31 | 2 + 4 | – |
| GV | Estonia | Services (recruiting and hiring) | 29 | 3 + 2 | – |
| SC | Argentina | Software as a service | 32 | 4 + 6 | 6 |
| AS | Venezuela | Health technology | 26 | 5 + 0 | 11 |
| CN | Mexico | Entertainment | 33 | 3 + 0 | 6 |
| LC | Argentina | Software as a service | 32 | 4 + 6 | 6 |
| VK | Argentina | Venture capital investment | 40 | – | – |
| MA | Chile | Software as a service | 32 | 2 + 1 | 6 |

were able to identify the present and missing elements that are contributing to the identity-building of female founders. All interviews were conducted during 2015.

Some of the results are illustrated by the data of Start-Up Chile applicants and beneficiaries, provided by the organization. This was an anonymized database containing the demographic information for each start-up team participating in the acceleration program during five years between March 2010 and March 2015.

## Procedure

The female entrepreneurs included in the sample were contacted by e-mail and invited to participate in an interview. Before the interview, signature of an informed consent form was required. It contained a full explanation of the objectives and scope of the study in compliance with established ethical policies. Researchers and the participants signed the consent form and a copy was provided to participants. All participants agreed to participate in audio-recorded interviews.

To fulfill the requirements of the research questions, each interview followed a semi-structured script with questions related to the following six topics: (1) motivation and previous experience as entrepreneur; (2) role models; (3) funding needs and sources; (4) team structure; (5) common obstacles; and (6) networks used.

The following is a sample of the kind of questions included in the personal interviews: 'Why and how did you decide to apply for Start-Up Chile funding?' 'What are the future expectations for your venture?' 'As a female start-up founder, did you confront special challenges raising capital?' Interviews with the entrepreneurs lasted between 40 minutes and one hour and 20 minutes. After the interview, each audio recording was transcribed verbatim and entered into the Atlas.ti v.7.0 software for qualitative analysis.

## Analysis

We have applied a grounded theory approach to our data, defined as 'the discovery of theory from data systematically obtained from social research' (Glaser and Strauss, 1967: 2). Briefly, a grounded theory approach consists in simultaneous collection and analysis of data, a creation of analytic codes and categories developed from data and not by pre-existing conceptualizations, inductive construction of abstract categories, theoretical sampling to refine categories, and writing analytical memos as the stage between coding and writing.

# Results

We observed that the first wave of female entrepreneurs in technology from Latin American countries shared some common characteristics as they responded to an underdeveloped entrepreneurial ecosystem.

## Female participation

*Being a woman as being part of a minority*

Table 2.2 shows female participation in the Start-Up Chile program. In the first 13 funding rounds, 445 women out of 2,765 participants were selected for Start-Up Chile, meaning that 16 percent of the participants were female. We include these data as they may serve as a proxy for the total female participation in the technology industry in Chile.

Table 2.3 shows the number of selected start-ups per funding round and the gender of the start-ups' leaders. There is a strong correlation with the results presented in Table 2.2, as 15 percent of the projects were led by women.

Moreover, the staff of Start-Up Chile (SUP) were proud to grant more opportunities to women (15 percent on average) than other accelerators do. Other accelerators such as Y Combinator in Silicon Valley did not ask applicants to specify gender on their application for many years. Although 19.5 percent of the start-ups funded by YC during 2014 had women on the founding team (Altman, 2014), we do not have information about start-ups actually led by women. The estimation is 2–3 percent (Munguia, 2015).

Table 2.4 shows that, despite the lower number of female participants, there was no significant difference between genders when comparing the number of female chief executive officers (CEOs) versus the total number of female participants. Women who held CEO positions represented 44 percent of the total number of

**Table 2.2**    Female participation in Start-Up Chile

| Year | Funding round | Participants | | | % by gender | |
|------|------|------|------|------|------|------|
| | | Male | Female | Total | Male | Female |
| 2010 | 0 | 21 | 2 | 23 | 91 | 9 |
| 2011 | 1 | 169 | 26 | 195 | 87 | 13 |
| 2011 | 2 | 187 | 34 | 221 | 85 | 15 |
| 2012 | 3 | 184 | 39 | 223 | 83 | 17 |
| 2012 | 4 | 163 | 40 | 203 | 80 | 20 |
| 2012 | 5 | 180 | 46 | 226 | 80 | 20 |
| 2013 | 6 | 205 | 36 | 241 | 85 | 15 |
| 2013 | 7 | 202 | 36 | 238 | 85 | 15 |
| 2013 | 8 | 162 | 40 | 202 | 80 | 20 |
| 2014 | 9 | 202 | 46 | 248 | 81 | 19 |
| 2014 | 10 | 222 | 34 | 256 | 87 | 13 |
| 2014 | 11 | 210 | 29 | 239 | 88 | 12 |
| 2015 | 12 | 213 | 37 | 250 | 85 | 15 |
| Total participants | | 2320 | 445 | 2765 | 84 | 16 |

**Table 2.3**    Number of selected start-ups and gender of leader

| Year | Funding round | Start-ups | | | % by gender | |
|------|------|------|------|------|------|------|
| | | Male leader | Female leader | Total projects | Male leader | Female leader |
| 2010 | 0 | 20 | 2 | 22 | 91 | 9 |
| 2011 | 1 | 96 | 11 | 107 | 90 | 10 |
| 2011 | 2 | 133 | 21 | 154 | 86 | 14 |
| 2012 | 3 | 85 | 15 | 100 | 85 | 15 |
| 2012 | 4 | 82 | 18 | 100 | 82 | 18 |
| 2012 | 5 | 85 | 16 | 101 | 84 | 16 |
| 2013 | 6 | 89 | 16 | 105 | 85 | 15 |
| 2013 | 7 | 82 | 18 | 100 | 82 | 18 |
| 2013 | 8 | 67 | 18 | 85 | 79 | 21 |
| 2014 | 9 | 74 | 26 | 100 | 74 | 26 |
| 2014 | 10 | 90 | 10 | 100 | 90 | 10 |
| 2014 | 11 | 89 | 10 | 99 | 90 | 10 |
| 2015 | 12 | 86 | 14 | 100 | 86 | 14 |
| Total teams | | 1078 | 195 | 1273 | 85 | 15 |

**Table 2.4**   Number of selected start-ups and gender of the leader

| Gender/Role | Participants | CEOs | CEOs vs Participants |
| --- | --- | --- | --- |
| Male | 2320 | 1078 | 46% |
| Female | 445 | 195 | 44% |
| Total | 2765 | 1273 | |

women who participated in the program, versus 46 percent in the case of male CEOs.

These numbers were apparent in every meeting, seminar with visiting consultants, networking event, meeting with investors, or demo day. [1] The evident low participation of women in the accelerator program was taken for granted, as it was similar to the situation of other accelerators and companies of the technology industry.

> Somebody from the audience came to me and said, 'I loved seeing a woman at a demo day.' Then I realized that although there were more women as members of the teams that participated in the competition, the one who pitched was always a man. (CM, Argentina, SUP Gen 11)

### Female founder as an element of differentiation

Tech ventures founders believed that having a female co-founder might benefit the company by giving the start-up some visibility:

> Beyond the fact that our start-up is about women's clothing, thinking strategically, when we had to decide who was going to remain as the public face of our project I said, 'It's better for us that I'll be the leader, there are only a few women in this field (tech entrepreneurship).' I do all of the pitches. (CM, Argentina, SUP Gen 11)

Female founders had two different attitudes regarding gender, but it was difficult to find female founders who were neutral to gender. At the very beginning, many if not all female founders were gender-blind. Then they started to experience obstacles with clients, suppliers and potential investors in Chile; then they began to realize that they had experienced gender discrimination in Chile. They first decided to react aggressively to this type of discrimination by defending feminism, gathering themselves to build a women's group, and building their own networks. Although some women understood that there were more benefits to being 'the only woman in the room', the majority tended to victimize themselves. For those women who decided to use gender as a differentiator, they gained several benefits for the company, for the team and for themselves (that is, self-confidence):

> As there are not many women in this field, I am easily remembered everywhere. (LF, United States, SUP Gen 1)

I never felt less for being a woman, in fact, I never felt any issues for being a woman. Instead, I always tried to it use it as an advantage to me. (LC, Argentina, SUP Gen 6)

## No appropriate role models

For this first wave of female entrepreneurs in technology, low female participation in the technology industry was the norm. Female founders had no appropriate role models to follow in the tech industry. There was a lack of role models representing a female entrepreneur, a female founder, a successful female entrepreneur, a successful founder in Latin America or a more 'balanced' entrepreneur. Any meeting or seminar a female entrepreneur went to was full of men, without women as keynote speakers. Some participants mentioned Sheryl Sandberg, Facebook chief operating officer, although her profile does not necessarily fit the role of a childless, young female founder.

Some female and male teachers did serve the role of motivator, enhancing women's careers. For many women, the real role model came from their families: the entrepreneurial activity of the romantic partner or the father and the multiple roles of the mother.

### The romantic partner as entrepreneur

I helped my husband when he started his entrepreneurship, and he helped me back when I started mine. He used to say, 'the most difficult part of being an entrepreneur is to be aware and take actions that nobody else will do for you'. (DG, Chile, SUP Gen 9)

### The father as entrepreneur

My dad was always an entrepreneur. Since I was a child, I saw him making millions and then failing to the point that we didn't even have food on our table. And then again, the whole success and failure cycle would repeat over and over. This had a big impact in the way I see things in life. For me, to have a corporate job with all its financial stability and predefined career path was always completely out of the picture. It's not that I was explicitly taught to think like that, it's just that my dad had the courage to take risks and I learnt that from him. I have skills to face uncertainty that others who are more conservative do not have. (SC, Argentina, SUP Gen 6)

### The mother as a working woman

I had a working mother. She was a science teacher. And she had friends that were also working mothers. She was always a fighter. (PC, Chile, not-accelerated)

## No network

For the first wave of female founders, there were no professional networks available. In the US, there are some networks in the Silicon Valley area, for example Women 2.0, Women Who Tech, Women Tech Founders, Girls in Tech, Women

Who Code. Girls in Tech and Women Who Code were foreign networks, born in the US, that initiated activities in Chile in 2013 and gained traction and visibility in the media over the last few years.

Moreover, female founders usually do not participate actively in these networks at the early stages of their start-up. Low network activity is explained by the fact that female founders are frantically working to build their start-ups and do not want to get distracted. Female networks also replicate gender patterns by not including men in the conversation.

> In Estonia, we have an organization called Big Sisters. I participate in almost every event they have. But most of our activities aren't exclusively female focused. Most of them are focused in start-ups, or in marketing topics . . . topics that don't have a gender. So, I haven't actually been part of a network intended only for women. (GV, Estonia, not-accelerated)

> I started to get closer to other female colleagues at Start-Up Chile . . . We have a group and we get together to speak about a bunch of things, not only personal stuff but about also the entrepreneurship process that we are going through as female entrepreneurs and it's very helpful . . . I think that we have reached a stage where what female empowering communities should do is to provide more down-to-earth tools, right? Mentorship, access to investors, technical knowledge, don't you think? If I want to participate in a funding round, what kind of paperwork do I need? And I think that many of these female empowering communities are still in the stage of 'don't be afraid, you can do it, we're here to help you,' right? More as motivators, and as emotional helpers than as providers of resources that will really help you get through with your business idea. (CN, Mexico, SUP Gen 6)

> I see a trend among all of my friends from the tech and start-ups environment, they have a strong commitment to motivate other female entrepreneurs, to tell their story to make themselves more visible, to inspire and help others to actively participate in this generation of female entrepreneurs. (SC, Argentina, SUP Gen 6)

At the same time, networks are not always perceived as 'helpful' for venture development:

> I believe that there is a very negative system of false help. That you have to go through accelerators that are going to help, that you have to have a mentor, and that everyone is willing to help you . . . I didn't receive help from anybody. The guy that started Mercadolibre didn't receive any help. The Groupon guys didn't receive any help. (VK, Argentina, Angel Investor)

## Teams

### Small teams

Start-up Chile application limits the number of team members to a maximum of three people. Table 2.5 shows that participants of the first 13 financing rounds

**Table 2.5**   Team size

| Team size | No. of teams | % of teams |
|---|---|---|
| One member | 309 | 24 |
| Two members | 446 | 35 |
| Three members | 518 | 41 |
| Total | 1273 | 100 |

**Table 2.6a**   Team leadership by gender and team size: one-member teams

| Team leader | No. of teams | % of teams |
|---|---|---|
| Male | 270 | 87 |
| Female | 39 | 13 |
| Total one-member teams | 309 | 100 |

**Table 2.6b**   Team leadership by gender and team size: two and three-member teams

| Team leader | No. of teams | % of teams |
|---|---|---|
| Male | 808 | 84 |
| Female | 156 | 16 |
| Total two- and three-member teams | 964 | 100 |

grouped in 1,273 teams that had one, two and three members in 24 percent, 35 percent and 41 percent of the sample, respectively.

Tables 2.6a and 2.6b show that team leadership by gender closely follows the gender participation presented in Table 2.2. Men are leaders of 84 percent of two and three-member teams.

Table 2.7 shows an analysis of gender composition of two and three-member teams: 65 percent of teams have male-only members, 3 percent of teams have female-only members, 32 percent of teams are mixed-gender.

It is interesting to contrast the small number of female-only teams shown in Table 2.7 with the leadership role that females adopt within mixed-gender teams. Table 2.8 shows that, within mixed-gender teams, 42 percent of teams are led by a female CEO.

Opening up the composition and leadership within three-member teams, Table 2.9 shows that female leadership is relevant in mixed-gender groups, with a female founder leading 82 percent of the teams that have two female members.

**Table 2.7**   Gender composition of two- and three-member teams

| Team composition | No. of teams | % of teams |
| --- | --- | --- |
| Only male members | 624 | 65 |
| Only female members | 31 | 3 |
| Mixed-gender members | 309 | 32 |
| Total two- and three-member teams | 964 | 100 |

**Table 2.8**   Leadership by gender composition within mixed-gender teams of two and three members

| Leader gender | Team size | | |
| --- | --- | --- | --- |
| | Two members | Three members | Total |
| Male | 74 | 104 | 178 |
| Female | 52 | 79 | 131 |
| Total teams | 126 | 183 | 309 |
| % Male leader | 59 | 57 | 58 |
| % Female leader | 41 | 43 | 42 |
| Total | 100 | 100 | 100 |

**Table 2.9**   Leadership by gender composition within mixed-gender teams of three members

| Leader gender | Team composition | | |
| --- | --- | --- | --- |
| | Two male, one female | One male, two female | Total |
| Male | 97 | 7 | 104 |
| Female | 47 | 32 | 79 |
| Total teams | 144 | 39 | 183 |
| % Male leader | 67 | 18 | 57 |
| % Female leader | 33 | 82 | 43 |
| Total | 100 | 100 | 100 |

Summarizing, Start-up Chile teams show that women prefer to work either individually or in mixed-gender groups. In these teams, females adopt the CEO position in 42 percent of cases.

*Trust-based teams*

The female founders who were interviewed built their teams based on trust. At the beginning, they formed a small team with friends with whom they had long relationships, or their romantic partner. They feel that trust-based partnerships reduce risk:

> I met my business partner in high school. Since back then he is somebody who I trust very much. Trust is key. He knows my bank account password. That level of trust, for sure. (MA, Chile, SUP Gen 10)

> It's not easy to have a business partner in entrepreneurship. You have to trust and get to know the other person so much as to get along on a journey that will have highs and lows. To be able to delegate, know about strengths and weaknesses, and say, 'okay, you take care of this . . . or how do we complement each other. It's not an easy job to start working right away in an entrepreneurship with somebody that you don't know. (PC, Chile, not-accelerated)

For some of them, their romantic partner or best friend seems to fit the business partner's requirement of trust:

> I started with my husband. He is still co-owner of the company, but in the day-to-day activities, it's only me as full time. He has another job. They told us that being copreneurs is a red flag for investors. (CM, Argentina, SUP Gen 11)

> My partner and I, we both quitted Groupon and started our own business. (DG, Chile, SUP Gen 9)

The criterion for team-building was not specialization in another area of the company, as experts recommend. This was not considered as a handicap, because later on they include developers as business partners:

> My business partner and I have been friends since we were 5 years old . . . our first company was a software development company. My partner did the sales and I did project management, and we met our new partners outsourcing part of our work as they were our vendors. And we said, 'why don't we work as partners?' In order to scale up in a much more solid way.' (SC, Argentina, SUP Gen 6)

## Building self-confidence

Female founders who were interviewed for this study acknowledge that their male counterparts are far more confident than they are. Part of their challenge is to become, or at least 'act', as a confident founder:

> We started without fear, empowered. You have to believe in yourself. My business partners are the two individuals that believe more in themselves in the world. That's not the problem. I am the one who stays behind saying, 'hey, what if this or that happens?' But the courage that we've had with our website has been great. I get infected by my partner's level of trust. They have an incredible courage. If they believe too much in something, I can't be a naysayer. (DG, Chile, SUP Gen 9)

You have to believe in yourself and get out there to make things happen. There will be times when you will not have a clue, and therefore, the idea is to have a solid support system, with good suppliers, good consultants, and good employees. (VK, Argentina, Angel Investor)

At the end of the day, your gender doesn't matter, the road of innovation and entrepreneurship is a hard road intended for those who have high levels of self-confidence and self-esteem. For those who wish to find opportunities. There are limits, for sure, the ones that you impose upon yourself. (AS, Venezuela, SUP Gen 11)

## Discussion

### Identity of the first wave of female techpreneurs

These women have created entirely original ventures. The start-up founders lack awareness of who they are (for example, business women, innovators, saleswomen), what they want to do (business model), or how they will do it (business plan or execution). Female founders are working on something they have never been taught to do (as well as male founders). The tech industry is, by definition, an uncertain path.

Our study revealed five elements that contribute to the female founder identity: female participation in the tech industry, role models, network, team and attitude, as shown in Figure 2.1.

First, being part of a well-known accelerator program gives entrepreneurs a social identity acknowledged by family, friends, other entrepreneurs, co-founders and investors. Being part of a 'minority' also makes female founders feel special. At the same time, they use their gender as a differentiation element which gives them an advantage because they become more memorable. This finding is in line with 'optimal distinctiveness theory' which states that individuals desire to attain an optimal balance of inclusion and distinctiveness within and between social groups and situations (Brewer, 2003).

Second, identity of the first wave of female founders in Latin America was 'self-made', highlighting attributes and virtues of many people they admired. Although most of their role models were not female founders, in order to illustrate and negotiate an entrepreneurial identity they often established provisional identities (Ibarra, 1999) through the early stages of the venture's formation. The cultural factor can also play a role. Peus et al. (2015) found in a sample of 76 mid- to upper-level female managers from China, India, Singapore and the US that a role model is a critical factor for career advancement and success. Although they were managers, and not entrepreneurs as in our sample, the finding is relevant for our discussion on role models for women. Peus et al. (2015) compared the female employees in those countries. In their results, while U.S. managers generally referred to role models from their professional lives, in China and India role models were usually taken from the private sphere (that is, the mother). Our Latin American data confirmed

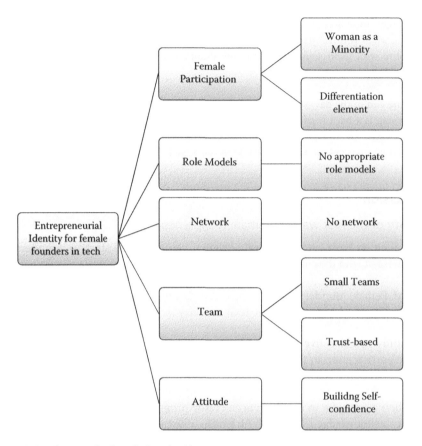

**Figure 2.1**    Elements for female founder identity

the results of Asian data, whose culture is family-oriented and not individualistic as in the U.S.

Third, female founders did not have emotional or business support from a network. The lack of network affected their socialization and adjustment to their role. On the other hand, they preferred to trust their own team instead of being distracted by actively participating in a network that was only just beginning at that time.

Fourth, contrary to the current academic advice of building an effective and functional team based on the specialization of each member, female founders preferred to build small and trust-based teams. Some female founders work with their romantic partner in the management team (Kuschel and Lepeley, 2016b). Although this type of team may seem to be a disadvantage at the onset of their entrepreneurial venture, it ultimately allowed them to leverage their self-confidence. The female founders worked to both gain legitimacy (through storytelling) and then maintain legitimacy (through feedback from their team) in the desired role of 'entrepreneur' (Somers, 1994; Kuschel and Lepeley, 2016b; Williams-Middleton, 2013).

Lastly, female founders reported that the struggles and challenges they have faced in building a successful company have, at the same time, enabled them to build self-confidence, which is a required asset to navigate through the uncertainties of the technology industry. We conclude that these five elements help women to construct their identity, which is an unstable result of these beliefs, people, and reinterpretation of facts (failures and successes).

## Conclusion

### Contribution

We have characterized the elements that female founders of technology ventures utilize to build their identity in the Chilean context. An understanding of entre-preneurial identity and identity construction will allow policy development and accelerating growth.

### Policy implications for early stages of entrepreneurial ecosystems

Many developing countries are trying to emulate the Chilean entrepreneurial eco-system. We suggest that these countries deploy initiatives to foster the construc-tion of social identity and the sense of belonging to a community among female entrepreneurs that not only funds start-ups but also provides them with advice from influential and effective leaders (Haslam and Reicher, 2007). Identity con-struction needs to be seen as equally important as entrepreneurial education and venture creation (Ollila and Williams-Middleton, 2013). Motivation and a frame-work of 'positive relationship between women and technology' in overall society will decrease the 'identity threat' and will assure the performance and persistence of women in STEM (Lee et al., 2015).

### Policy implications for advanced stages of entrepreneurial ecosystems

The entrepreneurial ecosystem in Chile has now developed into a new stage. In this new stage, the Chilean ecosystem provides the second wave of female found-ers with more resources. They have networking activities intended for women in business (for example, Mujeres Empresarias, Emprendedoras de Chile), and par-ticularly intended for women in technology ventures (for example, Girls in Tech). Business angels who invest in Chile are now gathered around a network called Chile Global Angels. Access to these networks has enabled an increasing number of female entrepreneurs to participate in entrepreneurial activities, helping to close the gender gap of participation widely reported in the technology industry.

## Suggestions for further research

A number of initiatives, companies and programs are diligently working to close the female entrepreneurs' participation gap. Although progress is certainly being made, some may argue that it has not been quick enough. For the industry to radically transform, it must also be influenced by the rise of successful women-led start-ups augmented by an influx of investment for their companies. Having more female tech executives will affect the pace of change. We suggest examining the impact of the first wave of female founders on further generations of women-led start-ups. Moreover, women in the business world are helping others to achieve their goals through mentoring, a move that could improve the outlook for women in technology.

Female entrepreneurial identity construction requires further investigation and discussion. The process of founding a business is, for most people, a period of transition entailing taking on a new role. Such a transition will often result in a change of values and beliefs. For some women, values ascribed to the entrepreneur will conflict with conventional feminine values. Our interviewees reported conflicting values, which need to be further explored and studied to find out whether, or how, this could affect identity construction. More research is needed on the dynamic identity claiming strategies that female tech entrepreneurs engage in to gain legitimacy (Lepisto et al., 2015).

### Note

1   A demo day is an accelerator event where the start-ups are presented to the investors. Each team (previously selected) presents their business model in a 'pitch' format (a two- to five-minute presentation).

## References

Ahl, H. (2006), 'Why research on women entrepreneurs needs new directions', *Entrepreneurship Theory and Practice*, 30(5), 595–621.

Altman, S. (2014), 'Diversity and startups', accessed February 8, 2016 at http://blog.ycombinator.com/diversity-and-startups.

Alvesson, M. and Y. Due Billing (2009), *Understanding Gender and Organizations*, 2nd edn. London: SAGE Publications.

Ashforth, B.E. (2001), *Role Transitions in Organizational Life: An Identity-Based Perspective*. Mahwah, NJ: Lawrence Erlbaum Associates Publishers.

Berger, E.S.C. and A. Kuckertz (2016), 'Female entrepreneurship in startup ecosystems worldwide', *Journal of Business Research*, 69(11), 5163–5168.

Blank, S. (2010), 'What's a startup? First principles', accessed February 8, 2016 at http://steveblank.com/2010/01/25/whats-a-startup-first-principles.

Brewer, M.B. (2003), 'Optimal distinctiveness, social identity, and the self', in M. Leary and J. Tangney (eds), *Handbook of Self and Identity* (pp. 480–491). New York: Guilford.

Bruni, A., S. Gherardi and B. Poggio (2005). *Gender and Entrepreneurship: An Ethnographic Approach*. London: Routledge.

Cohoon, J.M.G., V. Wadhwa and L. Mitchell (2010), 'Are Successful Women Entrepreneurs Different from Men?', Kansas City, MO: Ewing Marion Kauffmann Foundation of Entrepreneurship, accessed

September 11, 2017 at http://www.kauffman.org/~/media/kauffman_org/research%20reports%20 and%20covers/2009/07/successful_women_entrepreneurs_510.pdf.

Coleman, S. and A. Robb (2009), 'Characteristics of new firms: a comparison by gender', *Small Business Economics*, 33(4), 397.

Csorny, L. (2013), 'Careers in the growing field of information technology services', US Department of Labor, Bureau of Labor Statistics, accessed February 8, 2016 at http://www.bls.gov/opub/btn/ volume-2/careers-in-growing-fieldof-information-technology-services.htm.

Díaz-García, M.C. and F. Welter (2011), 'Gender identities and practices: interpreting women entrepre-neurs' narratives', *International Small Business Journal*, 31(4), 384–404.

Down, S. and L. Warren (2008), 'Constructing narratives of enterprise: clichés and entrepreneurial self-identity', *International Journal of Entrepreneurial Behaviour and Research*, 14(1), 4–23.

Dy, A.M., S. Marlow and L. Martin (2017), 'A web of opportunity or the same old story? Women digital entrepreneurs and intersectionality theory', *Human Relations*, 70(3), 286–311.

*The Economist* (2012), 'The lure of Chilecon Valley', accessed February 8, 2016 at http://www.economist. com/node/21564589.

Falck, O., S. Heblich and E. Luedemann (2012), 'Identity and entrepreneurship: do school peers shape entrepreneurial intentions?', *Small Business Economics*, 39(1), 39–59.

Gatewood, E.J., C.G. Brush, N.M. Carter, P.G. Greene and M.M. Hart (2009), 'Diana: a symbol of women entrepreneurs' hunt for knowledge, money, and the rewards of entrepreneurship', *Small Business Economics*, 32(2): 129–144.

Glaser, B.G. and A.L. Strauss (1967), *The Discovery of Grounded Theory: Strategies for Qualitative Research*. New York: Aldine de Gruyter.

Hamilton, E. (2006), 'Whose story is it anyway? Narrative accounts of the role of women in founding and establishing family businesses', *International Small Business Journal*, 24(3), 253–271.

Haslam, S.A. and S. Reicher (2007), 'Identity entrepreneurship and the consequences of identity failure: the dynamics of leadership in the BBC Prison Study', *Social Psychology Quarterly*, 70(2), 125-147.

Hytti, U. (2003), 'Stories of entrepreneurs: narrative construction of identities', Turku University dis-sertation, Publications of the Turku School of Economics and Business Administration, Series A.1, accessed September 11, 2017 at http://www.doria.fi/bitstream/handle/10024/98535/Ae1_2003hytti. pdf?sequence=2.

Ibarra, H. (1999), 'Provisional selves: experimenting with image and identity in professional adaptation', *Administrative Science Quarterly*, 44(4), 764-791.

Institute for Women's Policy Research (2016), 'Pathways to Equity: Narrowing the Wage Gap by Improving Women's Access to Good Middle-Skill Jobs', Washington: Institute for Women's Policy Research, accessed 14 November 2017 at https://iwpr.org/publications/pathways-to-equity-narrow ing-the-wage-gap-by-improving-womens-access-to-good-middle-skill-jobs/.

Johansson, A.W. (2004), 'Narrating the entrepreneur', *International Small Business Journal*, 22(3), 273-293.

Jones, R., J. Latham and M. Betta (2008), 'Narrative construction of the social entrepreneurial identity', *International Journal of Entrepreneurial Behavior and Research*, 14(5), 330–345.

Kenney, M. and D. Patton (2015), 'Gender, ethnicity and entrepreneurship in initial public offerings: illustrations from an open database', *Research Policy*, 44(9), 1773–1784.

Kuschel, K. and M.T. Lepeley (2016a), 'Women startups in technology: literature review and research agenda to improve participation', *International Journal of Entrepreneurship and Small Business*, 27(2/3), 333–346.

Kuschel, K. and M.T. Lepeley (2016b), 'Copreneurial women in start-ups: growth-oriented or lifestyle? An aid for technology industry investors', *Academia Revista Latinoamericana de Administración*, 29(2), 1–19.

Kuschel, K., M.T. Lepeley, F. Espinosa and S. Gutierréz (2017), 'Funding challenges of Latin American

Women Start-up Founders in the Technology Industry', *Cross Cultural & Strategic Management*, 24(2), 310-331.

Leatherbee, M. and C.E. Eesley (2014), 'Boulevard of broken behaviors: socio-psychological mechanisms of entrepreneurship policies', available at SSRN: https://ssrn.com/abstract=2488712.

Lee, J.K., A.T. Alston and K.B. Kahn (2015), 'Identity threat in the classroom: review of women's motivational experiences in the sciences', *Translational Issues in Psychological Science*, 1(4), 321–330.

Lepeley, M.T., E. von Kimakowitz and R. Bardy (2016), *Human Centered Management in Executive Education. Global Imperatives, Innovation, and New Directions*. London: Palgrave Macmillan.

Lepisto, D.A., E. Crosina and M.G. Pratt (2015), 'Identity work within and beyond the professions: toward a theoretical integration and extension', in A. Desilva and M. Aparicio (eds), *International Handbook of Professional Identities* (pp. 11–37). Rosemead, CA: Scientific & Academic Publishing.

Marlow, S., and M. McAdam (2015), 'Incubation or induction? Gendered identity work in the context of technology business incubation', *Entrepreneurship Theory and Practice*, 39(4), 791–816.

Morris, M.H., N.N. Miyasaki, C.E. Watters and S.M. Coombes (2006), 'The dilemma of growth: understanding venture size choices of women entrepreneurs', *Journal of Small Business Management*, 44(2), 221–244.

Munguia, H. (2015), '78 percent of Y Combinator startups have no female founders — and that's progress', accessed February 8, 2016 at http://fivethirtyeight.com/datalab/78-percent-of-y-combinator-startups-have-no-female-founders-and-thats-progress.

Nadin, S. (2007), 'Entrepreneurial identity in the care sector: navigating the contraditions', *Women in Management Review*, 22(6), 456-467.

Ollila, S. and K. Williams-Middleton (2012), 'Entrepreneurial identity construction – what does existing literature tell us?', paper presented at Institute of Small Business and Entrepreneurship Conference, accessed February 8, 2016 at http://publications.lib.chalmers.se/records/fulltext/162178/local_162178.pdf.

Ollila, S. and K. Williams-Middleton (2013), 'Exploring entrepreneurial identity construction: the case of an action-based entrepreneurship education', paper presented at Nordic Academy of Management (NFF) Conference 2013, Iceland, accessed February 8, 2016 at http://publications.lib.chalmers.se/records/fulltext/179509/local_179509.pdf.

Peus, C., S. Braun and K. Knipfer (2015), 'On becoming a leader in Asia and America: empirical evidence from women managers', *Leadership Quarterly*, 26, 55-67.

Rigg, C. and B. O'Dwyer (2012), 'Becoming an entrepreneur: researching the role of mentors in identity construction', *Education + Training*, 54(4), 319-329.

Somers, M.R. (1994), 'The narrative constitution of identity: a relational and network approach', *Theory and Society*, 23(5), 605-649.

Vesalainen, J. and T. Pihkala (2000), 'Entrepreneurial identity, intentions and the effect of the push-factor', *International Journal of Entrepreneurship*, 4, 111-136.

*Washington Post* (2014), 'Chile teaches the world a lesson about innovation', accessed February 8, 2016 at http://www.washingtonpost.com/news/innovations/wp/2014/06/11/chile-teaches-the-world-a-lesson-about-innovation.

Williams-Middleton, K. (2013), 'Becoming entrepreneurial: gaining legitimacy in the nascent phase', *International Journal of Entrepreneurial Behaviour and Research*, 19(4), 404-424.

# 3 Perception of success of men and women entrepreneurs: a social identity approach

*Rachida Justo,\* Cristina Cruz and Julio O. De Castro*

An important body of research on female entrepreneurship has focused on women's perceptions and expectations from the entrepreneurial experience (Bird and Brush, 2002; Cliff, 1998; Olson and Currie, 1992). On the one hand, several scholars have highlighted the importance of the women's non-monetary expectations from the business as a key to understand gender differences in business ownership patterns (e.g., MacNabb et al., 1993; Buttner and Moore, 1997; Fenwick and Hutton, 2000; Walker and Brown, 2004). Others, however, have found little gender-based variance in values and attitudes toward success (e.g., Catley and Hamilton, 1998; Kalleberg and Leicht, 1991; Shane et al., 1991).

Trying to reconcile both perspectives, this chapter subscribes to a post-structural feminist view which, rather than searching for universal sex differences, recognizes that men and women entrepreneurs have both similarities and differences that are prompted by specific contextual factors (Ahl, 2006; Cliff et al., 2004). Accordingly, we recognize that entrepreneurs' perceptions of success do not necessarily conform to established gender archetypes, but we examine under which conditions men and women entrepreneurs differ in the importance they attach to different success factors. We pay special attention to parenthood and argue that this contextual factor drives some important, yet often overlooked, heterogeneities that exist within men and women entrepreneurs (de Bruin et al., 2006; Hughes and Jennings, 2012; Hughes et al., 2012).

Using social identity theory (SIT) and insights drawn from the literature on women entrepreneurs, we contend that parenthood, and especially the presence of dependent children, is a powerful driver of change in entrepreneurs' perceptions of success for both men and women entrepreneurs, yet those effects are stronger for women entrepreneurs.

We provide four main contributions to the literature. First, we bring SIT into the entrepreneurship literature and to the examination of gender in entrepreneurship. SIT provides a useful approach to analyze sex differences in entrepreneurs' perceptions of success, one that allows us to decouple the analysis from approaches that rely on stereotypical examinations.

Second, we analyze the effect of the work–family interface on shifts in perceptions and values. Although the entrepreneurship literature provides empirical evidence of the relationship between family responsibilities and women's initial start-up motivation as a solution to the dual domains of work and family (Caputo and Dolinsky, 1998; Boden, 1999; DeMartino and Barbato, 2003; Marlow, 1997; Lombard, 2001), few studies have taken the analysis further to assess the impact on perceptions of success. Moreover, while it is taken for granted that for women entrepreneurs balancing work and family is fundamental, scholars have only recently started to consider men with respect to these issues (Ahl, 2006; Jennings and McDougald, 2007; Kalnins and Williams, 2014).

Third, we expand the measure of an entrepreneur's perception of success by including non-monetary measures of success under its different dimensions and by gathering perceptions from direct reports by the entrepreneur. Prior research has traditionally assessed success indirectly, from measures of motivation for start-up, which can be colored by other elements. Moreover, rather than grouping all non-monetary criteria under the same broad concept, we separate them into two distinct dimensions. The first is an 'intrinsic' and feminine dimension which relates to the importance of the entrepreneur's position in society, and status as a parent and as job provider. The second, an 'independence' dimension, is rather masculine in nature, which stresses freedom and self-realization as the main expectations from self-employment.

Lastly, by focusing on disentangling within-gender differences in business aspirations, we respond to calls from gender scholars to examine the heterogeneity present amongst women entrepreneurs (de Bruin et al., 2006; Hughes and Jennings, 2012; Hughes et al., 2012), and address how work–family concerns also affect male entrepreneurs. Building on SIT we add to the understanding of this heterogeneity. Specifically, we examine how women and men entrepreneurs' perception may be shaped by their individual-level characteristics, that is, the family context in which they are embedded (Hughes et al., 2012).

## Theoretical background and hypotheses

### Defining business success: intrinsic and extrinsic values

A growing number of scholars have called for an exploration of new definitions of business success, ones that extend beyond financial performance (Hudson et al., 2001; Walker and Brown, 2004). They contend that traditional measures of success do not account for non-monetary measures (Fenwick and Hutton, 2000; Still and Timms, 2000; Rogers, 2005). In particular, researchers have highlighted the importance of female non-monetary expectations from the business as a key to understanding gender differences in small business ownership patterns (MacNabb et al., 1993; Buttner and Moore, 1997; Fenwick and Hutton, 2000; Walker and Brown, 2004). However useful this perspective is, prior studies exploring attitudes and perceptions of success have found little gender-based variance in fundamental values (Catley and Hamilton, 1998; Eagly, 1995; Fagenson, 1993; Kalleberg and Leight, 1991; Shane et al., 1991).

We contend that confounding variables might be causing those conflicting results. While there seems to be consensus on categorizing financial achievement as masculine in nature, non-monetary goals are less clear-cut: they include multiple – yet differing – constructs such as job satisfaction, reputation and flexibility that could be included in either the feminine or the masculine category, according to how they are interpreted.

In assessing feminine and masculine categories we follow the research of Bird and Brush (2002), who define traditional entrepreneurial values as including 'financial success (survival, profits and wealth), power in demonstrations of personal efficacy and business competitive advantage, personal or ego gratification seen in autonomy accorded to the self-employed' (ibid.: 53). In this chapter we argue that these aspects are consistent with Bem's (1981) index of what is culturally accepted as masculine in nature. Bem's (1981) study shows indeed that concepts such as competitive advantage, ego or autonomy are considered to be masculine attributes. This contrasts with feminine values as described by Bird and Brush, who consider them as 'more existential than driven towards definable goals, reflective of the personal values of the founder and oriented toward well-being, cooperation and caring, self-determinations and preservation of relationships' (Bird and Brush, 1992: 53). This definition also coincides with Bem's femininity scale attributes.

Following this discussion, we seek to capture the multidimensional aspects of the subjective perception of success, by classifying previous indicators of non-financial criteria into two distinct attributes: the intrinsic dimension of perceived success, which we contend is feminine in nature; and the independence dimension, which we argue is related to masculine values. The intrinsic dimension of success refers to the individual's intention to have status, approval and recognition from their family, friends and from the business, and it is consistent with constructs used in previous studies on motivation, and labeled as recognition (Carter et al., 2003; Shane et al., 1991), or need for approval (Scheinberg and McMillan, 1988).

On the other hand, the independence dimension of success stresses the values of autonomy and self-achievement as primary criteria for assessing success. Previous studies on reasons for start-up have also used a similar construct to describe an individual's desire for freedom and control over their career and time (Carter et al., 2003; Birley and Westhead, 1994; Blaise et al., 1990).

We depart from traditional research in entrepreneurial success in that, given that both dimensions reflect non-monetary concepts, they would have been associated with women entrepreneurs, establishing an analogy between 'non-monetary' measures and gender stereotypes. However, our approach is consistent with research that objects to stereotypical feminine view of the firm, and with the systematic association of those dimensions with women (Cliff et al., 2004; Ahl,

2006). Advocates of this view argue that gender-stereotypic values do not always correspond to entrepreneurs according to their biological sex. In particular, they claim that men and women entrepreneurs have a mix of masculine and feminine values. The extent to which they will display one more than the other will depend on a variety of situational factors.

Among these factors, we focus on the effect of parenthood, given its central role in shaping personal values and its increasingly recognized influence on work–family interface. Therefore, we follow a family embeddedness perspective of entrepreneurship (Aldrich and Cliff, 2003), which recognizes a relationship between the entrepreneur's family value systems and the new venture's outcome, including performance and the subjective perception of success.

## Gender, parenthood and their effects on entrepreneurs' perceptions of success

Social identity theory (SIT) is utilized to examine when entrepreneurs are more likely to act consistently with their gender-stereotypic role, and when they are more likely to adopt attitudes more congruent with traditional entrepreneurial archetypes. The central assumption underlying social identity theory (Tajfel, 1974, 1978) is that while there are elements of self-identity that are derived from individual traits and interpersonal relationships (personal identity), there are many social settings in which people do not act as independent individuals. In these situations, people primarily think of themselves and others in terms of particular group memberships (for example, in terms of their professional or family roles), and tend to adopt 'group' behaviors and attitudes. This latter element of self-identity is called the 'social identity'. The social identity incorporates the notion that definitions of self can relate to multiple groups simultaneously, and that the relative degree to which people see each of these different identities as self-descriptive varies across different situations, and/or over time (Haslam et al., 2003).

A central premise of SIT is that people identify with groups that contribute to a positive sense of self, such as high-status or high-power groups (Ellemers, 1993; Haslam et al., 2000). In the case of competing social identities, people will use cultural associations of status-worthiness and competence as cues for self-definition. Thus, because of the positive cultural association of masculine entrepreneurial attributes, and the negative or neutral association attached to feminine subjective criteria (Ahl, 2006; Bruni et al., 2004), entrepreneurs will generally tend to identify primarily with masculine, extrinsic attitudes. Because of this, and due to the higher status attached to masculine entrepreneurial values, we expect women entrepreneurs to report masculine values, that is, ones that are similar to those of their male counterparts.

However, people's identification with higher-status groups is not the only operating mechanism, nor is it immutable. Changes in context can affect the content of group prototypes to which people refer, and hence lead to a change in self-concept and attitudes. In order to predict when certain group memberships will tend to become more powerful determinants of behavior than others, SIT also refers to salience mechanisms as a basis for self-conceptualization in a given context (Hogg and Terry, 2000).

We contend that role salience will have significant consequences on entrepreneurs' perceptions of success. Specifically, we claim that there are specific moments in an entrepreneur's life where family role is likely to become more salient than the entrepreneurial responsibilities, therefore inducing changes in self-concept and a greater identification with parental values and groups, as compared to entrepreneurial values and groups. In this case, the presence of dependents (children) acts as a powerful salience mechanism that provokes a shift towards family-role salience, with both male and female entrepreneurs expressing greater concern for intrinsic values rather than for extrinsic values. We denominate this behavior the 'parenthood effect'. In this situation, the similarities between male entrepreneurs and female entrepreneurs are the result of the former adopting a feminine perspective on business. As suggested by Cliff et al. (2004), archetypical feminine qualities are increasingly touted in popular managerial texts (see, e.g., Fondas, 1997), which leads the authors to conclude that perhaps they are being implemented in practice. In our case, men would also be affected by parenthood and internalize intrinsic perceptions of success.

Additional concerns may moderate identity enhancement motives and people's identification to the archetype of the ambitious, extrinsic-oriented entrepreneur. According to Ellemers et al. (2004):

> people are ready to identify with groups that compare unfavorably to other groups (e.g., low-status groups), to the extent that they believe in the potential of the group to improve its plight . . . or perceive their group's disadvantage as unjust – that is, where inter-group differences are illegitimate (ibid.: 463)

The authors specify that such behavior may be prompted by 'a work situation in which people are systematically excluded from certain rewards or opportunities on the basis of their category membership (e.g., their age, gender or ethnic background)'. In other words, people who endure work discrimination are induced to think of themselves in terms of low-status groups, and adhere to their beliefs and values.

A well-known phenomenon that might reflect the operation of this process is the glass ceiling. Male-dominated systems and authoritarian structures in organizational life are indeed known to affect women negatively as they attempt to ascend the corporate ladder (Buttner and Moore, 1997). Having vicariously or directly experienced discrimination in the workplace, women are then expected to identify more with their female colleagues and to express motivations and entrepreneurial goals that emphasize their belonging to this group. This would be a key reason why several studies (Mattis, 2004) portray female entrepreneurs as attaching importance to independence as a primary goal from self-employment. At this point, it is worth highlighting that independence is a masculine value, just as financial wealth is, but while male entrepreneurs will tend to emphasize the latter dimension of success, we hypothesize that female entrepreneurs will prioritize the aspects that improve their social status with respect to previous work experiences, that is, the independence dimension of success. In this case, the leap to self-employment might not increase their economic wealth, or at least not in the initial stages of the business, but it might significantly improve their empowerment and self-reliance.

The previous discussion points to the existence of a parenthood effect on the intrinsic dimension of success and a gender effect on the independence dimension. Formally stated:

*H1: The intrinsic dimension of success will be more important for entrepreneurs with dependent children than for entrepreneurs without dependent children.*

*H2: The independence dimension of success will be more important for female entrepreneurs than for male entrepreneurs.*

## The moderating effect of gender

Although we suggest that gender does not affect intrinsic perception of success per se, based on social identity theory we do argue, however, that gender moderates the relationship between parenthood and the intrinsic dimension of success. In particular, we propose that when family role becomes salient, women entrepreneurs will lean towards feminine values to a greater extent than men entrepreneurs. Thus, we contend that 'motherhood' – that is, the combined effect of women with dependent children – has its own unique implications beyond those associated with parenthood. Since theory argues that a salience mechanism must operate in order to produce a change in an individual's self-concept, we should account for the circumstances under which parenthood is likely to act more as a salient descriptor for women than for men. Ridgeway and Correll (2004) provide a good argument in this sense when they state: 'Anytime a woman in the workplace gives behavioral evidence of being a mother of dependent children, she will be categorized as primary caretaker, priming the status and competence implications of that role'. This will happen when a women worker becomes visibly pregnant (Halpert et al., 1993), leaves a meeting early to pick up her children from school or calls in absent due to a sick child. In the vast majority of work settings, her now-recognized role as mother will differentiate her from at least some other workers and/or will be seen as directly relevant to her job performance. 'As a result, the status implications of motherhood will be effectively salient in these settings' (Ridgeway and Correll, 2004: 693).

This salience will not be as strong for men as parents, since our cultural presumptions about mothers as primary caretakers are still firmly entrenched and fathers are mostly expected to provide financially for their children (Bernhardt, 1994; Deutsch and Saxon, 1998). Consequently, we hypothesize that woman entrepreneurs will not necessarily prioritize the intrinsic dimension of success unless there is a salient context – that is, motherhood – which pushes them to conform to what is socially expected from them.

Gender discrimination is also likely to become more systematic in this particular context, in which the presence of dependent children makes gender more salient. In line with the above-mentioned argument, we claim that this would make the independence dimension of success more important for female entrepreneurs with dependents.

Thus, the foregoing arguments suggest that there is a motherhood effect on both the intrinsic and the independence measures of entrepreneurs' success, and we hypothesize that:

*H3: The intrinsic dimension of success will be more important for women entrepreneurs with dependent children than for men entrepreneurs with dependent children.*

*H4: The independence dimension of success will be more important for women entrepreneurs with dependent children than for men entrepreneurs with dependent children.*

## Sample and methodology

Data for our study came from the Global Entrepreneurship Monitor (GEM) survey conducted in Spain in April 2005. The GEM study tracks entrepreneurship in more than 40 countries, including Spain, based on a representative telephone survey of the adult population. The GEM survey requests a broad array of information related to individuals' demographics, and business characteristics as well as attitudes and awareness of entrepreneurship in the different countries. Additional questions were included in the 2005 survey in order to capture perceived entrepreneurial success as well as parenthood characteristics.

In 2005, a survey was conducted on a sample of 19 384 individuals. A total of 1236 individuals (6.37 percent) were classified as entrepreneurs following the GEM methodology. Consistent with previous literature on gender and entrepreneurship, females were significantly under-represented in the entrepreneurial ranges (Franco and Winqvist, 2002). Our data yield a percentage of 10.2 percent entrepreneurs for women with respect to the general adult feminine population, against a 14.6 percent for the masculine population.

We assume that wealth generation is an important goal for every entrepreneur regardless of biological sex (Holmquist and Sundin, 1988; Kolvereid, 1996), and operationalize both the intrinsic and independence dimensions as bipolar measures, where non-monetary subjective values are assessed in opposition to profit and eco-nomic motivations. Indeed, Pfeffer and Salancik (1978: 246) explain that 'pay is a complex aspect of work, serving not only to justify the activity but also to convey worth, status and competence, as well as to provide for various goods and services obtained outside work'. Since people engage in social comparisons, pushing them to choose between monetary and non-monetary aspects of work might produce confusing answers and muddled results. For that reason, and instead of pushing entrepreneurs to choose between adopting or discarding extrinsic values, we asked them to assess the relative importance of non-monetary ones with respect to the former.

In order to measure the intrinsic dimension of perceived success, we used four items included in a scale developed by Walker and Brown (2004) which captures the importance of measuring business success in terms of traditional financial measures (making money) versus other alternative measures (personal satisfaction, pride in job or flexibility) using a five-point Likert scale. The four selected items capture the desire expressed by the entrepreneur to pursue social goals from entre-preneurial activity as opposed to financial goals, that is, making money. We inter-pret this dichotomy as the difference between 'intrinsic' versus 'extrinsic' values when measuring business success. The composite scale reached an acceptable level of internal consistency ($\alpha = 0.70$).

The independence dimension of perceived success was measured by means of a single item. In particular, respondents were asked to rate the importance of being their own boss as opposed to making money, using a five-point Likert scale with the anchors of $1$ = strongly disagree to $5$ = strongly agree. Although reliance on a single item is often questionable, single-item measures are considered to be rela-tively valid and have frequently been used in work attitudes literature (Ganzach, 1998).

*Woman*: sex was measured as a dummy variable that takes the values of $1$ if the entrepreneur is a woman, $0$ otherwise.

*Dependent children*: Parenthood was measured by a dummy variable coded $1$ if the entrepreneur has at least one dependent child and $0$ otherwise. A child was consid-ered as dependent if they are less than $18$ years old.

Control variables: To better isolate the effect of gender and parenthood on per-ception of success, we controlled for several potential confounding variables. Entrepreneurs' characteristics include owner *Age* (continuous variable), *Education* (a three-category variable coded $0$ = no education, $1$ = at least secondary educa-tion, $2$ = post-secondary education) and *Personal income* ($1$ = low, $2$ = medium, $3$ = high). Entrepreneur's dedication to the business, *Full-time entrepreneur*, was meas-ured as a dummy variable that takes the value of $1$ if she works full-time in the busi-ness, $0$ otherwise. Firm characteristics included *Employment size*, as represented by the number of employees at the time that the survey was conducted.

Additionally, four dummy variables were introduced to control for industry effects, since previous research has shown that industry characteristics may push entrepreneurs to develop strategies that are inconsistent with their personal values (Bird and Brush, 2002; Cliff, 2004; Olson and Currie, 1992). Following Bates (2002), we grouped industries into five categories: *construction, consumer goods, retailing, personal services* and *skilled services*.

*New business*: following GEM methodology, we create a dummy variable that indicates the stage of development of a venture, and takes the value of 1 if the firm owned by the entrepreneur is less than 42 months old, and 0 otherwise. In GEM terminology, this categorization differentiates between nascent and baby businesses, rated with a 1; and established businesses, those with 0. We group nascent and baby businesses under a single category labelled 'new businesses'.

Moreover, given that previous research has showed that self-reported motivations for start-up correlate with measures of success (Buttner and Moore, 1997; Carter et al., 2003), we included the motivation to start the business as a control variable in the analysis. Following the GEM classification, we distinguish between 'push' and 'pull' motivators. Push factors drive individuals towards business ownership out of necessity and are originally linked with dissatisfaction with one's current position (necessity entrepreneur). Pull factors attract individuals into entrepreneurship because of the future value behind the business opportunity (Ohran, 2004). The variable takes the value of 1 if the entrepreneur was motivated by pull factors (*opportunity* entrepreneur), 0 if motivated by push reasons (necessity entrepreneur). Lastly, *Overall satisfaction* with the job is taken into account, since previous research has shown that differences in job attitudes may be affected by satisfaction levels and that women entrepreneurs are consistently more satisfied than men entrepreneurs (Cooper and Artz, 1995). Specifically, to measure overall satisfaction, we asked respondents to specify their level of agreement or disagreement (based on a five-point Likert scale) with the statement 'I am satisfied with my job' (Appendix 3A.1).

## Analysis and results

Descriptive statistics and correlations appear in Table 3.1. The table indicates that the intrinsic dimension of success is correlated with opportunity entrepreneurship and with overall job satisfaction (positive). However, it shows no relationship with any of the variables measuring entrepreneur, firm or sector characteristics. On the other hand, the independence dimension shows significant correlation with the biological sex of the entrepreneur. The positive sign indicates that women rate higher than men on the independence dimension of success, in line with Hypothesis 2. The only other significant correlation related to the gender variable can be found with age. This result is consistent with previous studies on women entrepreneurs which show that women tend to start ventures at a later age than males, indicating a probable effect of pregnancy and early motherhood as a barrier to venture creation at a younger age.

**Table 3.1**  Descriptives and correlation

| Variables | Mean | St. dev. | 1 | 2 | 3 | 4 | 5 | 6 |
|---|---|---|---|---|---|---|---|---|
| 1 *Employment size* | 3.24 | 4.72 | | | | | | |
| 2 *Industry_construction* | 0.11 | 0.31 | 0.00 | | | | | |
| 3 *Industry_goods* | 0.12 | 0.32 | −0.02 | −0.13*** | | | | |
| 4 *Industry_personal services* | 0.08 | 0.26 | 0.00 | −0.10*** | −0.10*** | | | |
| 5 *Industry_retail* | 0.44 | 0.49 | −0.01 | −0.31*** | −0.32*** | −0.25*** | | |
| 6 *Industry_skilled services* | 0.26 | 0.47 | 0.03 | −0.21*** | −0.22*** | −0.17*** | −0.52*** | |
| 7 *Personal income* | 2.13 | 0.81 | 0.10** | 0.00 | −0.07* | 0.02 | −0.07* | 0.12*** |
| 8 *Education* | 3.54 | 1.25 | 0.03 | −0.06* | −0.07* | 0.16*** | −0.23*** | 0.26*** |
| 9 *Age* | 43.12 | 11.97 | 0.04 | 0.00 | 0.05 | −0.03 | 0.00 | −0.02 |
| 10 *Full-time entrepreneur* | 0.95 | 0.25 | 0.03 | −0.02 | 0.03 | −0.05 | 0.03 | −0.01 |
| 11 *Pure opportunity* | 0.63 | 0.48 | 0.00 | 0.01 | −0.01 | 0.01 | −0.02 | 0.02 |
| 12 *Overall satisfaction* | 3.75 | 1.02 | 0.01 | 0.00 | −0.01 | 0.00 | −0.02 | 0.03 |
| 13 *New business* | 0.32 | 0.46 | 0.02 | −0.06* | −0.03 | 0.08** | −0.04 | 0.05+ |
| 14 *Woman* | 0.42 | 0.49 | −0.01 | −0.03 | 0.04 | 0.04 | 0.00 | −0.04 |
| 15 *Dependent children* | 0.59 | 0.04 | 0.00 | 0.01 | 0.00 | 0.02 | −0.01 | −0.01 |
| 16 *Intrinsic scale* | 2.84 | 0.52 | 0.02 | 0.00 | −0.03 | −0.01 | −0.03 | 0.06+ |
| 17 *Independence* | 3.28 | 0.99 | −0.05 | 0.00 | −0.01 | −0.01 | 0.00 | 0.02 |

**Notes:**
N = 1234
+ $p \leq 0.10$, * $p \leq 0.05$, ** $p \leq 0.01$.

On the contrary, the entrepreneurial stage variable shows significant correlations with several of the proposed variables, pointing to the importance of distinguishing between entrepreneurs leading new businesses and those managing more established ones. As derived from the table, nascent and baby entrepreneurs are more likely to belong to personal services and less to industry services than more established entrepreneurs. Moreover, their income is lower and their level of education higher than that of established owners. Interestingly, compared to their established counterparts, they rate higher the intrinsic aspects of success as opposed to making money.

In general, the rest of the bivariate correlations are consistent with our expectations. Higher family income is associated with firms of bigger size. Moreover, highly educated entrepreneurs are younger and have the higher family income levels. In the same vein, belonging to industries that provide skill services is positively associated with both high income and education levels. No problem with multicollinearity seems to exist.

Hypotheses were tested using hierarchical regression analysis. As customary, control variables were entered first, followed by main effects. Multiplicative terms were added later to examine the hypothesized interactions. We calculated the vari-

| 7 | 8 | 9 | 10 | 11 | 12 | 13 | 14 | 15 | 16 | 17 |
|---|---|---|---|---|---|---|---|---|---|---|
| 0.26*** | | | | | | | | | | |
| 0.03 | −0.12*** | | | | | | | | | |
| −0.06+ | −0.10*** | 0.00 | | | | | | | | |
| 0.02 | 0.04 | −0.06* | −0.01 | | | | | | | |
| −0.03 | −0.02 | 0.05+ | 0.01 | 0.04 | | | | | | |
| −0.12*** | 0.07** | −0.09*** | −0.05+ | 0.17*** | 0.01 | | | | | |
| −0.04 | −0.01 | 0.07* | −0.03 | 0.01 | 0.06 | −0.04 | | | | |
| 0.00 | 0.11*** | −0.86*** | −0.02 | 0.05 | −0.03 | 0.08 | −0.10*** | | | |
| 0.05 | 0.02 | 0.00 | −0.05* | 0.09*** | 0.36*** | 0.02 | 0.04 | 0.05 | | |
| 0.00 | 0.03 | −0.02 | −0.04 | 0.02 | 0.01 | −0.06+ | 0.07* | 0.04 | 0.15*** | 1.00 |

ance inflation factor (VIF) after each regression to make sure the results were not subject to the threat of multicollinearity. Values were within acceptable limits for Hypotheses 1 to 4.

Table 3.2 shows the results for the determinants of the intrinsic dimension of success using the full sample. Model 1 is the base model that includes only control variables. This model shows that entrepreneurs who work part-time tend to attach higher value to the intrinsic aspects of success, when compared to those committed full-time to their business. This result is consistent with our arguments, since part-time entrepreneurs, having their financial needs covered by their actual jobs, look for different aspirations than just earning money when deciding to create their own business. In the same line, those entrepreneurs who decide to start a new business because of the attractiveness of the business idea, and not due to necessity, place a higher value on the intrinsic measure of success. Lastly, it is interesting to note that the coefficient for the overall job satisfaction is positive and highly significant. This result is indeed consistent with studies indicating that intrinsic motivation for employees maximizes heuristic performance, trust, satisfaction and well-being (Gagné and Deci, 2005).

Models 2 and 3 introduce sex and parenthood effects. As expected, women and men do not differ in terms of their evaluation of the intrinsic aspects of success, but parents with dependent children do. The positive significant coefficient for the dependent children variables indicates that parenthood makes a difference, with

**Table 3.2**    Effect of gender and parenthood on the intrinsic dimension of success

| | Dependent variable: *Intrinsic goals* | | | |
| --- | --- | --- | --- | --- |
| | Model 1 | Model 2 | Model 3 | Model 4 |
| *Employment size* | 0.010 | 0.011 | 0.009 | 0.007 |
| *Industry_construction* | 0.002 | 0.003 | 0.003 | 0.002 |
| *Industry_goods* | −0.008 | −0.008 | −0.011 | −0.010 |
| *Industry_skilled services* | 0.038 | 0.038 | 0.040 | 0.041 |
| *Industry_personal services* | −0.006 | −0.007 | −0.007 | −0.009 |
| *High income* | 0.051 | 0.051 | 0.050 | 0.053 |
| *Average income* | 0.060+ | 0.060+ | 0.057+ | 0.058+ |
| *Education_secondary* | 0.009 | 0.007 | 0.005 | 0.008 |
| *Education_primary* | 0.004 | 0.003 | 0.003 | 0.007 |
| *Age* | −0.015 | −0.016 | 0.030 | 0.018 |
| *Full-time entrepreneur* | −0.052* | −0.052* | −0.051* | −0.053* |
| *Motivation* | 0.068** | 0.068** | 0.068** | 0.069** |
| *Overall satisfaction* | 0.334*** | 0.333*** | 0.332*** | 0.332*** |
| *Woman* | | 0.019 | 0.023 | −0.036 |
| *Dependent children* | | | 0.070* | 0.017 |
| *Woman x Dependent children* | | | | 0.090* |
| R squared | 0.126 | 0.127 | 0.129 | 0.132 |
| R squared change | 0.126 | 0.000 | 0.003* | 0.003* |
| F | 13.586*** | 12.647*** | 12.079*** | 11.610*** |

**Notes:**
N = 1234. Standardized regression coefficients are shown in the table
+ $p \leq 0.10$, * $p \leq 0.05$, ** $p \leq 0.01$.

parent entrepreneurs with dependent children placing a higher value on the intrinsic dimension of success, providing support for Hypothesis 1. For Hypothesis 3, Model 3 provides clear support for it: the effect of parenthood is higher for women than for men entrepreneurs, confirming the hypothesized 'motherhood' effect.

Table 3.3 shows the results for Hypotheses 2 and 4, which relate to the independence dimension of success. As predicted, the 'desire to be one's own boss' (as opposed to earning money) is higher for women entrepreneurs, confirming Hypothesis 2. However, the interaction effect of sex and dependents is not significant in this case, so Hypothesis 4 is rejected.

**Table 3.3**  Effect of gender and parenthood on the independence dimension of success

|  | Dependent variable: *Independence goals* | | | |
|---|---|---|---|---|
|  | Model 1 | Model 2 | Model 3 | Model 4 |
| *Employment size* | −0.054* | −0.054* | −0.055* | −0.055* |
| *Industry_construction* | −0.002 | 0.000 | 0.000 | −0.001 |
| *Industry_goods* | −0.012 | −0.014 | −0.016 | −0.016 |
| *Industry_skilled services* | 0.006 | 0.008 | 0.009 | 0.010 |
| *Industry_personal services* | −0.010 | −0.012 | −0.012 | −0.013 |
| *High income* | −0.010 | −0.010 | −0.011 | −0.010 |
| *Average income* | −0.039 | −0.040 | −0.042 | −0.042 |
| *Education_secondary* | 0.176+ | 0.171+ | 0.169+ | 0.169+ |
| *Education_primary* | 0.170+ | 0.165+ | 0.165+ | 0.166+ |
| *Age* | −0.010 | −0.015 | 0.025 | 0.021 |
| *Full-time entrepreneur* | −0.031 | −0.029 | −0.028 | −0.029 |
| *Motivation* | 0.021 | 0.020 | 0.020 | 0.020 |
| *Overall satisfaction* | 0.014 | 0.010 | 0.009 | 0.010 |
| *Woman* |  | 0.069* | 0.072* | 0.054 |
| *Dependent children* |  |  | 0.059 | 0.043 |
| *Woman x Dependent children* |  |  |  | 0.027 |
| R squared | 0.009 | 0.014 | 0.016 | 0.016 |
| R squared change |  | 0.005* | 0.002 | 0.000 |
| F | 0.862 | 1.219* | 1.294* | 1.234* |

**Notes:**
N = 1234. Standardized regression coefficients are shown in the table.
+ p ≤ 0.10, * p ≤ 0.05, ** p ≤ 0.01, *** p ≤ 0.001.

## Discussion and conclusions

In this chapter we have analyzed how men and women entrepreneurs shift in their perceptions of two dimensions of success, the intrinsic dimension, which is more related to feminine values, and the independence dimension, which is more masculine in nature, as a consequence of parenthood. Our research provides evidence that these two dimensions, intrinsic and independence, respond to different logics and are related in different ways to social identity theory. In doing so we provide both a theoretical and an empirical examination of the logic behind non-monetary perceptions of success in the context of gender and entrepreneurship. In our research we take as given the centrality of wealth generation for entrepreneurs (both male and female), and the relative importance of each of these subjective criteria is assessed in this research with respect to economic (extrinsic) success.

In particular, our arguments and results provide a theoretically solid picture with respect to the role of dependents in the context of entrepreneurial perceptions of success. In the absence of dependents, women and men entrepreneurs behave in a similar fashion. Thus, the results indicate that women entrepreneurs do not necessarily place masculine (extrinsic) criteria in a secondary position with respect to intrinsic goals, unless the presence of dependent children induces them to do so.

A corollary of this finding is that men entrepreneurs are not inevitably oriented against the principle of giving to others as the literature has suggested (Adler, 1999; Miller, 1976). As entrepreneurs, they exhibit work expectations and values that are similar to those of their female counterparts. Once they become parents, both men and women reveal altruistic values such as the desire to help others and to achieve a work and family balance. Nevertheless, our findings indicate that parenthood is experienced differently by women and men entrepreneurs, the former exhibiting intrinsic values to a greater extent than the latter. Following SIT we contend that the differences are attributable to the diverse expectations that society places on the entrepreneur as the saliency of parenthood appears: for fathers, to be the economic provider; for mothers, to be the primary caretaker and nurturer.

These results are consistent with research by Cliff et al. (2004), which attempts to reconcile both perspectives by suggesting that female and male entrepreneurs differ in their rhetoric, but not in their inherent values and actual practices. While we agree with this argument, we add that the need to conform to social and cultural expectations, be this through simple speech or through real implementation, emerges when gender becomes salient. Thus by controlling for parenthood, our chapter helps to explain previous contradictions found between the studies that attach gender-stereotypic goals to entrepreneurs according to their sex, and those which reject this view.

In contrast, we found that gender had a direct impact on the independence dimension of success. As a result of the glass ceiling effect and discrimination experienced in the labor market, women entrepreneurs are more likely than men to value freedom and control over monetary rewards. What is interesting about these findings is that they clarify part of the existing confusion regarding women's expectations from self-employment. The characterization of entrepreneurship as a panacea for balancing work and family role responsibilities for women is a case in point. Scholars have indeed recently been calling this claim into question, and have proposed that although the self-employed experience higher freedom and job satisfaction than organizationally employed workers, the drive for economic security may also imply higher levels of work–family conflict and lower family satisfaction (Moore, 2005; Parasuraman and Simmers, 2001).

Why, then, are women increasingly entering self-employment? Our findings provide evidence that gaining balance in their professional career and personal relationship is not necessarily women's main expectation from business ownership.

Instead, they seem to value above all career autonomy and self-reliance. In this sense, women seem willing to 'forgo . . . both the traditional, male-based career path and the "Mommy track" and are instead building new paths by using entrepreneurial activities to expand their careers and relationships' (Sullivan and Mainiero, 2002: 8).

The results of our study provide a link back to the works of Goffee and Scase (1983) and Cromie and Hayes (1988) which classify women business owners' trajectories according to their orientations towards business performance and their families. While these studies suggested the existence of a 'Mummy track' for entrepreneurial women, their findings have not been validated by subsequent research, and researchers have not built on them to understand how parenthood affects male and female entrepreneurs' perceptions of success (Ohran, 2004).

We believe that our research provides empirical support for these typologies of women entrepreneurs, allows for the comparison of entrepreneurs of both sexes according to parenthood, and provides links to the different expectations that these groups may have from entrepreneurship. A number of questions regarding gender, perceptions of success and entrepreneurship remain to be examined. In particular, future research might try to analyze the formation of distinct entrepreneurial careers based on an individual's perceptions of life and their roles. Scholars might also study the implications of those perceptions for career stages and patterns for women and men entrepreneurs. Finally, and more importantly, future studies might want to examine the effect of modern family structure and dual-career families on entrepreneurial performance.

Our results could also provide interesting theoretical insights about the organizational policies and practices established by entrepreneurs. These will indeed tend to create work situations consistent with their own values. For example, motherhood and the higher value attached to the intrinsic dimension of success could help to explain why women more often than men will provide environments that allow employees to balance family and business life, or establish organizational cultures that minimize conflicts among employees (Robinson, 2001).

In the same vein, Rogers (2005) contends that an entrepreneur's commitment to work or family roles will affect the development of their business: 'women with family responsibilities will direct their marketing efforts according to the needs of the family. Travelling may be curtailed, business locations changed, opportunities rejected, personnel hired, all with the goal of maintaining a balance between work and family' (ibid.: 96). Although this affirmation sounds intuitive, further research is needed to investigate whether the entrepreneur's definition of success actually influences firm strategy and financial outcomes. In doing so, an analysis of sex differences could also prove insightful. So far, this argument has been used by some scholars to justify findings that women underperform in comparison to men (Du Reitz and Henrekson, 2000; Srinivasan et al., 1994), but this argument has not been empirically tested.

Moreover, the exploration of sex differences in perceptions of success may benefit from country comparisons, and examination of the effect of social and institutional factors related to culture, history, legislation, educational structures or family policies. Gender is the 'result of upbringing and social interaction and it varies in time and place' (Ahl, 2006, page 597), so a replication of our study in a distinct context should prove enriching.

Our results also provide interesting insights on management practice. First, prospective entrepreneurs' work aspirations and values should be put into the broader perspective of their present and future family life, acknowledging that people's commitment to a specific role (be it work- or family-related) reflects only a transitory set of priorities. Understanding which role prevails at each moment of their career development is important, because the different commitment to work and family spheres will affect the possibility of experiencing inter-role conflict. The latter has indeed been related positively to stress, and negatively to financial success and satisfaction (Rogers, 2005).

Second, the fact that gender, per se, does not distract entrepreneurs from focusing on financial profits also has important implications for bank loan officers, venture capitalists and informal investors. Indeed, the traditional view of women as seeking mainly non-monetary rewards from their business could have placed them at a disadvantage for receiving financial support. Our chapter shows that this is not necessarily true, and that all other factors held constant, women and men are 'made from the same cloth'.

Lastly, the results of our chapter point to the need for business owners' advisors and policy-makers to acknowledge entrepreneurs' changing requirements during their lives, and the unique challenges they face when they become parents. Help could be directed towards identifying coping strategies and sources of support to address work and family conflict. The issue is not only important for actual entrepreneurs; it also has implications in terms of future generations of businesspersons. As suggested by Schindehutte et al. (2003) the entrepreneurial parent's discontent or satisfaction with their career will later influence the extent to which their children consider entrepreneurship as a desirable professional option or not. Public and private agents should, however, avoid actions directed exclusively towards women and also involve men entrepreneurs, since our results indicate that for both the presence of dependents is a cause of changes in their perceptions of success. By concentrating solely on women entrepreneurs, they might otherwise perpetuate stereotypes of women as the only ones responsible for childcare (Ahl, 2006).

Finally, in studies of this nature, social desirability bias is always a concern. Like most previous research in this area, a limitation of our study is the possibility that entrepreneurs' answers have been affected by this bias. Further research should include alternative approaches towards gathering these sensitive and bias-prone data. Possibilities include more observational techniques (Helgesen, 1990), longitudinal tracking of entrepreneurs to assess perceptions over time, organizational informants (Cliff et al., 2004), or other techniques that allow us to capture perception and values at different times and under different contingencies.

Note

* Professor Justo acknowledges support received from the Ministerio de Economía y Competitividad de España through research project ECO2015-66146-R: El emprendimiento social desde un enfoque configuracional: Los determinantes individuales y contextuales de la acción estratégica y persistencia de los emprendedores sociales.

# References

Adler, N. (1999), 'Global leaders: women of influence', in G.N. Powell (ed.), *Handbook of Gender and Work*, Thousand Oaks, CA: SAGE Publications, 239–262.

Ahl, H. (2006), 'Why research on women entrepreneurs needs new directions', *Entrepreneurship Theory and Practice*, 30(5), 595–621.

Aldrich, H.E. and J.E. Cliff (2003), 'The pervasive effects of family on entrepreneurship: toward a family embeddedness perspective', *Journal of Business Venturing*, 18(5), 573–596.

Bates, T. (2002), 'Restricted access to markets characterizes women-owned businesses', *Journal of Business Venturing*, 17(4), 313–324.

Bem, S. (1981), *Bem Sex-Role Inventory*, Palo Alto, CA: Mind Garden.

Bernhardt, I. (1994), 'Comparative advantage in self-employment and paid work', *Canadian Journal of Economics*, 27(2), 273–289.

Bird, B. and C. Brush (2002), 'A gendered perspective on organizational creation', *Entrepreneurship Theory and Practice*, 26(3), 41–66.

Birley, S. and P. Westhead, P. (1994), 'A taxonomy of business start-up reasons and their impact on firm growth and size', *Journal of Business Venturing*, 9, 7–31.

Blaise, R., J. Toulouse and B. Clement (1990), 'International comparisons of entrepreneurial motivation based on personal equation, hierarchical analysis, and other statistical methods', paper presented at Proceedings of the 39th World Conference for Small Business, Washington, DC.

Boden, R.J., Jr (1999), 'Flexible working hours, family responsibilities, and female self-employment: gender differences in self-employment selection', *American Journal of Economics and Sociology*, 58(1), 71.

de Bruin A., C.G. Brush and F. Welter (2006), 'Introduction to the special issue: towards building cumulative knowledge on women's entrepreneurship', *Entrepreneurship Theory and Practice*, 30, 585–593.

Bruni, A., S. Gherardi and B. Poggio (2004), 'Doing gender, doing entrepreneurship: an ethnographic account of intertwined practices', *Gender, Work and Organization*, 11(4), 406–429.

Buttner, E.H. and D.P. Moore (1997), 'Women's organizational exodus to entrepreneurship: self-reported motivations and correlates with success', *Journal of Small Business Management*, 35(1), 34.

Caputo, R. and A. Dolinsky (1998). 'Women's choice to pursue self-employment: the role of financial and human capital of household members', *Journal of Small Business Management*, 36(3), 8–18.

Carter, N.M., W. Gartner, K.G. Shaver and E.J. Gatewood (2003), 'The career reasons of nascent entrepreneurs', *Journal of Business Venturing*, 18(1), 13–39.

Catley, S. and R. Hamilton (1998), 'Small business development and gender of owner', *Journal of Management Development*, 17(1), 75–82.

Cliff, J.E. (1998), 'Does one size fit all? Exploring the relationship between attitudes towards growth, gender and business size', *Journal of Business Venturing*, 13, 523–542.

Cliff, J.E., N. Langton and H.E. Aldrich (2004), 'Walking the talk? Gendered rhetoric vs. action in small firms', *Organization Studies*, 26(1), 63–91.

Cooper, A.C. and K. Artz (1995), 'Determinants of satisfaction for entrepreneurs', *Journal of Business Venturing*, 10(6), 439–457.

Cromie, S. and J. Hayes (1988), 'Towards a typology of female entrepreneurs', *Sociological Review*, 36(1), 87–113.

DeMartino, R. and R. Barbato (2003), 'Differences between women and men MBA entrepreneurs: exploring family flexibility and wealth creation as career motivators', *Journal of Business Venturing*, 18(6), 815–832.

Deutsch, F.M. and S.E. Saxon (1998), 'Traditional ideologies, non traditional lives', *Sex Roles*, 38(5–6), 331–362.

Du Rietz, A. and M. Henrekson (2000), 'Testing the female underperformance hypothesis', *Small Business Economics*, 14(1), 1–10.

Eagly, A.H. (1995), 'The science and politics of comparing women and men', *American Psychologist*, 50, 145–158.

Ellemers, N. (1993), 'The influence of socio-cultural variables on identity enhancement strategies', *European Review of Social Psychology*, 4, 27–57.

Ellemers, N., D. De Gilder and S.A. Haslam (2004), 'Motivating individuals and groups at work: a social identity perspective on leadership and group performance', *Academy of Management Review*, 29, 459–478.

Fagenson, E.A. (1993), 'Personal value systems of men and women entrepreneurs versus managers', *Journal of Business Venturing*, 8(5), 409–430.

Fenwick, T. and S. Hutton (2000), 'Women crafting new work: the learning of women entrepreneurs', paper presented at 41st Annual Adult Education Research Conference, Vancouver.

Fondas, N. (1997), 'Feminization unveiled: management qualities in contemporary writings', *Academy of Management Review*, 22(1), 257–282.

Franco, A. and K. Winqvist (2002), *Women and Men Reconciling Work and Family Life*, Brussels: European Communities, Eurostat.

Gagné, M. and E.L. Deci (2005), 'Self-determination theory and work motivation', *Journal of Organizational Behavior*, 26, 331–362.

Ganzach, Y. (1998), 'Intelligence and job satisfaction', *Academy of Management Journal*, 41(5), 526–539.

Goffee, R. and R. Scase (1983), 'Business ownership and women's subordination: a preliminary study of female proprietors', *Sociological Review*, 31(4), 625–648.

Halpert, J.A., M.L. Wilson and J.L. Hickman (1993), 'Pregnancy as a source of bias in performance appraisals', *Journal of Organizational Behavior*, 14(7), 649–663.

Haslam, S.A., T. Postmes and N. Ellemers (2003), 'More than a metaphor: organizational identity makes organizational life possible', *British Journal of Management*, 14, 357–369.

Haslam, S.A., C. Powell and J. Turner (2000), 'Social identity, self-categorization, and work motivation: rethinking the contribution of the group to positive and sustainable organizational outcomes', *Applied Psychology An International Review*, 49(3), 319–339.

Helgesen, S. (1990), *The Female Advantage: Women's Ways of Leadership*, New York: Doubleday.

Hogg, M.A. and D.J. Terry (2000), 'Social identity and self-categorization processes in organizational contexts', *Academy of Management Review*, 25(1), 121–140.

Holmquist, C. and E. Sundin (1988), 'Women as entrepreneurs in Sweden: conclusions from a survey', Frontiers of Entrepreneurship Research 1988, The Arthur M. Blank Center for Entrepreneurship Babson College, Babson Park, Massachusetts, 626–642.

Hudson, M., A. Smart and M. Bourne (2001), 'Theory and practice in SME performance measurement systems', *International Journal of Operations and Production Management*, 21(8), 1096–1115.

Hughes, K.D. and J.E. Jennings (2012), *Global Women's Entrepreneurship Research: Diverse Settings, Questions and Approaches*, Cheltenham, UK and Northampton, MA, USA: Edward Elgar Publishing.

Hughes, K.D., J.E. Jennings, C. Brush, S. Carter and F. Welter (2012), 'Extending women's entrepreneurship research in new directions', *Entrepreneurship Theory and Practice*, 36, 429–442.

Jennings, J.E. and M.S. McDougald (2007), 'Work–family interface experiences and coping strategies: implications for entrepreneurship research and practice', *Academy of Management Review*, 32, 747–760.

Kalleberg, A.L. and K.T. Leicht (1991), 'Gender and organizational performance: determinants of small business survival and performance', *Academy of Management Journal*, 34(1), 136–161.

Kalnins, A. and M. Williams (2014), 'When do female-owned businesses out-survive male-owned businesses? A disaggregated approach by industry and geography', *Journal of Business Venturing*, 29(6), 822–835.

Kolvereid, L. (1996), 'Prediction of employment status choice intentions', *Entrepreneurship Theory and Practice*, 21(1), 47–58.

Lombard, K.V. (2001), 'Female self-employment and demand for flexible, nonstandard work schedules', *Economic Inquiry*, 39(2), 214–238.

MacNabb, A., J. McCoy, P. Weinreich and M. Northover (1993), 'Using identity structure analysis (ISA) to investigate female entrepreneurship', *Entrepreneurship and Regional Development*, 5, 301–313.

Marlow, S. (1997), 'Self-employed women: new opportunities, old challenges', *Entrepreneurship and Regional Development*, 9(3), 199–210.

Mattis, M.C. (2004), 'Women entrepreneurs: out from under the glass ceiling'. *Women in Management Review*, 19(3), 154–163.

Miller, J. (1976), *Toward New Psychology of Women*, Boston, MA: Beacon Press.

Moore, D.P. (2005), 'Four career paths of women business owners', in S.L. Fielden and M. Davidson (eds), *International Handbook of Women and Small Business Entrepreneurship*, Cheltenham, UK and Northampton, MA, USA: Edward Elgar Publishing, 42–50.

Ohran, M. (2004), 'Why women enter into small business ownership', in S. Fielden and M.J. Davidson (eds), *International Handbook of Women and Small Business Entrepreneurship*, Cheltenham, UK and Northampton, MA, USA: Edward Elgar Publishing, 3–16.

Olson, S.F. and H.M. Currie (1992), 'Female entrepreneurs: personal value systems and business strategies in a male-dominated industry', *Journal of Small Business Management*, 30(1), 49–57.

Parasuraman, S. and C.A. Simmers (2001), 'Type of employment, work–family conflict and well-being: a comparative study', *Journal of Organizational Behavior*, 22(5), 551–568.

Pfeffer, J. and G. Salancik (1978), *The External Control of Organizations: A Resource Dependence Perspective*, New York: Harper & Row.

Ridgeway, C.L. and S.J. Correll (2004), 'Motherhood as a status characteristic', *Journal of Social Issues*, 60(4), 683–700.

Robinson, S. (2001), 'An examination of entrepreneurial motives and their influence on the way rural women small business owners manage their employees', *Journal of Developmental Entrepreneurship*, 6(2), 151.

Rogers, N. (2005). 'The impact of family support on the success of women business owners', in S.L. Fielden and M.J. Davidson (eds), *International Handbook of Women and Small Business Entrepreneurship*, Cheltenham, UK and Northampton, MA, USA: Edward Elgar Publishing, 91–102.

Scheinberg, S. and I.C. MacMillan (1988), 'An 11 country study of motivations to start a business', Frontiers of Entrepreneurship Research 1988, The Arthur M. Blank Center for Entrepreneurship Babson College, Babson Park, Massachusetts, 669–687.

Schindehutte, M., M. Morris and C. Brennan (2003), 'Entrepreneurs and motherhood: impacts on their children in South Africa and the United States', *Journal of Small Business Management*, 41(1), 94–107.

Shane, S., L. Kolvereid and P. Westhead (1991). 'An exploratory examination of the reasons leading to new firm formation across country and gender', *Journal of Business Venturing*, 6(6), 431–446.

Srinivasan, R., C.Y. Woo and A. Cooper (1994), 'Performance determinants for male and female entrepreneurs', paper presented at the Babson Entrepreneurship Research Conference, Babson College, Wellesley, MA.

Still, L.V. and W. Timms (2000), 'Women's business: the flexible alternative workstyle for women', *Women in Management Review*, 15(5/6), 272–283.

Sullivan, S.E. and L. Mainiero (2002), 'The protean careerist – development and innovation in the 21st century – new links not yet defined', All Academy of Management Show Program Symposium presentation, Denver, Colorado, August 13.

Tajfel, H. (1974), 'Social identity and intergroup behavior', *Social Science Information*, 13, 65–93.

Tajfel, H. (ed.) (1978), *Differentiating Between Social Groups: Studies in the Social Psychology of Intergroup Relations*, London: Academic Press.

Walker, E. and A. Brown (2004), 'What success factors are important to small business owners?', *International Small Business Journal*, 22(6), 577–594.

## Appendix 3A.1

This is a follow-up survey to the GEM survey regarding your business activity. Please indicate your level of agreement or disagreement with the following statements (from 1 = Completely disagree, to 5 = Completely agree):

1. I am satisfied with my job.
2. My personal satisfaction is more important than making a lot of money.
3. Feeling proud about my work is more important than making a lot of money.
4. Making a lot of money is more important than job flexibility.
5. Being able to provide jobs to others is more important than making a lot of money.
6. Making a lot of money is more important than being my own boss.
7. Social status is more important than making a lot of money.
8. Financial indicators are the best way to measure the success of a business.
9. Spending time with my family is more important than making a lot of money.

# 4 Aspirations of women entrepreneurs in poverty: the livelihood entrepreneur

*Smita K. Trivedi*

## Introduction

At 16, Palak[1] was betrothed to a man in a Gujarati (a large state in western India) village outside of Ahmedabad, different than her own. She was forced to drop out of school because her father believed her education was just taking money away from educational opportunities for her brothers. Two years later she had still never met her betrothed, but she had started to sell the clothes she had embroidered for years. This way, she was able to put one of her brothers through school with the money she made and she was quite proud of this. When asked about her dreams, she asked first why she should have them when they were not going to come true. After some prodding, Palak said her dream was to go back to school, become a model and never get married. But she said she knew none of that would ever happen so she was content and proud to be putting her brother through school with the money she made as an embroiderer.

Palak's world may seem foreign and distant enough that it does not concern you, such that you may neglect to think about her ever again. But Palak's story does matter to you; in fact, this chapter proposes that her story matters to the world. The world is interconnected as it has never been before, and the global economy is truly just that: global. Poverty, because of its effects on population, disease and pollution, affects us all whether we choose to think about it or not. While there may not be consensus on the best way to handle it, the fact that poverty is a grave, vast problem is not really under debate (Karlan and Appel, 2011). Scholars as well as society need to figure out how to address poverty and create a sustainable world for us all (Karlan and Appel, 2011: 3). This chapter is about poverty alleviation led by those living in poverty. It is about women – who have been identified by the outside world as impoverished – lifting themselves and their families out of poverty, using their already developed skills and strengths to build their own enterprises, and therefore helping the world. The chapter attempts to explain these women entrepreneurs' lives through the study of a well-established community-based enterprise based in India, and identifies them as livelihood entrepreneurs.

## Addressing poverty from the ground up

There are 702 million people living in extreme poverty (less than $1.25, purchasing power parity) in the world today (World Bank, 2015). With our current approaches to poverty eradication, it will take more than 100 years to lift these people out of poverty (Woodward, 2015). Seventy percent of the world's poorest people are women, and they lack access to basic credit, money and opportunities (ILO, 2008). Research indicates that giving women in poverty access to credit and business opportunities may be more beneficial to society in general than giving this access to men, because women tend to invest it in the future such as in the health and education of children (ILO, 2008; Premchander, 2003). Thus, this chapter will discuss women entrepreneurs – possibly a key factor in poverty reduction – from the ground up.

Entrepreneurship, in its common form, is 'the combination of a context in which an opportunity is situated, a set of personal characteristics required to identify and pursue this opportunity and the creation of a particular outcome' (Martin and Osberg, 2007). Social entrepreneurship, on the other hand, is loosely defined as entrepreneurship with the explicit intent of improving society or pooling resources to address a social need (Martin and Osberg, 2007; Ratten and Welpe, 2011). Many other forms of entrepreneurship have been studied in the literature. In Table 4.1, the author has compiled a list of their definitions, themes how they may be grouped, as well as indicated where research exists on that form of entrepreneurship with relation to women.

The author intends to contribute a new definition of 'entrepreneur' that has been largely overlooked in the current literature; one that is somewhere on a continuum between the concepts of social entrepreneurship and traditional entrepreneurship. An entrepreneur must first meet her family's basic needs before she can dream about expanding or helping others. But because the entrepreneurs are living in poverty themselves, they are helping the world just by helping themselves. Thus these entrepreneurs have a dual purpose of both achieving poverty reduction (for the entrepreneur herself and her family) as well as building broader opportunities in impoverished communities for the future.

In this chapter the author first introduces and develops this type of entrepreneur, called the livelihood entrepreneur, and explains how it differs from other forms of entrepreneurship due to the entrepreneur's goals in the context of poverty. The concept proposes that the livelihood entrepreneur herself has the opportunity to participate in the actions that affect her life and the lives of her family and community; and in this context is able to bring herself and her community out of poverty. The concept is developed by a series of propositions to differentiate livelihood entrepreneurs from other entrepreneurs. It seeks to examine women entrepreneurs' aspirations in a distinct context: that of poverty. Thus, the research question driving this study is: What are the distinguishing characteristics of women entrepreneurs living in the context of poverty?

Table 4.1  Different forms of entrepreneurship, their themes, and research on women for each form

| Theme | Type | Definition | Studies on women entrepreneurs |
|---|---|---|---|
| | Overall | 'any attempt at new business or new venture creation, such as self-employment, a new business organization, or the expansion of an existing business, by an individual, a team of individuals, or an established business' (Reynolds et al., 1999: 3); 'the combination of a context in which an opportunity is situated, a set of personal characteristics required to identify and pursue this opportunity and the creation of a particular outcome' (Martin and Osberg, 2007). | Women's businesses are becoming more commonplace throughout the world (Anthias and Mehta, 2003; Carter and Cannon, 1992; Heemskerk, 2003; Marlow, 1997; Serdedakis et al., 2003). |
| Motivation | Social entrepreneurship | 'combines the passion of a social mission with an image of business-like discipline, innovation, and determination commonly associated with, for instance, the high-tech pioneers of Silicon Valley' (Dees, 1998). | May be an intervention from outside the community such as the Self-Employed Women's Association (SEWA), a women's co-operative in India (Datta and Gailey, 2012); or may be from within the community, 'a process involving the innovative use and combination of resources to pursue opportunities to catalyze social change and/or address social needs' (Mair and Marti, 2006: 37). |
| | Opportunity-based | Where they have many options and they choose this one (Thurik and Wennekers, 2001; Wennekers et al., 2005; Wennekers et al., 2010); 'the pursuit of unexploited or underexploited business opportunities' (Acs, 2006). | Less evident in women in developing countries (Hernandez et al., 2012). |
| | Necessity-based | Individuals in developing countries who start small enterprises out of necessity (Brewer and Gibson, 2014); last resort where there are no other options left (Acs, 2006). | Women entrepreneurs' motivation is necessity (Buttner, 1993; Hisrich and Brush, 1983; Schrier, 1975), particularly if they are members of ethnic minorities (Smith-Hunter and Boyd, 2004). |
| | Subsistence | 'entrepreneurial actions undertaken by individuals living in poverty' (Viswanathan et al., 2014: 213). | Not used yet by others specifically for women, but there is a marketing study using women: Venugopal et al. (2015). |

| | | |
|---|---|---|
| Livelihood | 'a study of entrepreneurs living in poverty who create value for the world by sustaining their own family livelihoods and thus lift themselves out of poverty . . . Because these entrepreneurs are living in poverty themselves, they are helping the world just by helping themselves. Thus these entrepreneurs have a dual purpose of both achieving poverty reduction (for the entrepreneur herself and her family) as well as building broader opportunities in impoverished communities for the future' (Trivedi, 2014). | Self-Employed Women's Association (SEWA) entrepreneurs in India (Trivedi, 2014). |
| Ownership or operations | **Family business**<br>Business governed and/or managed with the intention to shape and pursue the vision of the business held by a dominant coalition controlled by members of the same family or a small number of families in a manner that is potentially sustainable across generations of the family or families (Chua et al., 1999). | Women not usually chosen to head up family business (Sharma et al., 1996: 22). Yet, 'globally, family-owned and family-controlled businesses have higher percentages of women in the c-suite – as well as in top management positions and on the board – than other types of companies' (Moran, 2015). |
| | **Community-based**<br>'a community acting cooperatively as both entrepreneur and enterprise of the common good' (Peredo and Chrisman, 2006: 310). | Study of intrapersonal resources and success in women's community-based enterprises (Katongole et al., 2015); there is much need for studies about gender in community entrepreneurship (Vestrum, 2016). |
| Size | **Micro-enterprise**<br>'Characteristics are: owner-operator with 10 employees or less, no separation of household and business finances, high percentage of women owners, fixed assets of US$20,000 or less, heavy reliance on family labor, limited access to the formal financial sector, little management and technical training, limited access to business support services' (IADB, 1998: 19). | Can help women out of poverty and gender constraints (Apitzsch, 2003; Wahid, 1994); does not necessarily alleviate poverty for low-income women (Strier, 2010). |

The author attempts to shed light on the aforementioned research question through an in-depth qualitative study of 134 women livelihood entrepreneurs associated with the education and training intervention SEWA (the Self-Employed Women's Association) in the context of impoverished communities in urban and rural communities around Ahmedabad, Gujarat, India. Conducted verbally and through a combination of semi-structured interviews, and a study of panel data, this research is about what hopes and dreams the women livelihood entrepreneurs have for themselves and their families, as well as their goals for the businesses they have built.

## The livelihood entrepreneur

Business in the twenty-first century is not just about making profit, but also about creating shared value, innovation and social cooperation (Freeman et al., 2007; Porter, 2011). Value may be created in many ways, but this chapter is most concerned with co-creating value for mutual benefit both for entrepreneurs living in poverty and thus also for society through poverty alleviation (Griffin, 2016; Prahalad and Ramaswamy, 2004; Simanis et al., 2008). However, to understand how entrepreneurs can help to alleviate poverty, we must first understand the context of poverty (Peredo and Chrisman, 2006; Peterson, 1988).

### What is poverty?

There are many definitions of both poverty and poverty alleviation. While most believe that poverty is only about economic means, some believe it is more than that: it is 'a deprivation of basic capabilities' (Anand et al., 2006; Drèze et al., 1997; Sen, 1999, 1997, 1973). The United Nations High Commission on Human Rights (UNHCHR) has a comprehensive definition: 'Poverty: a human condition characterized by the sustained or chronic deprivation of the resources, capabilities, choices, security and power necessary for the enjoyment of an adequate standard of living and other civil, cultural, economic, political and social rights' (UNHCHR, 2001). As of the twenty-first century, more than 2 billion people cannot meet their basic needs of food, shelter, clothing, access to health care, clean water, sanitation and education (Sachs, 2005). To humanize it further, approximately 27,000 children die every day from poverty, from absolutely preventable disease and starvation (Singer, 2009).

### Framework for poverty

The most widely accepted framework for poverty separates poverty into extreme, moderate and relative forms (Sachs, 2005; UN Millennium Project, 2006; UNDP, 2012). Extreme poverty is when one lives on less than US$1 per day, at purchasing power parity (ppp) (Sachs, 2005). Purchasing power parity means this is reflecting the kinds of things we would actually be able to buy for $1 in the United States, not items that a dollar can buy in the developing world (ibid.). Individuals who have an income of between US$1–US$2 per day (ppp) are considered to live in moderate poverty (ibid.). Those with a household income less than the national average in their country, and who lack resources that would be taken for granted on the average income in their country, are considered to be living in relative poverty (ibid.).

Conventionally, the motivation for business creation in the context of poverty is simple: if basic needs such as food, water and shelter are not met, higher-order needs cannot be met either (Maslow, 1943). However, what Maslow (and perhaps many in the Western world) presumes to be the lowest-level needs for someone living in poverty are not necessarily what the impoverished person perceives to be their first level of needs. This chapter thus challenges Maslow's theory that identifies impoverished people in a conventional manner, and instead considers poverty to be a 'varied and multidimensional' (Sen, 1973) deprivation, which includes access to basic needs, income, dignity, well-being and social capital (ibid.). If this definition of poverty is assumed, the process by which poverty is alleviated must be multidimensional as well.

## The end of poverty (solutions)

Poverty is clearly a problem that needs to be addressed, but there are extremely different points of view as to who should take on the responsibility to end it, and how. The conventional yet short-term solution was through basic needs assistance and foreign aid, such as in the Peace Corps. There are many other solutions, including empowerment, giving impoverished people more options in consumption and, finally, poverty alleviation from the ground up, which will be explored in the following paragraphs.

### Empowerment

While basic needs are certainly necessary in the direst conditions, the endless amount of money that has been sent down the 'aid' tube has not ended the problem of poverty (Karlan and Appel, 2011). Global humanitarian aid agencies began to get used to the idea of empowerment and 'teaching to fish' so as to create longer-term solutions. Academic definitions of empowerment are varied, meaning: the freedom to spend, and ability to share household responsibilities (Devi, 1982), taking responsibility, achieving self-confidence (Gielnik and Warren, 1995), enhancing power to make decisions (Devi, 1982; Gielnik and Warren, 1995), to achieve recognition, involvement and a sense of worth in jobs (Vogt and Murrell, 1990).

It is rare that those empowered would give back to their own communities of poverty, because education may be viewed as a 'way out', not a way to continue to build and create value, yet it still did produce the result of poverty alleviation within a community (Trivedi, 2005). In order to have a more macro poverty alleviation result, there should be a feedback loop of empowerment that would filter into the communities that need poverty alleviation most. There are interventions which do just this, and this chapter will explore one of them in more depth.

*Poverty alleviation as consumption*

In the last century, there have been some ideas about viewing the 'aspiring poor' as a lucrative emerging market (Prahalad and Hart, 2002). Since two-thirds of the world's population is poor, it does seem that in numbers there are many who would be able to consume more. But since the majority of those people have less than $1 (ppp) a day (Prahalad and Hart, 2002), the only types of product for which multinationals could view them as potential consumers would be those that are necessary to fulfill their basic needs, such as laundry detergent (Chandon and Guimaraes, 2007). While some scholars still assert that consumption can also alleviate poverty (Prahalad, 2011), there is skepticism as to whether or not viewing them as consumers is the way to 'alleviate poverty', or whether it is just shifting the definition of poverty and alleviating our guilt (Karnani, 2005).

## Why poverty alleviation from the ground up

There is a new surge to view these emerging markets not just as consumers, but as potential producers as well (Prahalad, 2011). C.K. Prahalad would argue that poverty alleviation is about improving access (both consumption and production) more specifically: 'Poverty alleviation is, simply, improving the disposable income for families – by reducing the costs of services, improving [their] quality, and releasing their time to do work that is productive' (Prahalad, 2011). Karnani (2007) posits that instead of selling to the poor, to alleviate poverty we must view them as businesses to buy from, and 'raise the real income of the poor'.

Recently, these ideas of improving consumption and production have progressed to be viewed as ground-up solutions to ending the poverty problem. 'Enabling local communities and individuals to convert their ideas into products and services – by blending modern science and technology, design and risk capital – constitutes the heart of grassroots innovation' (Gupta, 2013: 18). A laudable example of grassroots innovation is the HoneyBee Network, where innovators at the base of the economic pyramid can harness their ideas and make them accessible to others (Gupta, 2013).

Even William Easterly, a well-known anti-aid economist, has praised the ground-up solutions to poverty problems via 'searchers' who find the reality at the 'bottom' and find things that work (Easterly, 2006). This chapter explains some realities in this context, and highlights some that work by demonstrating when people find solutions from the bottom up. Thus, it begins with women living in poverty who are able to create livelihoods for themselves and their families.

## The purpose of entrepreneurship in the context of poverty

Seventy percent of the world's impoverished people are women, and they traditionally lack access to credit, jobs and money (ILO, 2015). Because women tend to invest in their children first (ILO, 2008; Premchander, 2003), addressing how women may receive that access to credit, jobs and money is important. In fact, closing gender gaps 'can enhance economic productivity, improve development outcomes for the next generation, and make institutions and policies more representative' (Revenga and Shetty, 2012). While much literature has focused on women's micro-enterprise, it has not demonstrated itself to be an exit out of poverty (Bates and Servon, 1998). Entrepreneurship has become more widely considered as 'critical to economic development and sustainability worldwide' (Kelley et al., 2014). Women's entrepreneurship in the developing-world context thus needs more research as a possible way to help eradicate poverty.

Insights from the entrepreneurship literature are lacking when it comes to uncertain environments, and more specifically in the context of poverty. Since uncertainty is at the heart of entrepreneurship, there are studies on how and when entrepreneurs bear uncertainty (McMullen and Shepherd, 2006), but these disregard those who lack basic needs such as food security and choice. Entrepreneurs are defined as those who create value by identifying and seizing opportunities in a particular context, and also hold certain personal attributes such as entrepreneurial spirit, are inspired, creative, courageous, possess fortitude, and take direct action (Dees et al., 2001; Drucker, 1995; Low and MacMillan, 1988; Martin and Osberg, 2007; Schumpeter, 1975).

Early entrepreneurship literature focused on entrepreneur characteristics to explain outcomes (Aldrich and Wiedenmayer, 1993; Gartner, 1988; Tolbert et al., 2011), and assumed that the main goal of new venture (value) creation was profit (Chrisman et al., 1998; Peredo and Chrisman, 2006). Eventually there was a lot more on social entrepreneurship (Desa and Basu, 2013; Spear, 2006), and literature began to look at the top-down microcredit policies that would fund entrepreneurs in the developing world (Schreiner and Woller, 2003; Dowla, 2006). More recently there has begun to be more literature on bottom-up approaches to microcredit (Imai et al., 2012; Khandker, 2005), where the idea is to help livelihood entrepreneurs come up with their own goals and approaches to how they may lift themselves out of poverty.

As academics we should test our assumptions, because the current knowledge about entrepreneurship may not apply to entrepreneurs who live in a multidimensional uncertainty like poverty. In the same vein, social entrepreneurship literature assumptions may not apply either, because people who have not yet met their most basic needs may not choose to explicitly help society with their mission (Martin and Osberg, 2007). Thus it is imperative that we study entrepreneurs in economic uncertainty because of lack of access and resources, in order to continue our pursuit of economic progress and knowledge. In the entrepreneurship literature currently there is a disconnection between looking at the micro (the individual) and the macro (overall societal betterment), and thus the author examines the individual entrepreneur herself as the unit of analysis.

An entrepreneurship theory that is closely related to the new concept of livelihood entrepreneurship is called the community-based enterprise (CBE), proposed to be a way to attain sustainable local development (Peredo and Chrisman, 2006). In this case, the meaning of sustainable local development is to improve the quality of life and meet the needs of those in the local community – which includes poverty reduction – while still preserving the environment (Rees, 1998; Smith, 1994). The characteristics of a CBE include basing new ventures on local community skills, dependence on community participation, and a multiplicity of goals (Peredo and Chrisman, 2006). A multiplicity of goals is also present in the concept of livelihood entrepreneurship, and is therefore a good place to begin. Finally, CBEs 'treat the entrepreneur and the enterprise as embedded in a network of relationships . . . [and] the community . . . [is] endogenous to the enterprise and the entrepreneurial process' (Peredo and Chrisman, 2006: 310).

However, there are clear differences between CBEs and livelihood entrepreneurs as well. While CBEs offer a multiplicity of goals for the entrepreneur, livelihood entrepreneurship is more specific: stability and survival of the family, creation of a livelihood for the family, is the aspiration. It is a CBE, but specific to subsistence marketplaces (Sridharan and Viswanathan, 2008; Viswanathan and Rosa, 2007; Viswanathan et al., 2010). There have been qualitative studies to further differentiate the contexts and cultures of subsistence consumer-merchants (SCMs) in South India that give some insight in unstable environments (Viswanathan et al., 2010).

## Livelihood creation

While studying poverty alleviation in more depth, the author sat with students in India who would be classified as 'street' or 'slum' children, discussing power, and those students explained that for their families (who are living in poverty), family livelihood is the goal. This means that making sure that their families have a steady stream of basic needs (not just for today and tomorrow) was most important, and was prioritized above all else. Furthermore, poverty alleviation is about people who are trying to make changes in their lives on a daily basis: it is not just a theoretical notion, it is about real individuals, their families and their daily lives:

*Proposition 1: For the livelihood entrepreneur, the goal of her business is to create a livelihood for herself and her family.*

Livelihood entrepreneurship is a means to alleviate poverty that creates value by empowering and creating livelihoods for and by the very people who need it most. This is a study of entrepreneurs who live in poverty and create value for the world by sustaining their own family livelihoods, identified here as livelihood entrepreneurs.

Current entrepreneurship literature is still just beginning to include observations of entrepreneurs who are living in extreme poverty, especially through studies of micro-enterprise (Strier, 2010; Bates and Servon, 1998). The author assumes that the study of entrepreneurship is to 'explain and facilitate the role of new enterprise in furthering economic progress' (Low and MacMillan, 1988), and that it is therefore imperative that furthering economic progress be studied in all parts of society, especially among the most downtrodden. The new concept of livelihood entrepreneurship could fill the gap in the literature about entrepreneurs who are living in poverty and lifting themselves out of it.

The entrepreneurship literature has distinguished between necessity-based and opportunity-based nascent entrepreneurship (Brewer and Gibson, 2014; Kelley et al., 2014). Most would imagine that those living in poverty are all necessity-based entrepreneurs, those individuals who create businesses primarily because of involuntary job loss and the scarcity of vacancies (Thompson, 2003). This chapter seeks to distinguish livelihood entrepreneurship from concepts such as those aforementioned and CBE. Livelihood entrepreneurship does not have to do with the beginnings of entrepreneurial activity; it may have begun either as necessity-based (a last resort where there are no other options left) or as opportunity-based forms of nascent entrepreneurship (where there are many options and one is chosen) (Wennekers et al., 2005; Wennekers et al., 2010). Nor does livelihood entrepreneurship deal with the macro-level sustainable development issue, as CBEs do (Peredo and Chrisman, 2006). While livelihood entrepreneurship is about survival, it is not just about subsistence, because it has the additional embedded component of helping the world without the intention of helping the world (Sridharan et al., 2014; Viswanathan et al., 2014; Viswanathan and Rosa, 2007; Viswanathan et al., 2010). Livelihood entrepreneurship is about sustainability on many levels: sustaining the venture that an entrepreneur has already created, as well as sustaining their own lives and the lives of their families.

Livelihood entrepreneurship is the most basic form of entrepreneurship that has to occur first for those living in poverty, before the traditional entrepreneurship, or social entrepreneurship, tends to occur. First, the basic needs (livelihood creation) of an entrepreneur need to be fulfilled, before there can be an intent to move toward other needs (such as expansion):

*Proposition 2: The livelihood entrepreneur is currently not interested in expanding her business.*

Social entrepreneurship, in particular, goes beyond the initial stages and thus sets itself apart because it is where the basic needs of that entrepreneur most likely have already been met. Social entrepreneurship may not apply to livelihood entrepreneurs, because only a person who has met their most basic needs may choose to explicitly help society with their mission (Martin and Osberg, 2007). While some social entrepreneurs do come from the 'Other 90%' (Gupta, 2013) most social entrepreneurs come from social and economic wealth (Zahra et al., 2009). This chapter therefore proposes that entrepreneurs living in the context of poverty do not intend to help broader society in the way a social entrepreneur does:

*Proposition 3: The livelihood entrepreneur is not motivated by the intention to help broader society with her business.*

The livelihood entrepreneur herself has the opportunity to participate in the actions that affect her life and the lives of her family and surrounding community, and in this context it means being able to bring herself and her community out of poverty:

*Proposition 4: The livelihood entrepreneur aspires to help herself, her family, and her immediate surrounding community.*

Because the CBE is so deeply connected to the livelihood entrepreneur, this chapter explains livelihood entrepreneurship through the study of a well-established CBE. In this particular study, the author does not examine the specific CBEs (micro-enterprises) of the livelihood entrepreneurs themselves, but rather an overarching CBE that has intervened to help these livelihood entrepreneurs establish their own micro-enterprises.

## Research design: methodology and setting

The 'new commons' approach to development (Hawken, 2007) provides that since people who live at base of the pyramid (BoP) do not have the resources to lift themselves out of poverty, the 'top of the pyramid', those with the resources, can improve BoP access through both consumption and production. However, the top of the pyramid does not know exactly how to help.

In this chapter the author makes the assumption that improving the quality of livelihood by giving people access to choices, opportunity and social capital is the essence of poverty alleviation (Sen, 1985). Social capital is the ability to use one's relationships as well as the network of the relationships (Granovetter, 1985; Levin, 2008; Nahapiet and Ghoshal, 1998). In a previous study by the author, through careful examination of a few networks in which a trade union in India called SEWA has been an intervention, it seems that women have gained skills and social capital because of the organization (Trivedi, 2014). This study therefore assumes that the social capital of a women entrepreneur in the context of poverty affects her ability to lift herself out of poverty, since this is one of the primary advantages that the SEWA intervention gives women (Trivedi, 2014).

New approaches in BoP strategy are appealing, and include business co-ventures, which create shared value for those in poverty and those who are at the top of the pyramid as well (Porter, 2011; Simanis et al., 2008). These new business co-ventures are when those at the BoP are not just consumers or producers, but partners in the co-creation of value (Griffin, 2016; Hawken, 2007; Simanis et al., 2008). In order to co-create, the top of the pyramid must understand the context of poverty and how there have been successes, to sustain livelihoods. The top of the pyramid must also understand that those living in poverty do not identify themselves as impoverished, but rather identify themselves as change-makers. The intention for this qualitative study is to aid that better understanding of livelihood entrepreneurs' experiences, and to help explain what these successful women actually want.

## Research setting

### India

As a foreigner traveling the world from the United States, poverty always seems shocking and apparent when first seen in Asia, Latin America and Africa. For many, poverty is particularly overwhelming in India, due to the concentration of poverty as well as dense overpopulation throughout the country. For this reason, this study is based in India. Additionally, this research focuses on women because, while the gender gap is narrowing, there are still more men than women globally who are active entrepreneurs (Kelley et al., 2014: 7). However, the likelihood of entrepreneurs being female is close to equal or higher than that of being male in ten countries, all of which are developing (Kelley et al., 2014: 8). The type of entrepreneurship that exists in these countries must be significantly different for this to occur. Since India is not one of these nations where the ratio of female to male entrepreneurs is high, it makes sense to study women entrepreneurs with low incomes in India, to gain more knowledge about Indian women entrepreneurs (Kelley et al., 2014: 83).

### Ethnic entrepreneurship and social networks

If we explore the theory of CBE and those of ethnic entrepreneurship (Aldrich and Waldinger, 1990; Bonacich, 1973; Light and Rosenstein, 1995; Waldinger et al., 1990), it is found that there are some culturally embedded institutions that shape the founding of new enterprises (Brandl and Bullinger, 2008; Tolbert et al., 2011). This indicates that we must look at not just new enterprises creating livelihoods in the context of poverty, but also those that may have cultures that nurture entrepreneurship; thus the necessity to specify a cultural group or ethnicity arises. This chapter explores livelihood entrepreneurship in the context of India, one of the four BRIC countries (Brazil, Russia, India China), and has been an emerging market of interest over the last several decades (Palepu et al., 2010). However, India has many different states with different cultures and different economic and social policies, so it is necessary to narrow down further. The author chose Gujarat as the research setting because of its liberal economic policies, and because it is a state in India from where many entrepreneurs have originated (Kalnins and Chung, 2006; Tsui-Auch, 2005).

### Gujarat

As most economies in the world began, the history of India's economy began with small businesses. More specifically, in modern South Asian history, Gujarati and Marwadi merchants, entrepreneurs and bankers (Hindu, Jain and Muslim) traded and established businesses throughout India, and they without a doubt helped India's economy extensively (Leonard, 2011). Gujarat or Rajasthan would therefore be an ideal place to start when beginning a research study on Indian entrepreneurship.

*Women*

Using women as the primary participants is justified because India has a lower percentage of necessity-based early-stage male entrepreneurs than female, when on average there is a higher percentage of early-stage female entrepreneurs throughout the rest of the world (Singer et al., 2014: 85). Historically, research has demonstrated that women have not had equal access to financial resources (Brush et al., 2002; Kelley et al., 2014). While this inequality is also historically accurate for Indian women, there is in addition a distinct history of resilience and civil disobedience as well (for example, the Chipko movement). Hindus worship female forms of their Ultimate Being and the Indian government has had female prime ministers and heads of party. There are parts of India where a matriarchal society has existed and still does (for example, Hindus in Kerala). For all of these reasons, Indian women would be a unique and interesting set of respondents for this particular entrepreneurship study.

*SEWA*

In Indian women's studies literature, it is discussed that the best strategy to empower women is through organizing and strengthening their roles in community-based women's groups (Gulati, 1993). In fact, in the particular case of women living in poverty, the group approach has proven to be most effective for income generation (Nair, 1996). Thus, this is a study of female livelihood entrepreneurs, using the Self-Employed Women's Association (SEWA) network intervention located in and around Ahmedabad, Gujarat.

SEWA is a trade union of female laborers and entrepreneurs who are living in poverty (SEWA, 2012). The organization is a well-known bounded network. The women who are a part of the SEWA union receive training, subsidies and loans from SEWA. Most importantly, they meet other women in their same line of work in different villages, and get to talk about what different techniques are successful and those that are not for their particular area. They build their weak ties, and this is most helpful for their success (Granovetter, 1983; Trivedi, 2014). There are special circumstances where SEWA also gives the women goods, and even amenities such as shelter or bathrooms. SEWA field workers are mostly women and men from the local communities themselves, so the trust is built-in from the very beginning. Women in the SEWA network have equal access to the financial resources that historically have not been available to them (SEWA, 2012).

## Data

The targets of the survey are female adults, currently or previously a part of the SEWA network or trade union. Women entrepreneurs in the SEWA network are involved in many different types of work, primarily what their villages specialize in. SEWA helps to build their capacity and helps to build their networks, so that they may learn how to turn their work into thriving businesses. Different types of work that SEWA helps with include fabric embroidery and other fabric artisans, animal husbandry, salt production (through labor), street vending (selling vegetables, food and some miscellaneous tourist items) and farming.

At the initial stage, SEWA identified five different trades to study from the many different types of entrepreneurs that SEWA worked with: the professions chosen were animal husbandry, farming, salt working, fabric embroidery and street vending. The trades decided upon were based on villages that had not been evaluated, researched or visited by foreigners, in order to convey their value to SEWA. The desired sample size of participants was determined to be 125, therefore as a next step the author pre-determined 25 participants per profession. First, the author looked at SEWA's panel data for each of those five types of entrepreneurs in the specific regions. Then the author conducted a personal interview with each participant between October 2013 and December 2013. Each interview lasted between 15 and 60 minutes long.

The total sample size for this study was 134 respondents in the SEWA network. While the population size is unknown, the number of women in the SEWA network in urban Ahmedabad alone (not including surrounding villages which were part of the sample) was more than 179 000. The sample was approximately evenly distributed between the five different trades (animal husbandry, farming, salt production, street vending and fabric embroidery). Each village the author went to specialized in one or more of the different entrepreneurial trades identified. Each participant had attended meetings at SEWA, the trade union and co-operative that had either trained them in skills or built their networks through meeting with other village women who were in the same line of work. The mean education level of all participants in the study was two years of school, and 68 percent of the population sampled had no schooling at all.

The mean family income for all of the respondents at the time of the survey was 166 rupees per day, which is approximately US$2.75. The mean income for all respondents before they joined SEWA was 61.4 rupees per day, which is approximately US$1. The number of people living under one roof with the respondent was an average and median of six people, and the maximum was 15 people, while the minimum was one person.

Table 4.2 displays some of the characteristics of the study sample. Also, it is important to note that 80 percent of the participants were from rural geographic areas, and only 20 percent were from urban areas.

**Table 4.2**  Summary of sample characteristics (% or mean)

|  | Mean (from 134 total) | Median | Max | Min | % |
|---|---|---|---|---|---|
| Age | 41.9 | 40 | 65 | 18 | |
| Education | 2.07 years | 0 | 11 | 0 | |
| None | | | | | 67.9 |
| 1–4 years | | | | | 6.59 |
| 5–6 years | | | | | 8.95 |
| 7–8 years | | | | | 10.4 |
| 9–12 years | | | | | 5.97 |
| Tenure at SEWA | 11.22 | 12 | 26 | 1 | |
| Work tenure | 21.27 | 20 | 60 | 2 | |
| Single | | | | | 2.2 |
| Engaged to be married | | | | | 0.75 |
| Married | | | | | 86 |
| Widow | | | | | 11.1 |
| Number living under one roof | 6.044 | 6 | 15 | 1 | |
| Family income per day | 226.4 | 166.66 | 2000 | 0 | |
| Income before SEWA | 61.444 | 41.666 | 555.567 | 0 | |
| Rural | | | | | 79.85 |
| Urban | | | | | 20.15 |
| Street vendors | | | | | 20 |
| Animal husbandry | | | | | 20 |
| Fabric workers | | | | | 20 |
| Salt workers | | | | | 18.66 |
| Farmers | | | | | 19.4 |
| Retired | | | | | 1.5 |

## Research design

The author asked SEWA to supply panel data to validate family income differences before and after joining SEWA, but the qualitative study is the primary mode of inquiry via entrepreneur experiences. The author used survey method with the respondents to collect qualitative data about their basic attributes as well as those related to the research question. Since the research question was about distinguishing characteristics, and the author proposed that livelihood entrepreneurs are distinct because of their goals and personal dreams and aspirations, the questions specifically asked were: 'What goals do you have for your business?' and 'What are your personal hopes and dreams for yourself?' Additionally, the author asked about the SEWA intervention itself and wanted to know what it gave these women. The author asked, 'What did SEWA give you?' and coded the answers.

*Procedure*

The author received Institutional Review Board (IRB) approval after creating a set of questions that indicated constructs and then translated the questions into Gujarati and back to English to cross-check. While quantitative studies help to demonstrate theoretical models, a qualitative study can give deeper insight as to what is necessary for the particular groups studied to succeed. This qualitative study addresses some (very few) characteristics of the entrepreneurs who have been successful in the context of poverty. The SEWA intervention may or may not be directly involved in this success, but asking livelihood entrepreneurs to explain it in their own words was insightful. From the sample characteristics (see Table 4.2), we see that the mean income of the sample data respondents went from ~US$1 a day to ~US$2.75 per day after joining SEWA, so participation in the union seems to possibly have some effect on their success.

The author conducted semi-structured interviews with open-ended questions. The author asked about participants' attributes first, which developed Table 4.2 (sample characteristics). Then the author asked an open-ended set of questions focused on their aspirations and goals, and how they had changed over time. The author hoped to enhance understanding on how Indian women livelihood entrepreneurs' aspirations and goals may be different than those of other types of entrepreneurs. In the method, the author allowed for emergent patterns. The entrepreneurs interviewed were those who had expanded their networks through SEWA and had successfully built businesses in the context of poverty. First, the author started with the *aagevaan*, or the organizer of the group; usually the first woman to join SEWA in the village. Then the author met with the women she had called to her home to meet with the author. Each of the women was asked how their life had changed because of SEWA, and what they wanted in life and for their businesses. After the data were collected, the author coded the responses by finding general patterns of frequency and codes, and comparing the different villages and different types of work. Each of the responses was put into a different category: for hopes and dreams, they were coded into both the business and personal; for personal, including the entrepreneur herself and others, just the entrepreneur herself, just others, and finally those refusing to give any response. The results are in Table 4.3.

For goals, they were coded based on content: money, expansion, another business in the future, the idea of moving forward (coming ahead in Gujarati), wanting more things (anything material), infrastructure, things personally, things more specific to the future of the business, more work, comfort while working, livelihood-related, and none. The results are in Table 4.4.

## Results and implications

While quantitative studies help to demonstrate theoretical models, a qualitative study can yield deep insight. Distinguishing characteristics of the livelihood entrepreneur were revealed through this qualitative study. The first proposition related to

**Table 4.3** Summary of hopes and dreams

| Categories/ Entrepreneur business | Vendors | Animal husbandrists | Fabric artisans | Salt workers | Farmers | Total | % |
|---|---|---|---|---|---|---|---|
| Business and Personal | 6 | 1 | 6 | 3 | 4 | 20 | 0.14925 |
| Personal: me and others | 7 | 5 | 9 | 2 | 6 | 29 | 0.21641 |
| Only others | 7 | 9 | 7 | 12 | 9 | 44 | 0.3283 |
| Only me | 5 | 9 | 4 | 4 | 2 | 24 | 0.1791 |
| None | 2 | 3 | 1 | 4 | 7 | 17 | 0.1268 |
| Totals | 27 | 27 | 27 | 25 | 28 | 134 | 1 |

**Table 4.4** Summary of business aspirations

| Goal | No. of participants who mentioned | % of total number of participants | Approx. % |
|---|---|---|---|
| m = money | 11 | 0.082089552 | 8 |
| e = expansion | 18 | 0.134328358 | 13 |
| se = another business in future | 1 | 0.007462687 | <1 |
| a = come ahead | 8 | 0.059701493 | 6 |
| t = things | 13 | 0.097014925 | 10 |
| i = infrastructure | 3 | 0.02238806 | 2 |
| p = personal things | 3 | 0.02238806 | 2 |
| sp = future things specific to business | 19 | 0.141791045 | 14 |
| w = more work | 9 | 0.067164179 | 7 |
| c = comfort while working | 1 | 0.007462687 | <1 |
| L = livelihood | 4 | 0.029850746 | 3 |
| N = None | 68 | 0.507462687 | >50 |

business goals being about livelihoods for these entrepreneurs (see Table 4.4). Only 49 percent of participants articulated goals for their businesses, and only 14 percent said they would be interested in expansion. Proposition 2 proposed that expansion was not yet part of livelihood entrepreneurs' aspirations, and this was true for most (but not all). If we delve deeper, this means that more than 50 percent of participants did not reply with aspirations for their businesses. One even said specifically that she would prefer to only have the business that she has now, and would not like any more (that it was 'enough'). Approximately 3 percent of participants replied that the goal they had was just to maintain their livelihoods. One of those four respondents said that she just wanted to be able to put food on the table every day. While this is not a large number who explicitly stated that livelihoods were their goals, the fact that less than 15 percent mentioned expansion and more than 50 percent did not have goals for their businesses implies that both hypotheses are worth exploring further. The third proposition was about the livelihood entrepreneur not explicitly stating she wanted to help society. This was not mentioned in any of the participants' goals or hopes and dreams, except for one, who mentioned peace but only for her surrounding community. While certainty cannot be claimed about these entrepreneurs' goals, this gives deeper insight into the goals of livelihood entrepreneurs.

The fourth proposition was about who exactly the entrepreneurs intend to help. When asked about personal hopes and dreams (see Table 4.3), 57 percent of participants spoke about their hopes and dreams for their children (even when asked repeatedly about themselves). Thirty-three percent of all participants spoke only of others, and said nothing about themselves at all; and 22 percent spoke of a mix between their own personal hopes and dreams and those of others, who were in every case specifically their family and community members. Approximately 15 percent spoke of their business in combination with their own personal hopes and dreams (that sometimes included others as well). Thirteen percent either would not answer this question or actually stated that they had no hopes or dreams. This indicates that while we cannot be certain that livelihood entrepreneurs aspire to help themselves, their family and their immediate community members, it seems to have held true within this dataset.

These findings imply that aspirations are culturally and perhaps even socio-economically contextual, because while these women had been successful and able to lift themselves out of poverty, very few women (14 percent) spoke of expanding their businesses, and many did not speak about dreams for their own futures. The study also clearly outlined how respondents felt that SEWA had helped them build their livelihoods (four of the respondents even mentioned the translation for 'livelihoods' when asked what SEWA had given them). Since 48 percent of participants in this study credited SEWA for their education or training for work, it seems the SEWA intervention was an education intervention. The livelihood entrepreneur may need this type of intervention in order to succeed.

## Future directions and conclusion

### Future directions

Because of the conceptual introduction of livelihood entrepreneurship, the author may be able to further clarify the concept through future research. First, there is an opportunity to look more closely at community-based interventions like SEWA and observe how exactly they helped to train and empower these women. In particular, the study of the network that SEWA was able to build for these women is of interest.

Second, there is an opportunity to examine the definition of poverty more closely by examining the different changes that occurred for these successful entrepreneurs.

What happened? Did they change their behavior? Was there an increase in social capital? Was there an increase in access to basic needs? Or was the increase primarily in economic status?

Third, it would be an interesting conceptual project to identify the different 'rungs' of emergent entrepreneurs, and whether they might be distinguished by the level of poverty the entrepreneurs hail from. The few women who did have aspirations for the future of their enterprises in this study demonstrate that there is a ladder, and it could be defined more clearly in the entrepreneurship literature. Finally, there is an obvious opportunity to compare livelihood entrepreneur aspirations and goals to those of traditional entrepreneurs or social entrepreneurs, in order to distinguish this type of entrepreneur further.

*Conclusion*

In this chapter, the goals and aspirations of these successful women livelihood entrepreneurs are evaluated in an attempt to explain how they may be distinguished from other entrepreneurs, and identified as change-makers rather than women living in poverty. The author concludes that they are different in that they do not have the same goals for their businesses as other entrepreneurs do, and their intention is only to help themselves and their families, not to help the world. In this way, the proposed distinction between traditional and social entrepreneurs appears to be valid. Since the women in this study were all part of a thriving network of SEWA women, it is important to note that this may be an integral aspect of successful entrepreneurship at the base of the pyramid.

The study of livelihood entrepreneurs is just beginning. For now, we may recognize there is a new type of woman entrepreneur: one who lifts herself and her family from poverty and stimulates her developing-country economy. This, in turn, has many positive effects on development and the world.

Note

1   Names have been changed to protect privacy.

# References

Acs, Z. (2006), 'How is entrepreneurship good for economic growth?', *Innovations*, 1(1), 97–107.

Aldrich, H.E. and R. Waldinger (1990), 'Ethnicity and entrepreneurship', *Annual Review of Sociology*, 16(1), 111–135.

Aldrich, H.E. and G. Wiedenmayer (1993), 'From traits to rates: an ecological perspective on organizational foundings', *Advances in Entrepreneurship, Firm Emergence, and Growth*, 1, 145–195.

Anand, S., F. Peter and A. Sen (2006), *Public Health, Ethics, and Equity*. Oxford: Oxford University Press.

Anthias, F. and N. Mehta (2003), 'The intersection between gender, the family and self-employment: the family as a resource', *International Review of Sociology/Revue internationale de sociologie*, 13(1), 105–116.

Apitzsch, U. (2003), 'Gaining autonomy in self-employment processes: the biographical embedded-ness of women's and migrants' business', *International Review of Sociology/Revue Internationale de Sociologie*, 13(1), 163–182.

Bates, T. and L. Servon (1998), 'Microenterprise as an exit route from poverty: recommendations for programs and policy makers', *Journal of Urban Affairs*, 20(4), 419–441.

Bonacich, E. (1973), 'A theory of middleman minorities', *American Sociological Review*, 38(5), 583–594.

Brandl, J. and B. Bullinger (2008), 'Entrepreneurship als institution: Gesellschaftlicher kontext und individuelle perspektiven', *Sozialwissenschaftliche Aspekte des Gründungsmanagements* in Die Entstehung und Entwicklung junger Unternehmen im gesellschaftlichen Kontext, Hannover, 52–68.

Brewer, J. and S. Gibson (eds) (2014), *Necessity Entrepreneurs: Microenterprise Education and Economic Development*. Cheltenham, UK and Northampton, MA, USA: Edward Elgar Publishing.

Brush, C.G., N. Carter, P.G. Greene, M.M. Hart and E. Gatewood (2002), 'The role of social capi-tal and gender in linking financial suppliers and entrepreneurial firms: a framework for future research.', *Venture Capital*, 4(4), 305–323.

Buttner, E. (1993), 'Female entrepreneurs: how far have they come?', *Business Horizons*, 36(2), 59–65.

Carter, S. and T. Cannon (1992), *Women as Entrepreneurs: A Study of Female Business Owners, Their Motivations, Experiences and Strategies for Success*. London: Academic Press.

Chandon, P. and P.P. Guimaraes (2007), *Unilever in Brazil (1997–2007): Marketing Strategies for Low-Income Consumers*. Fontainebleau: INSEAD.

Chrisman, J. J., A. Bauerschmidt and C.W. Hofer (1998), 'The determinants of new venture perfor-mance: an extended model', *Entrepreneurship Theory and Practice*, 23(1), 5–29.

Chua, J.H., J.J. Chrisman and P. Sharma (1999), 'Defining the family business by behavior', *Entrepreneurship: Theory and Practice*, 23(4), 19–39.

Datta, P.B. and R. Gailey (2012), 'Empowering women through social entrepreneurship: case study of a women's cooperative in India', *Entrepreneurship Theory and Practice*, May, 569–587.

Dees, J.G. (1998), 'The meaning of "social entrepreneurship"', Stanford University, Draft Report for the Kauffman Center for Entrepreneurial Leadership.

Dees, J.G., J. Emerson and P. Economy (2001), *Enterprising Nonprofits: A Toolkit for Social Entrepreneurs*. New York: Wiley.

Desa, G. and S. Basu (2013), 'Optimization or bricolage? Overcoming resource constraints in global social entrepreneurship', *Strategic Entrepreneurship Journal*, 7(1), 26–49.

Devi, U.L. (1982), *Status and Employment of Women in India*. New Delhi: B.R. Publishing Corp.

Dowla, A. (2006), 'In credit we trust: building social capital by Grameen Bank in Bangladesh', *Journal of Socio-Economics*, 35(1), 102–122.

Drèze, J., A.K. Sen and World Institute for Development Economics Research (1997), *Indian Development: Selected Regional Perspectives*. Delhi; New York: Oxford University Press.

Drucker, P. (1995), *Innovation and Entrepreneurship*. New York: Harper Business.

Easterly, W.R. (2006), *The White Man's Burden: Why the West's Efforts to Aid the Rest Have Done So Much Ill and So Little Good*. New York: Penguin Press.

Freeman, R.E., J.S. Harrison and A.C. Wicks (2007), *Managing for Stakeholders: Survival, Reputation, and Success*. New Haven, CT: Yale University Press.

Gartner, W.B. (1988), '"Who is an entrepreneur?" is the wrong question', *American Journal of Small Business*, 12(4), 11–32.

Gielnik, C. and S. Warren (1995), *Empowering Yourself: Self Development for Women*. New Delhi: Universities Press.

Granovetter, M. (1983), 'The strength of weak ties: a network theory revisited', *Sociological Theory*, 1, 201–233.

Granovetter, M. (1985), 'Economic action and social structure: the problem of embeddedness', *American Journal of Sociology*, 91, 481–510

Griffin, J.J. (2016), *Managing Corporate Impacts: Co-creating Value*. Cambridge: Cambridge University Press.

Gulati L. (1993), *In the Absence of their Men: The Impact of Male Migration on Women*. New Delhi: SAGE Publications.

Gupta, A.K. (2013), 'Tapping the entrepreneurial potential of grassroots innovation', *Stanford Social Innovation Review*, 11(3), 18–20.

Hawken, P. (2007), *Blessed Unrest: How the Largest Movement in the World Came into Being, and Why No One Saw it Coming*. New York: Viking.

Heemskerk, M. (2003), 'Self-employment and poverty alleviation: women's work in artisanal gold mines', *Human Organization*, 62(1), 62–73.

Hernandez, L., N. Nunn and T. Warnecke (2012), 'Female entrepreneurship in China: opportunity- or necessity-based?', *International Journal of Entrepreneurship and Small Business*, 15(4), 411–434.

Hisrich, R.D. and C.G. Brush (1983), 'The woman entrepreneur: implications of family, educational, and occupational experience', in J.A. Hornaday, J.A. Timmons and K.H. Vesper (eds). *Frontiers of Entrepreneurship Research* (pp. 255–270). Wellesley, MA: Babson College.

Imai, K.S., R. Gaiha, G. Thapa and S.K. Annim (2012), 'Microfinance and poverty – a macro perspective', *World Development*, 40(8), 1675–1689.

Inter-American Development Bank (1998), 'The microenterprise sector in Latin America and the Caribbean', *Promoting Growth with Equity* (pp. 1–27). Accessed September 13, 2017 at https://publications.iadb.org/handle/11319/4728.

International Labour Organization (ILO) (2008), 'Small changes big changes: women in microfinance', ILO Gender, Equality and Diversity Branch, Geneva, March 27. Accessed 10 June 2016 at http://www.ilo.org/wcmsp5/groups/public/@dgreports/@gender/documents/meetingdocument/wcms_091581.pdf.

International Labour Organization (ILO) (2015), 'Women at work'. Accessed September 13, 2017 at http://www.ilo.org/wcmsp5/groups/public/---dgreports/---dcomm/documents/publication/wcms_067595.pdf.

Kalnins, A. and W. Chung (2006), 'Social capital, geography, and survival: Gujarati immigrant entrepreneurs in the US lodging industry', *Management Science*, 2(2), 233–247.

Karlan, D.S. and J. Appel (2011), *More than Good Intentions: How a New Economics is Helping to Solve Global Poverty*. New York: Dutton.

Karnani, A. (2005), 'Misfortune at the bottom of the pyramid', *Greener Management International*, 51, 99–110.

Karnani, A. (2007), 'The mirage of marketing to the bottom of the pyramid: how the private sector can help alleviate poverty', *California Management Review*, 49(4), 90–111.

Katongole, C., J.C. Munene, M. Ngoma, S. Dawa and A. Sserwanga (2015), 'Entrepreneur's intrapersonal resources and enterprise success among micro and small scale women entrepreneurs', *Journal of Enterprising Culture*, 23(4), 405–447.

Kelley, D., C. Brush, C., P. Greene, M. Herrington, A. Ali and P. Kew (2014), 'Special report: women's entrepreneurship', *Global Entrepreneurship Monitor*. Wellesley, MA: Center for Women's Leadership at Babson College.

Khandker, S. (2005), 'Microfinance and poverty: evidence using panel data from Bangladesh', *World Bank Economic Review*, 19(2), 263–286.

Leonard, K.I. (2011), 'Family firms in Hyderabad: Gujarati, Goswami, and Marwari patterns of adoption, marriage, and inheritance', *Comparative Studies in Society and History*, 53(4), 827–854.

Levin, D. Z. (2008), 'Trust', in S.R. Clegg and J.R. Bailey (eds), *International Encyclopedia of Organization Studies* (pp. 1573–1579). Thousand Oaks, CA: SAGE Publications.

Light, I.H. and C.N. Rosenstein (1995), *Race, Ethnicity, and Entrepreneurship in Urban America*. New York: Aldine de Gruyter.

Low, M.B. and I.C. MacMillan (1988), 'Entrepreneurship: past research and future challenges', *Journal of Management*, 14(2), 139–161.

Mair, J. and I. Marti (2006), 'Social entrepreneurship research: a source of explanation, prediction, and delight', *Journal of World Business*, 41(1), 36–44.

Marlow, S. (1997), 'Self-employed women – new opportunity challenges?', *Entrepreneurship and Regional Development*, 9(3), 199–210.

Martin, R.L. and S. Osberg (2007), 'Social entrepreneurship: the case for definition', *Stanford Social Innovation Review*, 5(2), 28–39.

Maslow, A. (1943), 'A theory of human motivation', *Psychological Review*, 50(4), 370–396.

McMullen, J.S. and D.A. Shepherd (2006), 'Entrepreneurial action and the role of uncertainty in the theory of the entrepreneur', *Academy of Management Review*, 31(1), 132–152.

Moran, G. (2015), 'Exclusive: this is the type of business most likely to promote women leaders'. Accessed at http://fortune.com/2015/06/18/family-business-women-leaders.

Nahapiet, J. and S. Ghoshal (1998), 'Social capital, intellectual capital, and the organizational advantage', *Academy of Management Review*, 23(2), 242–266.

Nair, T.S. (1996), 'Entrepreneurship training for women in the Indian rural sector: a review of approaches and strategies', *Journal of Entrepreneurship*, 5(1), 81–94.

Palepu, K.G., R.J. Bullock and T. Khanna (2010), *Winning in Emerging Markets: A Road Map for Strategy and Execution*. Boston, MA: Harvard Business Press.

Peredo, A.M. and J.J. Chrisman (2006), 'Toward a theory of community-based enterprise', *Academy of Management Review*, 31(2), 309–328.

Peterson, R. (1988), 'Understanding and encouraging entrepreneurship internationally', *Journal of Small Business Management*, 26(2), 1.

Porter, M.E. (2011), 'Creating shared value', *Harvard Business Review*, 89(1/2), 62–77.

Prahalad, C.K. (2011), 'The big picture', Preface, in T. London and S. Hart (eds), *Next Generation Business Strategies for the Base of the Pyramid* (pp. xxvi–xxxii). Upper Saddle River, NJ: Pearson Education.

Prahalad, C.K. and S.L. Hart (2002), 'The fortune at the bottom of the pyramid', *Strategy + Business*, 26, 1–14.

Prahalad, C.K. and V. Ramaswamy (2004), *The Future of Competition: Co-creating Unique Value with Customers*. Boston, MA: Harvard Business School Press.

Premchander, S. (2003), 'NGOS and local MFIs – how increase poverty reduction through women's small and micro-entrreprise', *Futures*, 35, 361–378.

Ratten, V. and I.M. Welpe (2011), 'Special issue: community-based, social and societal entrepreneurship', *Entrepreneurship and Regional Development*, 23(5/6), 283–286.

Rees, G. (1998), *Economic Development*, 2nd edn. Basingstoke: Macmillan.

Revenga, A. and S. Shetty (2012), 'Empowering women is smart economics', *Finance and Development*, 49(1), 40–43.

Reynolds, P.D., M. Hay and S.M. Camp (1999), *Executive Report. Global Entrepreneurship Monitor*. Boston, MA: Babson College and London Business School.

Sachs, J. (2005), *The End of Poverty: Economic Possibilities for Our Time*. New York: Penguin Press.

Schreiner, M. and G. Woller (2003), 'Microenterprise in the first and third worlds', *World Development*, 31(9), 1567–1580.

Schrier, J.W. (1975), 'Entrepreneurial characteristics of women' in J. W. Schrier and J. Susbauer (eds) *Entrepreneurship and Enterprise Development: A Worldwide Perspective*, Milwaukee, WI: Centre for Venture Management, 66–70.

Schumpeter, J.A. (1975), *Capitalism, Socialism and Democracy*. New York: Harper.

Sen, A. (1973), *On Economic Inequality*. Oxford: Clarendon Press.

Sen, A. (1985), *Commodities and Capabilities*. Amsterdam: North-Holland.

Sen, A.K. (1997), *Resources, Values, and Development*. Cambridge, MA: Harvard University Press.

Sen, A. (1999), *Development as Freedom*. New York: Knopf.

Serdedakis, N., G. Tsiolis, M. Tzanakis and S. Papaioannou (2003), 'Strategies of social integration in the biographies of Greek female immigrants coming from the former Soviet Union: self-employment as an alternative', *International Review of Sociology/ Revue Internationale de Sociologie*, 13(1), 145–162.

SEWA (2012), 'Ahmedabad, India', www.sewa.org.

Sharma, P., J.J. Chrisman and J.H. Chua (eds) (1996), *A Review and Annotated Bibliography of Family Business Studies*. Assinippi Park, MA: Kluwer Academic Publishers.

Simanis, E., S. Hart and D. Duke (2008), 'Base of the pyramid protocol: beyond "basic needs" business strategies', *Innovations*, 3(1), 57–84.

Singer, P. (2009), *The Life You Can Save: Acting Now to End World Poverty*. New York: Random House.

Singer, S., J.E. Amoros and D.M. Arreola (2014), *Global Report, Global Entrepreneurship Monitor*. Boston, MA: Babson College and London Business School.

Smith, C. (1994), *Economic Development, Growth, and Welfare*. Basingstoke: Macmillan.

Smith-Hunter, A.E. and R.L. Boyd (2004), 'Applying theories of entrepreneurship to a comparative analysis of white and minority women business owners', *Women in Management Review*, 19(1), 18–28.

Spear, R. (2006), 'Social entrepreneurship: a different model?', *International Journal of Social Economics*, 33(5/6), 399–410.

Sridharan, S. and M. Viswanathan (2008), 'Marketing in subsistence marketplaces: consumption and entrepreneurship in a south Indian context', *Journal of Consumer Marketing*, 25(7), 455–462.

Sridharan, S., E. Maltz, M. Viswanathan and S. Gupta (2014), 'Transformative subsistence entrepreneurship: a study in India', *Journal of Macromarketing*, 34(4), 486–504.

Strier, R. (2010), 'Women, poverty, and the microenterprise: context and discourse', *Gender Work and Organization*, 17(2), 195–218.

Thompson, J.D. (2003), *Organizations in Action: Social Science Bases of Administrative Theory*. New Brunswick, NJ: Transaction Publishers.

Thurik, R. and S. Wennekers (2001), 'A note on entrepreneurship, small business and economic growth', *Small Business and Economic Growth* (January 2001, 11), ERIM Report Series Reference No. ERS-2001-60-STR.

Tolbert, P.S., R.J. David and W.D. Sine (2011), 'Studying choice and change: the intersection of institutional theory and entrepreneurship research', *Organization Science*, 22(5), 1332–1344.

Trivedi, S. (2005), 'Smita in India', *Blog*, accessed at sktrivedi.blogspot.com.

Trivedi, S. (2014), 'Creating livelihoods: Indian women entrepreneur networks in the context of poverty', Doctoral dissertation, George Washington University, Washington, DC.

Tsui-Auch, L.S. (2005), 'Unpacking regional ethnicity and the strength of ties in shaping ethnic entrepreneurship', *Organization Studies*, 26(8), 1189.

UN Millennium Project (2005), *Investing in Development*. New York: UN Secretary General and UN Development Group, accessed November 17, 2017 at http://www.who.int/hdp/publications/4b.pdf.

UNDP (2017), *Millennium Development goals: Eight Goals for 2015*. Geneva: United Nations Development Programme, accessed November 17, 2017 at http://www.undp.org/content/undp/en/home/sdgoverview/mdg_goals.html.

UNHCHR (2001), 'Substantive issues arising in the implementation of the International Covenant on Economic, Social and Cultural Rights: poverty and the International Covenant on Economic, Social and Cultural Rights', Geneva: Committee on Economic, Social and Cultural Rights, accessed Novemver 17, 2017 at http://www2.ohchr.org/english/bodies/cescr/docs/statements/E.C.12.2001.10 Poverty-2001.pdf.

Venugopal, S., M. Viswanathan and K. Jung (2015), 'Consumption constraints and entrepreneurial intentions in subsistence marketplaces', *Journal of Public Policy and Marketing*, 34(2), 235–251.

Vestrum, I. (2016), 'Integrating multiple theoretical approaches to explore the resource mobilization process of community ventures', *Journal of Enterprising Communities: People and Places in the Global Economy*, 10(1), 123–134.

Viswanathan, M., R. Echambadi, S. Venugopal and S. Sridharan (2014), 'Subsistence entrepreneurship, value creation, and community exchange systems: a social capital explanation', *Journal of Macromarketing*, 34(2), 213–226.

Viswanathan, M. and J.A. Rosa (2007), 'Product and market development for subsistence marketplaces: consumption and entrepreneurship beyond literacy and resource barriers', in M. Viswanathan and J.A. Rosa (eds), *Product and Market Development for Subsistence Marketplaces*. Oxford: Elsevier, pp. 1–17.

Viswanathan, M., J.A. Rosa and J.A. Ruth (2010), 'Exchanges in marketing systems: the case of subsistence consumer-merchants in Chennai, India', *Journal of Marketing*, 74(3), 1–17.

Vogt, J.F. and K.L. Murrell (1990), *Empowerment in Organizations*. San Diego, CA: University Associates.

Wahid, A. (1994), 'The Grameen Bank and poverty alleviation in Bangladesh', *American Journal of Economics and Sociology*, 53(1), 1–15.

Waldinger, R., R. Ward, H. Aldrich and J. Stanfield (1990), 'Ethnic entrepreneurs: immigrant business in industrial societies', University of Illinois at Urbana-Champaign's Academy for Entrepreneurial Leadership Historical Research Reference in Entrepreneurship.

Wennekers, S., A. Van Stel and M. Carree (2010), *The Relationship between Entrepreneurship and Economic Development: Is it U-shaped?*. Hanover, MA: Now Publishers.

Wennekers, S., A. Van Wennekers, R. Thurik and P. Reynolds (2005), 'Nascent entrepreneurship and the level of economic development', *Small Business Economics*, 24(3), 293–309.

Woodward, D. (2015), 'Incrementum ad absurdum: global growth, inequality and poverty eradication in a carbon-constrained world', *World Social and Economic Review*, 4. Accessed September 13, 2017 at http://wer.worldeconomicsassociation.org/files/WEA-WER-4-Woodward.pdf.

World Bank (2015), *Global Monitoring Report 2015/2016; Development Goals in an Era of Demographic Change*. Accessed September 13, 2017 at www.worldbank.org/gmr.

Zahra, S.A., E. Gedajlovic, D.O. Neubaum and J.M. Shulman (2009), 'A typology of social entrepreneurs: motives, search processes and ethical challenges', *Journal of Business Venturing*, 24(5), 519–532.

# PART II

Behaviors

# 5 On becoming an entrepreneur: unpacking entrepreneurial identity

*Eliana Crosina**

> *entrepreneurial identities serve as powerful entities that propel entrepreneurial actions . . .*
> *the study of entrepreneurial roles and identities offers tremendous potential for research*
> *in our field*

(Murnieks and Mosakowski, 2007: 1, 7)

## Introduction and chapter scope

As this opening quote indicates, the study of entrepreneurial identity constitutes a promising area of research. Identity, in fact, has been found to influence entrepreneurs' thoughts and actions including, most notably, how they evaluate opportunities (e.g., Fauchart and Gruber, 2011) and how they respond to adversity (e.g., Powell and Baker, 2014) as they prepare to launch and run their organizations. Thus, a closer understanding of the content and formation, as well as the upkeep (or change) of entrepreneurial identity, may afford important insights into the broader new venture creation process.

Despite recognizing entrepreneurial identity as something central to the behaviors entrepreneurs engage in, to date, scholars have paid limited attention to it, particularly in terms of what it entails (that is, its content), how people may develop it (that is, the process they may follow to build it), and the potential differences gender may play in the construction of the identities of women and men entrepreneurs. Indeed, if research on entrepreneurial identity is still limited on the whole, research that deals specifically with issues of identity and its construction among women entrepreneurs is even sparser (see the work of Bruni et al., 2004; Díaz García and Welter, 2013; Lewis, 2013; and that of Marlow and McAdam, 2015, for notable exceptions). Making matters worse, the research that does exist on entrepreneurial identity to date (e.g., Murnieks and Mosakowski, 2007; Hoang and Gimeno, 2010; Fauchart and Gruber, 2011; Navis and Glynn, 2011; Powell and Baker, 2014) provides varying definitions of entrepreneurial identity, leaving what it 'is', and ultimately how it may affect behavior, still somewhat unclear.

Taken together, a better appreciation for the identities (and their construction) among male and female entrepreneurs constitutes an important and promising endeavor, both theoretically and practically. From a theoretical standpoint, this chapter argues that this focus has the potential to challenge some of the 'bases' (see Cardador and Pratt, 2006), or some of the 'raw materials' that scholars have seen individuals leverage to build their work identities, including certain pre-existing social groups and roles. From a practical standpoint, a better understanding of entrepreneurial identity (including its formation and upkeep) may afford new insights into entrepreneurs' actions, including those shared by male and female entrepreneurs, as well as those that may set them apart.

Because research that focuses on entrepreneurial identity largely overlooks how entrepreneurial identity forms and evolves (including areas of potential differ-ence and/or overlap among men and women entrepreneurs), this chapter borrows insights from sister disciplines that have addressed identity and its construction. First, it reviews existing literature that has attempted to clarify what entrepre-neurial identity consists of – highlighting why and how exactly this matters – that is, the various ways in which entrepreneurial identity influences entrepreneurs' thoughts and actions.

Second, it addresses how entrepreneurial identity may come to be. Insights from the identity work literature in particular – a growing body of work that focuses on 'individuals' active construction of identity in social contexts' (Pratt et al., 2006: 237) – offer a promising start to make sense of how entrepreneurial identity might form. Because this literature has largely focused on what professionals do to gain, maintain or de-emphasize their work identities, this chapter compares identity work dynamics among professionals with identity work dynamics among entre-preneurs, highlighting those features of identity and its construction that may be distinctive for women entrepreneurs. Finally, it suggests avenues for, and chal-lenges associated with, future research, including aspects that may be of particular significance when studying entrepreneurial identity among women entrepreneurs.

## Entrepreneurial identity: overview of existing literature

> in the identity literature scarce attention has been paid to entrepreneurship as a site of identity creation and interpretation. This is ironic because entrepreneurship may offer one of the most visible instances of identity
>
> (Navis and Glynn, 2011: 480)

Existing literature that addresses entrepreneurial identity has, over the years, advanced various definitions of it. For example, Stanworth and Curran (1976: 104) described entrepreneurial identity as the 'several possible constellations of mean-ings which may form the core of the entrepreneur's self-definition of the entre-preneurial role'; while Vesalainen and Pihkala (2000: 113) noted 'entrepreneurial identity . . . as a person's inclination to adopt a certain type of occupational entre-preneurial role'.

Unlike Stanworth and Curran (1976) and Vesalainen and Pihkala (2000), who respectively focused on individuals' meanings around, and on their propensity to take on, an entrepreneurial role, Watson (2009) and Nadin (2007) portrayed entrepreneurial identity as a social resource, discursive and symbolic, that entrepreneurs strategically deploy primarily to gain legitimacy. Watson (2009), specifically, showed how entrepreneurial identity may be dynamically negotiated as family members engage in conversations about their roles in the future of their business; while Nadin (2007) discussed how female business owners in the care sector play up their gender to convey their identities as thoughtful entrepreneurs.

More recently, Powell and Baker (2014: 1406) talked about founder[1] identity as encompassing multiple sub-identities that are 'chronically salient' to entrepreneurs in their daily work. They also argued that founder identities entail a combination of role and social identities, and that congruence (or lack thereof) between how founders see themselves, and who they aspire to be, influences their behaviors. At the core of their conceptualization of founder identity is the idea that entrepreneurs carefully devise 'role identities to express their social identities' (Powell and Baker, 2014: 1408).

Kašperová and Kitching (2014: 438) cast 'entrepreneurial identity as a set of concerns emergent from the embodied practices of agents committed to new venture creation and management in relation to their natural, practical, and social environments'. In their theorizing, entrepreneurs need to show commitment to their role to obtain validation from external stakeholders (including their customers, investors and collaborators.) In elaborating what founder role identities can do, Hoang and Gimeno (2010) showed how different combinations of founder role centrality and role complexity shape individuals' capacity to engage in founding activities, as well as their responses to negative feedback (Hoang and Gimeno, 2010: 41). Finally, Navis and Glynn (2011) offered a broader definition of entrepreneurial identity, also accounting for entrepreneurs' claims around their organizations and markets. Table 5.1 summarizes these various, as well as other, definitions.[2]

As these selected examples implicitly indicate, there appears to be little consensus to date about entrepreneurial identity, in terms of both what it comprises as well as how one may develop it. This is in part because extant definitions of entrepreneurial identity range considerably in scope, from some that focus solely on the entrepreneur, to others that also encompass the entrepreneur's team, their business, and the markets in which they operate. Summarizing the state of research in the field, Laakkonen (2012: 62–63) noted that: 'When it comes to entrepreneurial identity . . . the scholarly literature of entrepreneurship has brought out many concepts that have a strong semblance to it . . . entrepreneurial identity has [however] not been given a . . . definition per se.'

Interestingly, despite the limited agreement around what entrepreneurial identity 'is', and on how it may come to be, scholars almost unanimously consider entrepreneurial identity as a key input to entrepreneurs' thoughts and actions, thus implicitly

**Table 5.1**    Selected definitions of entrepreneurial identity

| Authors & Publication References | Definitions |
| --- | --- |
| Stanworth & Curran (1976: 104) | '...the several possible constellations of meanings which may form the core of the entrepreneur's self definition of the entrepreneurial role...' |
| Vesalainen & Pihkala (2000: 113) | '...entrepreneurial identity can be defined as a person's inclination to adopt a certain type of occupational entrepreneurial role.' |
| Nadin (2007: 465) | [Entrepreneurial identity is framed as the constellation of] '...symbolic spaces through the occupation of which they [entrepreneurs] seek legitimacy and acceptance...' |
| Watson (2009: 255) | ''Entrepreneurial identity' can thus be conceptualized as something like a cultural stereotype – a characterization of a 'persona' that a particular individual may, for example, have attached to them by others... or may embrace as part of their notion of self... We thus treat the idea of an entrepreneurial identity as a discursive resource, something that is part of the 'linguistic repertoire' (Potter and Wetherall, 1987) of contemporary society that people, in different ways, in different circumstances and with different degrees of emphasis make use of in their social interactions...' |
| Shepherd & Haynie (2009: 1251) | '...we define the **business owner identity** as the *set of behavioral expectations associated with the business owner role*...' |
| Hoang & Gimeno (2010: 42) | '...an individual's thoughts, feelings, and beliefs about oneself in the founder role...' |
| Navis & Glynn (2011: 480) | *'...the constellation of claims around the founder, new venture, and market opportunity as to 'who we are' and 'what we do''* |
| Powell & Baker (2014: 1409) | '...we broadly define founder identity as 'the set of identities that is chronically salient to a founder in her or his day-today work.'' |
| Kašperová & Kitching (2014: 438) | [Entrepreneurial identity is cast as] '... a set of concerns emergent from the embodied practices of agents committed to new venture creation and management in relation to their natural, practical, and social environments.' |

converging on what entrepreneurial identity 'does'. To illustrate, Fauchart and Gruber (2011: 936) described how founders' identities shape the market opportunities they pursue, as well as the capabilities and resources they deploy to bring their ideas to fruition; and Powell and Baker (2014) framed identity as a lens that influences how entrepreneurs respond to adversity, advancing specifically that it is the structure of founders' identities that determines their response to it (see also Shepherd and Haynie, 2009). Finally, Sarasvathy (2001) and Ireland and Webb (2007) talked about entrepreneurial identity almost as a 'seed' fueling the new venture creation process. In Sarasvathy's (2001: 250) words, entrepreneurs start out with 'three categories of means', including 'who they are'. Taken together, it is important to unpack entrepreneurial identity to better understand entrepreneurial thought and action. To this end, Vesalainen and Pihkala (2000: 124) noted that when considering 'the promotion of entrepreneurship, the development of entrepreneurial identities becomes one of the most important areas of action'.

Another point of convergence among students of entrepreneurial identity seems to be the flexible, tenuous nature of entrepreneurial identity; one that requires active 'work' or upkeep on the part of individuals (e.g., Rae, 2004; Downing, 2005; Shepherd and Haynie, 2009; Farmer et al., 2011). That said, we still do not know much about how such an identity may exactly form and be sustained, and more specifically what differences, if any, gender may make in how men and women go about constructing their respective entrepreneurial identities. To this end, Ollila et al. (2012: 1) lamented that: 'There exists literature regarding identity and entre-preneurship, but limited publications of these areas in combination. In particular, nothing has been proposed regarding the process by which nascent entrepreneurs construct identity.'

Understanding how entrepreneurial identity is constructed and maintained is therefore important, for both theoretical and practical reasons. Theoretically, this focus has the potential to problematize 'traditional bases' of identity construction. According to Cardador and Pratt (2006: 174), the primary of 'bases' of identity construction are relational, behavioral or symbolic; and include, specifically, pre-existing social groups and roles, as well as symbols and artifacts.[3] In other terms, identity originates from a person's organizational or occupational group, their occupational roles, from the physical objects that comprise their work environ-ments, as well as from the narratives and meanings that surround them.

The first two of these bases – that is, pre-existing social groups (e.g., Tajfel, 1978, 1982a, 1982b; Tajfel and Turner, 1979) and roles (e.g., Stryker, 1980; Stryker and Serpe, 1982) – at least on the face of it, appear problematic to account for the experiences of entrepreneurs because no clearly defined groups and/or roles are available for them to join or to take on, especially at the beginning of their journeys. Thus, with no or limited supporting systems to rely on, they must craft their work identities while at the same time building their respective work contexts (see also Weick, 1979). This leaves us with symbols and artifacts as possible 'bases' of identity construction.[4]

These matters become even more complex when we consider the role of gender alongside entrepreneurial identity. To this end, several scholars (e.g., Bruni et al., 2004; Díaz García and Welter, 2013; Lewis, 2013; Marlow and McAdam, 2015) have cast entrepreneurial identity as something that entrepreneurs may stress or de-emphasize, together with their gender, to gain legitimacy for themselves and for their ventures. This research frames gender as a socially constructed category that women in particular selectively draw upon when setting up and running their busi-nesses. Further, it portrays 'identity work' (or the process of identity construction) and 'gender work' ('doing' and 'redoing' gender) as inextricably connected (Díaz García and Welter, 2013).

Practically, given that entrepreneurial identity shapes entrepreneurial perception and behavior, a better understanding of entrepreneurial identity may help us to gain new insights into each entrepreneurial motivation and action, including those motivators and behaviors that men and women possibly share, and/or others that may set them apart. The paragraphs that follow build on the arguments sketched so far leveraging ideas from identity scholars who have addressed issues of identity construction in a range of work contexts, and particularly among professionals. This discussion also highlights what may be unique and/or different when it comes to the identities of women entrepreneurs.

## Identity theories at a glance: building the foundations from sister disciplines

### Identity and identity work

At the individual level, identity may be thought of as 'a self-referential description that provides contextually appropriate answers to the question "Who am I?"' (Ashforth et al., 2008: 327). Over the past 30 years or so, scholars have come to use the term 'identity work' or 'identity construction' to denote the range of activities people engage in to actively construct, maintain or de-emphasize their work identity. Snow and Anderson (1987: 1348), for instance, noted that identity construction relies on '(a) procurement or arrangement of physical settings and props; (b) cosmetic face work or the arrangement of personal appearance; (c) selective association with other individuals and groups; and (d) verbal construction and assertion of personal identities.' Later, Sveningsson and Alvesson (2003) advanced that identity work is concerned with what people think and do to ultimately foster their self-coherence and positive distinctiveness.

Sveningsson and Alvesson's framing implies that identity work is motivated by individuals' need to achieve and preserve an overall positive sense of self. In their review, Lepisto et al. (2015) discuss continuity, authenticity, belonging, self-esteem, efficacy, coherence and meaning as additional motives for identity work; and highlight that identity construction generally takes place in situations where such motives are challenged (see also Ashforth, 2001; Alvesson et al., 2008). 'Identity motives', as such, may be thought of as the fundamental reasons for identity work (Lepisto et al., 2015).

Existing research that has begun to address identity work among women entrepreneurs has highlighted three primary motives as driving the construction of their identities: (1) gaining legitimacy and acceptance from their stakeholders (in part to secure the resources they need to set up and run their businesses; see Bruni et al., 2004); (2) securing and maintaining self-coherence and authenticity in expressing 'who they are' through their organizations (see Lewis, 2013); and (3) managing the 'gender gap' (see Díaz García and Welter, 2013) .

With respect to legitimacy, Marlow and McAdam (2015: 792) noted that: 'For women, claiming entrepreneurial legitimacy is particularly challenging given the ethos of masculinity which informs this discourse and the associated identity work it prompts.' As this quote implies, entrepreneurship is not a 'gender-neutral phenomenon' (e.g., Jennings and Brush, 2013: 679). To the contrary, entrepreneurial activity is shaped by the broader social systems in which entrepreneurs are embedded. Thus, shared beliefs with respect to appropriate behaviors for men and women influence both how and what entrepreneurs may do to build positive identities.

Moreover, because 'the normative entrepreneur is assumed to be "essentially more masculine than feminine"' (Collins and Moore, 1964: 5), Marlow and McAdam (2015: 793) noted that 'normative constructions of femininity do not fit well with the historical or contemporary iterations of entrepreneurial identity'. This suggests that women entrepreneurs, in comparison to their male counterparts, may need to engage in more, and potentially different, forms of identity work in order to be taken as seriously.

Finally, to determine appropriate identity work strategies, women must be aware of the gender perceptions within the sectors they may be interested in entering, in order to figure out how to 'negotiate the dissonance between their ascribed femininity and the masculinity inherent within entrepreneurship' (Marlow and McAdam, 2015: 794).

As inferred so far, when 'identity motives' are somehow activated, individuals deploy a range of strategies – including cognitive, verbal and physical – in efforts to gain, maintain, grow or de-emphasize a given work identity. Cognitive strategies have to do with people's active reframing of a given set of circumstances. To illustrate, Pratt et al. (2006) showed how medical residents engage in each identity, splinting, patching or enriching (that is, leaning on an established identity until the new identity fully forms, combining identities to make a new and better one, and adding depth and nuance to their existing identities) to cope with the strenuous demands of their residency program (see also Kreiner et al., 2006).

Verbal strategies, as the term suggests, involve the purposeful deployment of discourse. To this end, Ibarra and Barbulescu (2010: 135) described how individuals in transition leverage different 'narratives and other rhetorical strategies' to preserve a sense of coherence and continuity during destabilizing phases of their careers (see also Fine, 1996; Alvesson and Willmott, 2002; Sveningsson and Alvesson, 2003; Watson, 2008).

Physical tactics entail the use of artifacts as well as performances. For instance, Elsbach (2003) noted organizational members' different responses to non-territorial work arrangements,[5] and specifically their actions to assert and maintain positive distinctiveness; and Pratt and Rafaeli (1997) brought to the fore the role of dress in expressing nurses' deeply held beliefs regarding their work roles and identities.

Emerging research on the strategies women entrepreneurs deploy to build and maintain their entrepreneurial identities varies considerably. For example, Bruni et al. (2004) showed that their identity work may entail the purposeful conceal-ment of female founders' identities, as well as balancing home and work-related roles through the strategic deployment of narratives and actions. Díaz García and Welter's (2013) research on Spanish women entrepreneurs, and Marlow and McAdam's (2015) work chronicling the experiences of women founders part of a high-tech incubator, described, on the one hand, these women engaging in differ-ent behaviors to support existing gender differences; while on the other hand, they drew attention to women's unique expertise to challenge such differences. Finally, Lewis's (2013) study of English female entrepreneurs showed that these women, in efforts to preserve their self-authenticity, rejected a 'masculine' approach to business, accentuated their femininity, and stressed their professionalism. Taken together, in all of these examples, irrespectively of the specific strategies women deployed, their identity and gender work were inextricably connected.

## Comparing the careers of professionals and entrepreneurs: challenging traditional 'bases' of identity construction?

As this discussion so far alludes to, despite a growing focus on identity work among entrepreneurs, issues of identity construction have to date largely been among professionals – that is, among members of occupational groups who undergo shared and protracted socialization – including, for instance, medical residents (Pratt et al., 2006), consultants and investment bankers (Ibarra, 1999) and police officers (Van Maanen, 1973, 1975).

Because entrepreneurs' and professionals' careers differ considerably, it is not sur-prising that the straightforward applicability of traditional identity perspectives – most notably, social identity theory and identity theory – may be problematic to account for the formation and upkeep of entrepreneurial identity. The paragraphs that follow summarize some of the ways in which entrepreneurs' and professionals' experiences differ, reflect on why and how this may be the case, and examine, in particular, issues of identity development among women entrepreneurs.

To start, entrepreneurs face significant uncertainty and, broadly speaking, lack the structured support (organizational and professional) that professionals have access to, starting from the beginning of their careers (Von Nordenflycht, 2010). To this end, Gartner et al. (1992) noted the extensive equivocality involved in launching new organizations. Entrepreneurs ultimately seek to resolve some of this equivocality by creating what Weick (1979) defined as 'patterns of interlocked behaviors' and, more specifically, by 'talking and act as "as if" equivocal events were non-equivocal' (Gartner et al., 1992: 17).

Moreover, entrepreneurs' specific goals and ambitions, as well as the narratives they may deploy to build their respective work contexts, are likely to vary, in part due to the discretion that entrepreneurial careers afford, and more broadly due to the social-embeddedness of entrepreneurship. To this end, research by Jennings and Brush (2013) summarizes the various ways in which gender influences entrepreneurial intention and action. This work shows that women may be driven by different motives (compared to their male counterparts) in their entrepreneurial efforts, and that they may face unique possibilities as well as hurdles. These include, for example, starting their firms moved by a desire to achieve better work–family balance (rather than the pursuit of economic gains), as well as dealing with competing demands imposed by their dual roles as mothers and entrepreneurs (for a detailed review, see Powell and Eddleston, 2008; Eddleston and Powell, 2012; Powell and Greenhaus, 2012; Jennings and Brush, 2013).

A final feature that sets entrepreneurs' and professionals' careers apart is the absence of shared and established paths to advancement, marked by public milestones and coronated via ceremonies of various sorts (see Greenwood et al., 2002). This is, at least in part, because entrepreneurs set their own goals and objectives, and infuse words such as 'advancement' or 'progress' with ther own meanings. As such, 'advancement' and 'progress' may hold different understandings, and evoke different sets of actions for different people.

Taken together, we may infer broad heterogeneity in the factors that may contribute to bolster, or conversely to challenge, entrepreneurs' identities, based on: (1) why they became entrepreneurs in the first place; and (2) a range of other aspects (including their specific family situations) that may weigh (positively or negatively) on their ability to dedicate themselves to their businesses. Given such heterogeneity and overall equivocality, traditional identity perspectives (social identity theory and identity theory), and the 'bases' of identity they espouse (pre-existing social groups and roles, respectively), may not account well for issues of identity formation and upkeep among entrepreneurs.

Social identity theory, in particular, deals with the structure of identity as related to people's group membership (e.g., Tajfel, 1978, 1982a, 1982b; Tajfel and Turner 1979). Because social identity theory speaks to how individuals relate to one or more collectives, this identity perspective inherently emphasizes the role of impersonal relationships based on group membership, as 'bases' of identity construction (Cardador and Pratt, 2006).

At the core of social identity theory is the idea that a given social group – such as, for instance, one's nationality or political affiliation – provides a definition for one's identity (Tajfel and Turner, 1979). As such, according to social identity theory, people draw selectively upon their membership in different groups to define themselves, and ultimately to achieve identities that are self-enhancing.

Entrepreneurs, by definition, may not rely on an existing or well-defined organization to craft their work identities. Instead, they must develop their work identities while at the same time defining their respective work contexts; figuratively speaking, while 'drawing the contours' of their organizations. Thus, due to the lack of pre-defined groups for nascent entrepreneurs to join at the start of their careers, social identity theory appears problematic to account for their experiences. Moreover, insights from research on minimal groups (e.g., Tajfel et al., 1971) suggest that the mere adoption of a label (such as 'entrepreneur') may suffice for individuals to self-categorize as members of a given collective. It is unclear, however, whether this may apply to entrepreneurs, partly because their respective circumstances may or may not allow for evaluative intergroup comparisons, making the label 'entrepreneur' equivocal.

While these consideration apply to both men and women entrepreneurs, female founders, unlike their male counterparts, have been described as relying on their families and on their gender as additional 'bases' for self-categorization. Family, specifically, has been depicted as a group from which women entrepreneurs draw the resources and/or the support they may need to establish and sustain their businesses; as well as, conversely, something that may constrain their initiative and the development of their entrepreneurial identity (see Bruni et al., 2004; Jennings and Brush, 2013). Gender has also been cast as an important social category that brings women together, and that they differentially engage with (for instance, by emphasizing or downplaying their femininity) based on the circumstances and/or the sectors they operate in (see Ahl, 2006).

Whereas social identity theory discusses a prominent relational base of identity, identity theory discusses a behavioral base, linking what people do to 'who they are'. More specifically, identity theory deals with the structure of people's identities as related to the various roles they play in society (see Stryker, 1980; Stryker and Serpe, 1982). According to identity theory scholars, thus, the self is made up of multiple role identities, and people's actions are influenced by how committed they are to a given role identity, and how salient such a role identity is. Role identities that are higher (relative to others) in the hierarchy of salience tend to be more self-defining than those near the bottom of such hierarchy (Hogg et al., 1995). While identity theory provides meaningful insights into people's behaviors who are part of structured occupations, where the various roles one is expected to take on are well defined and often laid out from the start of one's career, it appears somewhat problematic to account for the experiences of entrepreneurs who, almost by definition, must craft their roles as they figure out what steps to take with their emerging organizations (see Gartner et al., 1992).

When it comes to women entrepreneurs, the study of role identities is further complicated by the fact that some women entrepreneurs must also juggle their roles as mothers as they establish and grow their organizations (see Bruni et al., 2004). The salience of their identities as mothers may influence not only how they see themselves as entrepreneurs, but also the extent to which they 'take family considerations into account when making work decisions' and thus in how they may set up and run their businesses (Powell and Greenhaus, 2012: 325).

Taken together, due to the high equivocality that launching and running a new organization entails, traditional 'identity bases' (Cardador and Pratt, 2006) –

established groups and roles – may not account well for how entrepreneurs construct their identities, especially at the outset of their careers (Gartner et al., 1992). Moreover, a focus on women entrepreneurs raises additional questions with respect to how social categories such as family and gender, as well as their possible roles as mothers, may shape the construction and development of their entrepreneurial identities.

## Identity construction among entrepreneurs: focusing on what entrepreneurs do and where

Given the heterogeneity of entrepreneurs' experiences, looking at what entrepreneurs do as well as the work environments in which they are embedded (including, specifically, the objects and tools entrepreneurs may use, how they occupy their respective work areas, as well as the extent to which they may or not appropriate resources) constitutes a promising starting point to better understand identity formation and upkeep among entrepreneurs.

This idea builds on a longstanding body of research in the entrepreneurship field that has recognized the merits of a behavioral approach to the study of entrepreneurs and their ventures (Gartner, 1989), and the powerful role of space (broadly defined) in influencing the choices in which entrepreneurs engage (e.g., Knight, 1921; Schumpeter, 1934) and the types of organizations they launch (e.g., Stinchcombe, 1965; Johnson, 2007). Moreover, it leverages emerging literature in management that examines the relationship between workspace, artifacts and identity (e.g., Pratt and Rafaeli, 1997; Elsbach and Pratt, 2007).

Scholars of entrepreneurial identity have indeed begun to recognize the need to engage in a closer examination of entrepreneurial behaviors to better understand each the content, formation and upkeep of entrepreneurial identity. Kašperová and Kitching (2014: 446), specifically, have invited research that takes into account not only what entrepreneurs say, or the stories they tell to gain resources, but also what they do. In their words, 'more explicit consideration of non-linguistic practices can produce new insights into the effects of embodiment on entrepreneurs' capacities, concerns and actions'.

Thus, to better appreciate entrepreneurial identity in terms of its content, development and maintenance (how it may come to be, and then be sustained), a promising approach is to look at the situated actions entrepreneurs take over time: what entrepreneurs do and where, as they attempt to launch and run their businesses. Specifically, emphasis should be placed not only on entrepreneurs' choices and on their behaviors, but also on the range of resources their respective contexts provide. Thornton, to this end, advanced that: 'Unless context is taken into account, the links between the actions of individuals in founding new organizations . . . are likely to remain elusive' (Thornton, 1999: 24); and Chen et al. (1998) stressed the importance, particularly for nascent entrepreneurs, to be embedded in supportive (psychologically and otherwise) environments. They noted, specifically, that 'Communities can work toward creating an efficacy enhancing environment by making resources both available and visible, publicizing entrepreneurial successes, increasing the diversity of opportunities, and avoiding policies that create real or perceived obstacles' (Chen et al., 1998: 296).

These ideas invite reflection around specific features (physical and social) of the work environments that female and male entrepreneurs may find helpful (or not) while figuring out what it means to be entrepreneurs, launching and running their organizations. The respective salience of their various role identities (including, for example, their possible role identities as parents and/or spouses) will likely shape what they may deem supporting or inhibiting of their efforts (see also Ahl, 2006; Powell and Greenhaus, 2012).

Figure 5.1 depicts visually the five key sources of entrepreneurial identity this chapter has introduced so far; that is, the five building blocks entrepreneurs may differentially deploy to construct, maintain or de-emphasize their identities as entrepreneurs. They are: entrepreneurs' gender; their new ventures; their respective work environments (where they do their work and surrounded by whom); the behaviors they engage in to set up and run their organizations; as well as their occupational meaning (or the meanings they ascribe to 'being entrepreneurs').

These five sources are represented in the figure as overlapping and linked by double-sided arrows to denote their interconnectedness and mutual influence, and are arranged in a circle to portray their fluidity. For example, at the outset of their entrepreneurial journeys, nascent entrepreneurs may wish to play up or conceal facets of their identities (such as their gender) in efforts to gain legitimacy for their emerging businesses. The environment in which they are embedded is likely to play a role in what exactly they may do, when and how. Differently, more experienced entrepreneurs may rely on the connections they have developed in their respective fields (part of their social work environments) to claim positive identities. Thus, depending on a range of contextual and individual factors (such as environmental stimuli and experience), one or more of the circles in Figure 5.1 may become salient, and guide entrepreneurs' actions. As these examples allude to, the activation of one (or more) of these five sources is influenced by, and at the same time shapes, the others.

While the circles in Figure 5.1 as building blocks of entrepreneurial identity are unlikely to vary across individuals, there may be differences within and across genders, in the specific content of and emphasis given to each. For example, there may be variation in what entrepreneurs believe it means to be entrepreneurs (their occupational meanings) based on their career goals and objectives, as well as on the salience of their broader entrepreneurial identity relative to the other identities they may hold (for example, being a parent). Likewise, their behaviors as entrepreneurs will partly depend on the set of resources and constraints they may perceive and/or face in their respective personal and work contexts. This way, the unique challenges that confront women entrepreneurs – including being taken seriously, gaining access to capital, and dealing with childcare responsibilities (Brush, 1997; Powell and Eddleston, 2008) – are likely to weigh on the formation of their identities, and thus on their actions as entrepreneurs.

## Entrepreneurial identity: taking stock and looking forward

As discussed at the outset of this chapter, no universal definitions exist to date of 'the entrepreneur', or of entrepreneurial identity. Borrowing from the identity work literature, which has cast identity as fluid, this chapter suggests that framing entrepreneurial identity as a dynamic process may help scholars to embrace multiple conceptualizations of it, and in so doing, engage in theoretically and empirically generative conversations. This approach invites us to look at entrepreneurs in action, as they each contemplate, work toward, launch and operate their businesses (see also Gartner et al., 1992).

This way, entrepreneurial identity may be seen as *the host of self-referential claims and actions that are associated with launching and running new organizations*. As this working definition suggests, entrepreneurial identity is closely coupled with the development of entrepreneurs' firms. Howorth et al. (2005: 38) support this idea. In summarizing the findings of their research, they noted, specifically, that: 'Entrepreneurs' identities were wrapped up with those of their organisation and they also found it difficult to separate what they are from what they do'.

Thus, contextual and individual factors that influence one's business development have the potential to shape one's self-understandings and actions as an

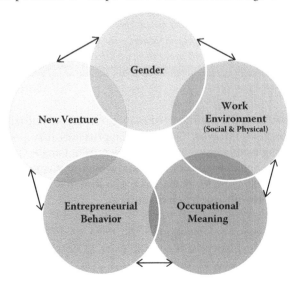

**Figure 5.1**    Key sources of entrepreneurial identity construction

entrepreneur. Examples of such factors include the various social and/or professional groups one may belong to, the broader institutional context one is embedded in, as well as one's expertise – to mention just a few. Of particular importance in order to advance current research on women entrepreneurs (and their identities) is to shed light on such factors; what Ahl (2006) referred to as the 'invisible' social structures that shape behavior. Surfacing the values, assumptions and expectations underlying the systems in which entrepreneurs are embedded will help us to gain a more contextualized understanding of why entrepreneurs (women and men) construct their identities as they do, as well as the specific content of their identities.

As Figure 5.1 shows, entrepreneurs' organizations constitute a key source of their identities. This distinguishing feature of entrepreneurial identity calls for the concurrent examination of entrepreneurs' self-understandings, of their actions, as well as of their ventures. Looking, for example, at the field one's organization is in, at the firm's value proposition, and at how it is managed, is likely to speak to the founder's expertise, preferences and work style – often expressions of one's identity. This approach implicitly shifts the focus from gender as 'a key explanation' of women's entrepreneurial behavior, to gender as one of the many socially constructed inputs in the creation of entrepreneurial firms – that is, as a source of entrepreneurs' identities (Ahl, 2006; Figure 5.1).

## How to study entrepreneurial identity?

> *The garden of entrepreneurial theories is ready for a variety of seeds from many different disciplines and perspectives. As our field emerges, it might begin to look more like a weed patch, rather than a neatly cultivated garden. At this stage in our development, 'weediness' should be encouraged ... In our acquisition of theoretical requisite variety, we may not, at this stage, possess the wisdom to accurately differentiate between weeds and flowers – those ideas that are intellectually vapid versus those ideas that will prove to be useful. Only through continued discussion, dialogue, and practice ... can our theories about the nature of emergence be cultivated.*
> (Gartner et al., 1992: 17)

As this quote illustrates, the multifaceted nature of entrepreneurial identity makes studying it a complex endeavor. Qualitative approaches may prove particularly effective in surfacing its dynamic nature. In the words of Langley and colleagues, in fact, they can help scholars to unpack 'how and why things emerge, develop, grow, or terminate over time' (Langley et al., 2013: 1), ultimately affording rich descriptions and insights of the phenomenon of interest.

Similarly, Gartner (1989: 64) recognized the need to embrace research methodologies that 'will do justice to the complexity of entrepreneurship', particularly because 'The creation of an organization is a very complicated and intricate process, influenced by many factors [and] ... The entrepreneur is not a fixed state of existence' (Gartner, 1989: 64). Specifically, he pleaded with scholars to engage in fieldwork to better understand founders as they create and launch their organizations.

More recently, Hamilton (2014) advocated for moving beyond the study of narratives, by embracing methodologies that may help to capture entrepreneurs' actions. Kašperová and Kitching (2014: 447), specifically, advanced that we should 'explore physical capabilities, including the use of artefacts, and the consequences for identity and action' through 'ethnographic methods'. This approach may ultimately help scholars to understand 'how entrepreneurs, as embodied agents, interact with their natural, practical and social environments'. Taken together, to better understand entrepreneurial identity we may consider engaging in in-depth longitudinal field work, focusing on aspects such as entrepreneurs' work practices, their attitudes, environments and relationships. Differently put, promising future research may shed light on the sources of identity construction highlighted in Figure 5.1 and, specifically, how entrepreneurs may emphasize them as their experiences evolve. To capture them as thoroughly as possible, scholars should plan to collect multiple sources of data. To this end, Gartner et al. (1992: 21) noted that 'more diverse data collection methods, particularly qualitative and ethnographic methods, would add valuable and unique insights to understanding entrepreneurship'. And, further, that 'theories on entrepreneurial behavior would benefit from more studies that utilize a variety of data-collection methods that describe what entrepreneurs do'.

Observations and interviews over time appear particularly appropriate to gain an in-depth contextualized understanding of entrepreneurial identity and its construction. As far as observations are concerned, an unstructured approach (Spradley, 1979) seems best suited (at least to start) to remaining open to emerging themes. Given the well-documented importance of the context in which entrepreneurs are embedded in shaping their cognitions and actions, careful attention should be paid to entrepreneurs' physical work environments, and to the host of relationships such environments inhibit and/or enable.

As far as interviews are concerned, they have frequently been deployed to study and explain how individuals, across occupations, develop and maintain their work identities (e.g., Ibarra, 1999; Pratt et al., 2006). This is largely because interviews can lend additional insights into people's thoughts, opinions and feelings that may otherwise be difficult to see and capture. Combined with observations, they may provide a more complete account of how entrepreneurs think, and of how they feel, as they engage in a host of activities to transform their business ideas into opportunities.

### Challenges

There is no shortage of possibilities when it comes to entrepreneurial identity, particularly because focused research on the topic is still at an early stage. Along with opportunities, however, also come some difficulties, ranging from conceptual to more practical.

From a conceptual standpoint, discerning entrepreneurial identity from other processes that are intrinsic to new venture creation may be challenging because of the close interdependence of entrepreneurial action and identity. Teasing entrepreneurial identity apart from entrepreneurial behavior is important to understand the motives underlying entrepreneurs' actions. While there is no one clear way to tackle this challenge, scholars (and reviewers) may find some reassurance in studies that leverage multiple sources of data and, specifically, that capture both people's self-understandings and their behaviors.

From a methodological and more practical standpoint, to study entrepreneurial identity as a process, scholars should consider engaging in longitudinal research, from when aspiring entrepreneurs contemplate their ventures, to when they reach some critical decision point with their organizations that may alter their choices and/or their career paths altogether. Besides being time-consuming, such an approach may be problematic due to the very nature of entrepreneurial activity. Entrepreneurs, in fact, spend most of their time working on transforming their ideas into businesses. This requires an enormous amount of energy and dedication, leaving little, if any, time to spare for other activities. As such, scholars should invest their time and efforts at the outset of their research projects to build positive and strong relationships with their informants. This may involve engaging in participant observations, or finding other ways to reciprocate entrepreneurs for their time and efforts.

*Opportunities*

Because focused research on entrepreneurial identity is at an early stage, there are many opportunities for new conceptual and empirical work. Conceptually, scholars who embrace entrepreneurial identity as a process might be interested in teasing out how exactly the process unfolds, or the specific steps that comprise it. This may involve, for example, examining the range of individual and environmental conditions under which certain events, activities and self-views are likely to emerge. To illustrate, looking at both entrepreneurs' personal and professional relationships may shed light on how the social milieu surrounding entrepreneurs shapes their identities. Because no one single model is likely to account for the experiences of different entrepreneurs, there will be ample room for theoretical elaboration.

Given that 'entrepreneurial identity' encompasses such a broad domain, scholars may choose to focus on developing (theoretically and/or empirically) specific facets of it. Some, for instance, might consider exploring issues of entrepreneurial identity formation; that is, how individuals come to see themselves and act as entrepreneurs. Others may want to look at entrepreneurial identity upkeep – how entrepreneurs actively nurture their identities as they go through different phases with their organizations – or, conversely, entrepreneurial identity deletion: what entrepreneurs may do to eliminate or de-emphasize their entrepreneurial identity.

Empirically, scholars may design their studies to look at the role of specific influences on each entrepreneurial identity creation, maintenance and/or elimination.

To illustrate, to tease out the role of a given workspace in entrepreneurial identity development, for instance, they may opt to study entrepreneurs who are part of a given shared workspace over time, and compare their thoughts and actions with those of entrepreneurs who work in different contexts: at various 'entrepreneurial hubs', or in their own private spaces.

Moreover, scholars may compare and contrast how men and women work on building their entrepreneurial identities, exploring the resources they leverage, and the steps they take to gain an understanding of what being an entrepreneur entails. This may involve specifying different models of entrepreneurial identity formation and upkeep for male and female entrepreneurs: a particularly promising area for future research. Indeed, despite a growing interest in issues of gender and entrepreneurial identity co-construction, we still know relatively little about it. Particularly, we do not know much about how, during their new venture creation journeys, women and men entrepreneurs leverage their gender to gather the resources they need; and how, confronted with challenges, they may maintain positive identities.

In conducting such comparative work, we should not assume however that all women and all men are similar in their intentions and approaches. To gain a solid understanding of entrepreneurial identity, thus, we should equally attend to both within- and across-gender differences (Eddleston and Powell, 2012). This may favor the discovery of finer-grained differences or, potentially, enable us to report on non-differences which rarely seem to have been the subject of scholars' attention.

In addition, given that existing research has highlighted three central motives – gaining legitimacy, securing and/or maintaining self-coherence and authenticity, and managing the gender gap – as driving the constructions of women entrepreneurs' identities, scholars may wish to map how, if at all, women's identity work strategies and the content of their entrepreneurial identities vary in conjunction with the motive(s) that activated their identity work in the first place.

We may also wish to compare the identity work tactics and practices of nascent and more seasoned entrepreneurs, or those of first-time and serial entrepreneurs, to grasp the role of experience in entrepreneurial identity development and maintenance – both within and across genders. Finally, exploring the role of business failure and success in entrepreneurial identity development appears to be another germane avenue for future research. Questions that seem particularly promising include: When, if at all, may failure serve as a positive catalyst for the development of men and women entrepreneurs' identities (and for that of their organizations)? How, if at all, may success become detrimental to the advancement of people's entrepreneurial projects and identities?

Taken together, considering entrepreneurial identity as a dynamic process enables us to think about it expansively and opens the doors to new questions, as well as to potentially generative cross-disciplinary conversations.

## Conclusion

To summarize, this chapter reviews in brief what we know about entrepreneurial identity, as well as existing literatures that address identity and its construction more broadly. It shows how traditional 'bases' of identity (often discussed in the context of professionals) may be problematic to account for the experiences of entrepreneurs, and of women entrepreneurs in particular. As such, it advocates for a closer examination of entrepreneurs' actions over time, as well as for greater focus on their respective work contexts. It also argues for the importance of shedding light on the 'invisible' social structures that shape – supporting and/ or constraining – entrepreneur's behaviors; it offers some thoughts for future research; and highlights a few of the many possibilities (and inherent challenges) associated with the study of entrepreneurial identity. My hope is that this chapter will inspire others to join me (and my colleagues in this volume) in this generative conversation.

### Notes

\*   I am very grateful to Candy Brush, Patti Greene, Mike Pratt, Jean Bartunek, Katherina Kuschel and Juan Pablo Labra for their helpful comments on earlier drafts of this chapter.

1   In their extant conceptualizations of entrepreneurial identity, scholars have on occasion used the words 'founder' and 'entrepreneur' interchangeably.

2   The purpose of this table is to selectively showcase definitions of entrepreneurial identity to illustrate the breadth of existing conceptualizations.

3   Following Schein (1990: 111), my definition of artifacts includes 'everything from the physical layout, the dress code, the manner in which people address each other, the smell and feel of the place . . . to the more permanent archival manifestations such as company records, products, statements of philosophy, and annual reports'.

4   This does not discount the possibility of personal relationships and non-role behaviors as contributing to the development of entrepreneurial identity.

5   By 'non-territorial work arrangements' I refer to workspaces in which employees do not have a dedicated seat, but rather take over space on a 'first come, first served' basis (see Elsbach, 2003).

## References

Ahl, H. (2006), 'Why research on women entrepreneurs needs new directions', *Entrepreneurship Theory and Practice*, 30(5), 595–621.

Alvesson, M., K.L. Ashcraft and R. Thomas (2008), 'Identity matters: Reflections on the construction of identity scholarship in organization studies', *Organization*, 15(1), 5–28.

Alvesson, M. and H. Willmott (2002), 'Identity regulation as organizational control: Producing the appropriate individual', *Journal of Management Studies*, 39(5), 619–644.

Ashforth, B. (2001), *Role Transitions in Organizational Life: An Identity-Based Perspective*. Mahwah, NJ: Lawrence Erlbaum Associates.

Ashforth, B.E., S.H. Harrison and K.G. Corley (2008), 'Identification in organizations: An examination of four fundamental questions', *Journal of Management*, 34(3), 325–374.

Bruni, A., S. Gherardi and B. Poggio (2004), 'Doing gender, doing entrepreneurship: An ethnographic account of intertwined practices', *Gender, Work and Organization*, 11(4), 406–429.

Brush, C.G. (1997), 'Women-owned businesses: Obstacles and opportunities', *Journal of Developmental Entrepreneurship*, 2(1), 1–24.

Cardador, M.T. and M.G. Pratt (2006), 'Identification management and its bases: Bridging management and marketing perspectives through a focus on affiliation dimensions', *Journal of the Academy of Marketing Science*, 34(2), 174–184.

Chen, C.C., P.G. Greene and A. Crick (1998), 'Does entrepreneurial self-efficacy distinguish entrepreneurs from managers?', *Journal of Business Venturing*, 13(4), 295–316.

Collins, O.F. and D.G. Moore (1964), *The Enterprising Man*. East Lansing, MI: Michigan State University.

Díaz García, M.C. and F. Welter (2013), 'Gender identities and practices: Interpreting women entrepreneurs' narratives', *International Small Business Journal*, 31(4), 384–404.

Downing, S. (2005), 'The social construction of entrepreneurship: Narrative and dramatic processes in the coproduction of organizations and identities', *Entrepreneurship Theory and Practice*, 29(2), 185–204.

Eddleston, K.A. and G.N. Powell (2012), 'Nurturing entrepreneurs' work–family balance: A gendered perspective', *Entrepreneurship Theory and Practice*, 36(3), 513–541.

Elsbach, K.D. (2003), 'Relating physical environment to self-categorizations: Identity threat and affirmation in a non-territorial office space', *Administrative Science Quarterly*, 48(4), 622–654.

Elsbach, K.D. and M.G. Pratt (2007), 'The physical environment in organizations', *Academy of Management Annals*, 1(1), 181–224.

Farmer, S.M., X. Yao and K. Kung-Mcintyre (2011), 'The behavioral impact of entrepreneur identity aspiration and prior entrepreneurial experience', *Entrepreneurship Theory and Practice*, 35(2), 245–273.

Fauchart, E. and M. Gruber (2011), 'Darwinians, communitarians, and missionaries: The role of founder identity in entrepreneurship', *Academy of Management Journal*, 54(5), 935–957.

Fine, G.A. (1996), 'Justifying work: Occupational rhetorics as resources in restaurant kitchens', *Administrative Science Quarterly*, 41(1), 90–115.

Gartner, W.B. (1989), '"Who is an entrepreneur?" is the wrong question', *Entrepreneurship Theory and Practice*, Summer, 47–68.

Gartner, W.B., B.J. Bird and J.A. Starr (1992), 'Acting as if: Differentiating entrepreneurial from organizational behavior', *Entrepreneurship: Theory and Practice*, 16(3), 13–32.

Greenwood, R., R. Suddaby and C.R. Hinings (2002), 'Theorizing change: The role of professional associations in the transformation of institutionalized fields', *Academy of Management Journal*, 45(1), 58–80.

Hamilton, E. (2014), 'Entrepreneurial narrative identity and gender: A double epistemological shift', *Journal of Small Business Management*, 52(4), 703–712.

Hoang, H. and J. Gimeno (2010), 'Becoming a founder: How founder role identity affects entrepreneurial transitions and persistence in founding', *Journal of Business Venturing*, 25(1), 41–53.

Hogg, M.A., D.J. Terry and K.M. White (1995), 'A tale of two theories: A critical comparison of identity theory with social identity theory', *Social Psychology Quarterly*, 58, 255–269.

Howorth, C., S. Tempest and C. Coupland (2005), 'Rethinking entrepreneurship methodology and definitions of the entrepreneur', *Journal of Small Business and Enterprise Development*, 12(1), 24–40.

Ibarra, H. (1999), 'Provisional selves: Experimenting with image and identity in professional adaptation', *Administrative Science Quarterly*, 44(4), 764–791.

Ibarra, H. and R. Barbulescu (2010), 'Identity as narrative: Prevalence, effectiveness, and consequences of narrative identity work in macro work role transitions', *Academy of Management Review*, 35(1), 135–154.

Ireland, R.D. and J.W. Webb (2007), 'A cross-disciplinary exploration of entrepreneurship research', *Journal of Management*, 33(6), 891–927.

Jennings, J.E. and C.G. Brush (2013), 'Research on women entrepreneurs: Challenges to (and from) the broader entrepreneurship literature?', *Academy of Management Annals*, 7(1), 663–715.

Johnson, V. (2007), 'What is organizational imprinting? Cultural entrepreneurship in the founding of the Paris Opera', *American Journal of Sociology*, 113(1), 97–127.

Kašperová, E. and J. Kitching (2014), 'Embodying entrepreneurial identity', *International Journal of Entrepreneurial Behavior and Research*, 20(5), 438–452.

Knight, F.H. (1921), *Risk, Uncertainty and Profit*. New York: Hart, Schaffner & Marx.

Kreiner, G.E., E.C. Hollensbe and M.L. Sheep (2006), 'Where is the "me" among the "we"? Identity work and the search for optimal balance', *Academy of Management Journal*, 49(5), 1031–1057.

Laakkonen, A. (2012), 'Construction of the entrepreneurial identity in the family business context – a cross-cultural study', *Jyväskylä Studies in Business and Economics*, 108, 1–297.

Langley, A., C. Smallman, H. Tsoukas and A.H. Van de Ven (2013), 'Process studies of change in organization and management: Unveiling temporality, activity, and flow', *Academy of Management Journal*, 56(1), 1–13.

Lepisto, D.A., E. Crosina and M.G. Pratt (2015), 'Identity work within and beyond the professions: toward a theoretical integration and extension', in A. Desilva and M. Aparicio (eds), *International Handbook of Professional Identities*. Rosemead, CA: Scientific and Academic Publishing, pp. 11–37.

Lewis, P. (2013), 'The search for an authentic entrepreneurial identity: Difference and professionalism among women business owners', *Gender, Work and Organization*, 20(3), 252–266.

Marlow, S. and M. McAdam (2015), 'Incubation or induction? Gendered identity work in the context of technology business incubation', *Entrepreneurship Theory and Practice*, 39(4), 791–816.

Murnieks, C. and E. Mosakowski (2007), 'Who am: I? Looking inside the "entrepreneurial identity"', *Frontiers of Entrepreneurship Research*, 25(5). Accessed September 14, 2015 at http://digitalknowl edge.babson.edu/fer/vol27/iss5/5.

Nadin, S. (2007), 'Entrepreneurial identity in the care sector: navigating the contradictions', *Women in Management Review*, 22(6), 456–467.

Navis, C. and M.A. Glynn (2011), 'Legitimate distinctiveness and the entrepreneurial identity: Influence on investor judgments of new venture plausibility', *Academy of Management Review*, 36(3), 479–499.

Ollila, S., K. Williams Middleton and A. Donnellon (2012), 'Entrepreneurial identity construction: What does existing literature tell us?', Institute for Small Business and Entrepreneurship Annual Conference, Dublin, Ireland.

Powell, E.E. and T. Baker (2014), 'It's what you make of it: Founder identity and enacting strategic responses to adversity', *Academy of Management Journal*, 57(5), 1406–1433.

Powell, G.N. and K.A. Eddleston (2008), 'The paradox of the contented female business owner', *Journal of Vocational Behavior*, 73(1), 24–36.

Powell, G.N. and J.H. Greenhaus (2012), 'When family considerations influence work decisions: Decision-making processes', *Journal of Vocational Behavior*, 81(3), 322–329.

Pratt, M.G. and A. Rafaeli (1997), 'Organizational dress as a symbol of multilayered social identities', *Academy of Management Journal*, 40(4), 862–898.

Pratt, M.G., K.W. Rockmann and J.B. Kaufmann (2006), 'Constructing professional identity: The role of work and identity learning cycles in the customization of identity among medical residents', *Academy of Management Journal*, 49(2), 235–262.

Rae, D. (2004), 'Entrepreneurial learning: A practical model from the creative industries', *Education + training*, 46(8/9), 492–500.

Sarasvathy, S.D. (2001), 'Causation and effectuation: Toward a theoretical shift from economic inevitability to entrepreneurial contingency', *Academy of Management Review*, 26(2), 243–263.

Schein, E. (1990), 'Organizational culture', *American Psychologist*, 45, 109–119.

Schumpeter, J.A. (1934) (Reprinted in 1962), *The Theory of Economic Development: An Inquiry into Profits, Capital, Credit, Interest and the Business Cycle*. Cambridge, MA: Harvard University Press.

Shepherd, D. and J.M. Haynie (2009), 'Family business, identity conflict, and an expedited entrepreneurial process: A process of resolving identity conflict', *Entrepreneurship Theory and Practice*, 33(6), 1245–1264.

Snow, D.A. and L. Anderson (1987), 'Identity work among the homeless: the verbal construction and avowal of personal identities', *American Journal of Sociology*, 92(6), 1336–1371.

Spradley, J.P. (1979), *The Ethnographic Interview*. New York: Holt, Rinehart & Winston.

Stanworth, M.J.K. and J. Curran (1976), 'Growth and the small firm – an alternative view', *Journal of Management Studies*, 13(2), 95–110.

Stinchcombe, A. (1965), 'Social structure and organizations', in J. March (ed.), *Handbook of Organizations*. Chicago, IL: Rand McNally, pp. 142–193.

Stryker, S. (1980), *Symbolic Interactionism: A Social Structural Version*. Menlo Park, CA: Benjamin/ Cummings Publishing Company.

Stryker, S. and R.T. Serpe (1982), 'Commitment, identity salience, and role behavior: Theory and research example', in W. Ickes and E.S. Knowles (eds), *Personality, Roles, and Social Behavior*. New York: Springer-Verlag, pp. 199–218.

Sveningsson, S. and M. Alvesson (2003), 'Managing managerial identities: Organizational fragmentation, discourse and identity struggle', *Human Relations*, 56(10), 1163–1193.

Tajfel, H. (1978), 'The achievement of group differentiation', in H. Tajfel (ed.), *Differentiation between Social Groups: Studies in the Social Psychology of Intergroup Relations*. London: Academic Press, pp. 77–98.

Tajfel, H. (1982a), 'Instrumentality, identity and social comparisons', in H. Tajfel (ed.), *Social Identity and Intergroup Relations*. Cambridge: Cambridge University Press, pp. 483–507.

Tajfel, H. (1982b), 'Social psychology of intergroup relations', *Annual Review of Psychology*, 33(1), 1–39.

Tajfel, H., M.G. Billig, R.P. Bundy and C. Flament (1971), 'Social categorization and intergroup behaviour', *European Journal of Social Psychology*, 1(2), 149–178.

Tajfel, H. and J.C. Turner (1979), 'An integrative theory of intergroup conflict', in W.G. Austin and S. Worchel (eds), *The Social Psychology of Group Relations*. Monterey, CA: Brooks-Cole, pp. 33–47.

Thornton, P.H. (1999), 'The sociology of entrepreneurship', *Annual Review of Sociology*, 25, 19–46.

Van Maanen, J. (1973), 'Observations on the making of policemen', *Human Organization*, 32(4), 407–418.

Van Maanen, J. (1975), 'Police socialization: A longitudinal examination of job attitudes in an urban police department', *Administrative Science Quarterly*, 20(2), 207–228.

Vesalainen, J. and T. Pihkala (2000), 'Entrepreneurial identity, intentions and the effect of the push-factor', *International Journal of Entrepreneurship*, 4, 105–129.

Von Nordenflycht, A. (2010), 'What is a professional service firm? Toward a theory and taxonomy of knowledge-intensive firms', *Academy of Management Review*, 35(1), 155–174.

Watson, T.J. (2008), 'Managing identity: Identity work, personal predicaments and structural circumstances', *Organization*, 15(1), 121–143.

Watson, T.J. (2009), 'Entrepreneurial action, identity work and the use of multiple discursive resources the case of a rapidly changing family business', *International Small Business Journal*, 27(3), 251–274.

Weick, K.E. (1979), *The Social Psychology of Organizing*. New York: Random House.

# 6 Feminist entrepreneurial identity: reproducing gender through founder decision-making

*Catherine Elliott and Barbara Orser*

## Introduction

Scholars have reported the need to build explanatory theory with respect to the influence of gender in the venture creation process (Marlow et al., 2009; Henry et al., 2015; Warren, 2004). Some argue that feminist theory is a robust perspective from which to examine the experiences of entrepreneurs (Ahl, 2004; Bird and Brush, 2002; Fischer et al., 1993; Mirchandani, 1999). However, there are few empirical studies that have explicitly drawn on feminism or feminist experiences to inform the entrepreneurship literature (Ahl and Marlow, 2012). As such, there remains a need to further develop theory that is informed through systematic, empirical research (Orser and Elliott, 2015; Ahl and Marlow, 2012; Ahl, 2004). In response, this chapter examines how feminist entrepreneurial identity (FEI) is expressed through founder decision-making. Recommendations for future research are advanced. The relevance of the study objectives and theoretical underpinnings are demonstrated in several ways.

First, the chapter contributes to an emerging area of academic inquiry about how gender is constructed within entrepreneurial identity (Bruni et al., 2004; Down and Warren, 2008; Eddleston and Powell, 2008; Fenwick and Hutton, 2000; Warren, 2004). Identity theory explains the ways in which individuals conceptualize 'Who am I?' within social and institutional settings (Pratt and Foreman, 2000: 18). Given the centrality of founders within the venture creation process, identity theory is applicable in linking individual (founder or owner) identity and organizational (the enterprise) identity, a relationship that has been described as reciprocal (Pratt and Foreman, 2000) and socially constructed (García and Welter, 2011; Fauchart and Gruber, 2011). Identity theory complements the principles of feminist theory and research, work that strives to 'understand women in their social context' (Bourne, 2007: 121) documenting their lived experiences. Identity theory responds to criticism of research about women entrepreneurs predicated on neoliberal economic theory (Ahl, 2004, 2006), theory that emphasizes the value of pecuniary outcomes without consideration of gender inequalities and alternative (non-pecuniary) motives for enterprise creation (Warren, 2004). Neoliberal entrepreneurship theory has also tended to 'silence' the feminine within entrepreneurial identity (Nadin, 2007: 456), viewing the masculine entrepreneur as the norm against which all entrepreneurial activity is judged (Ahl and Marlow, 2012). Identity theory responds to the call for dynamic approaches that provide insight into how gender is produced, and reproduced, rather than what it is (García and Welter, 2011; Deaux and Major, 1987; Marlow et al., 2009; Orser and Leck, 2010).

Second, while feminist criticism of the entrepreneurship literature has been instrumental in highlighting the marginalization of women by mainstream economic and entrepreneurship research (Walker et al., 2004; Yohn, 2006) and the inequitable impact of capitalism for women (Mirchandani, 1999; Yohn, 2006), certain tenets of feminist criticism are dated. For example, scholars of socialist feminism have typically ignored the significant engagement of women in entrepreneurship and the associated socio-economic benefits that have been afforded to some through business ownership (Orser and Elliott, 2015). The chapter considers how entrepreneurship might inform feminist theory and practice.

Third, documenting feminist values and how 'being female' is constructed within entrepreneurial identity may assist some founders in recognizing and validating their own 'identity work'; the personal synergies, tensions and conflicts that they experience (for example, within themselves and among family, employees, suppliers and clients) (Ahl and Marlow, 2012; García and Welter, 2011). It may also assist in illuminating those feminine assets or 'feminine capital' that contribute in a positive way to entrepreneurial success (Orser and Elliott, 2015).

The chapter presents findings from a research program that examines feminist entrepreneurs (FEs) and how their feminist values are expressed through entrepreneurial action. As the founders engage in entrepreneurial sense-making, they construct their feminist entrepreneurial identity. In this chapter, we build on published findings that have reported on how entrepreneurs express feminist values in governance structures and relationships (respectively, Orser et al., 2013; Orser and Elliott, 2015) to examine how feminist entrepreneurial identity (FEI) is constructed through founder decision-making associated with resource acquisition and market positioning. A conceptual model that captures the consolidated research findings is presented.

To do so, this chapter is organized in the following manner. The literature review opens with a description of definitions and assumptions employed within the study framework. Identity theory and studies that have empirically examined the association among gender, 'being female', and entrepreneurial identity are described. We then present the fieldwork and results. Finally, a synthesis of observations, conceptual model, study limitations and conclusions are presented.

## Literature review

### Definitions and assumptions

For the purpose of this chapter, 'identity' is defined as how one perceives 'self' (Burke, 2006; Pratt and Foreman, 2000). Entrepreneurial identity refers to how one perceives self within the venture creation process. It is assumed that gender is a social construction (Ahl, 2004, 2006), and that gender is recognized as a salient identity category (Burke, 2006; Limerick and O'Leary, 2006; Ridgeway, 2006). Gender is therefore 'enacted through the individual's own process of identity formation, as well as her interaction with the world' (Welch et al., 2008: 116). In this research, we are applying a social constructivist lens, which emphasizes the process of social interaction in all human cognition and knowledge production (Vygotsky, 1978). Following this subjectivist epistemology, all meaning-making activities (including entrepreneurial actions and identity construction and reconstruction) are viewed to be inherently socio-cultural, continuous and relational.[1]

'Feminism is defined as the recognition of men's and women's unequal conditions and the desire to change this' (Ahl, 2004: 16). Feminism embraces perceptions about women's unique needs, their subordination, differences of power within social interactions, and the need for strategies to improve the well-being of girls and women (Gattiker and Larwood, 1986; Nabi, 2001). Feminism focuses on inequitable power relations that subordinate women's interests to those of men, as well as how the social and economic roles of women are defined in relation to male norms (Ahl, 2004; Frye, 1983; Weedon, 1987). 'Feminist entrepreneurs' (FEs) are defined as 'change agents who employ entrepreneurship to improve girls' and women's quality of life and well-being' (Orser and Elliott, 2015: 214).

As noted above, we assume that the construction of entrepreneurial identity is a social process, and one that is intrinsically gendered (Bruni et al., 2004; de Bruin et al., 2006; Fenwick and Hutton, 2000; Limerick and O'Leary, 2006; Warren, 2004). However, unlike previous studies that have assumed that feminist theoretical criticism speaks on behalf of women's entrepreneurial experiences (Weedon, 1987), this study examines how feminist entrepreneurial identity is expressed through entrepreneurial action, and specifically, strategic decision-making. We suggest that this approach softens the prescriptive academic application of feminist theory to women's lived experiences, taking a more grounded approach. To explore the research question and related definitions and assumptions, the following section presents a review of the literature about entrepreneurial identity, gender and feminism.

### Entrepreneurial identity

Identity theory suggests that identities create 'sets of meaning' or 'standards' that link to patterns of behavior within a social environment (Burke, 2006: 82). The construction of identity is purposeful, sometimes contradictory, inherently linked to organizational identity, and situated in a social context (Pratt and Foreman, 2000;

Priola, 2004; Ridgeway, 2006). Entrepreneurship scholars have suggested that there are identity connections among the entrepreneur, her idea or opportunity, and the resulting business (Cardon et al., 2005), including her management style, organizational structure and governance (Orser et al., 2013). For example, 'when people are involved in entrepreneurship, they are also involved in identity construction, where social categories such as gender and ethnicity are implicated' (Essers and Benschop, 2009: 406). Entrepreneurial identity, therefore, is dynamic, multilayered and relational, as individuals make sense of their social and economic environment and culture (Down and Warren, 2008; Warren, 2004). Focused on the early stages of enterprise development, Down and Warren (2008) suggest that entrepreneurial identity is used to establish organizational and self-legitimacy; entrepreneurs are skilled at managing and manipulating perceptions of identity in order to achieve desired outcomes. As noted by Fauchart and Gruber (2011: 936), founders' social identity affects new firm creation, whereby strategic decisions have important 'imprinting effects'.

## Gender and entrepreneurial identity

Gender is one of multiple influences within the construction of identity (Pratt and Foreman, 2000). Gender-linked behaviors are flexible and context-dependent (Deaux and Major, 1987). Gender is reflected in expectations as individuals construct and continually negotiate their own identities. Processes of self-verification and self-presentation are naturally interwoven; people monitor their behavior against both internal (private self-identity) and external (public identity) standards as they strive to attain their interaction goals. 'Gender related behavior may be motivated by either self-presentation or self-verification concerns' (Deaux and Major, 1987: 371).

A number of studies have sought to examine gender and entrepreneurial identity. Drawing on adult learning theory, Fenwick and Hutton (2000) describe the emergent nature of entrepreneurial identity, as female business owners 'craft' their work environment. Identity changes as owners produce and clarify knowledge. Tensions center on issues such as control (the need to relinquish control to others in order to grow), and the desire to defy traditional gender expectations (the meaning of 'being female', the feminine, work–family balance, motherhood, and what constitutes a successful enterprise). Warren (2004: 43) uses life histories to explore the ways in which women 'process . . . to becoming an entrepreneur'. For example, women described the need to legitimize multiple identities including gender, being a professional and being an entrepreneur. Some were ambivalent or negative about the term 'entrepreneur', as the construct conflicted with the ability to 'fit their careers around their family' and 'entrepreneur' was associated with 'game playing' and 'jumping through hoops' (Warren, 2004: 43).

The above studies are consistent with reports that describe conflict between 'being female' and one's entrepreneurial self-image. For example, within the private healthcare sector, Nadin (2007) reports that entrepreneurial identity clashed with other identities such as being female and a caregiver. Verheul et al. (2005: 511) report that gender has a direct effect on business owners' perceptions of entrepreneurial self-image, such that 'Women were less likely than men to perceive themselves as entrepreneurs.' The authors also observed that women were less likely to attribute enterprise success to themselves compared to men; and the term 'entrepreneur' itself had male connotations for some women. Essers and Benschop (2009: 403) document similar results, whereby female Muslims experienced conflict among faith, gender and entrepreneurial identity. As Ahl (2004, 2006) points out, discourses around entrepreneurship and archetypes of the 'heroic entrepreneur' are inherently masculine. The masculine becomes a normative construct against which all entrepreneurial activity is judged: women are seen as 'other', and their activity, by comparison, needs 'fixing' (Ahl and Marlow, 2012: 544). García and Welter (2011) used an interpretive analysis to study how women entrepreneurs interact with these normative expectations in the construction and reconstruction of their gendered identities. They identified a variety of experiences in which respondents perceived dissonance between the discourse of womanhood and that of entrepreneurship. Women entrepreneurs were continually 'doing identity work' to negotiate their entrepreneurial identities within a context of conflicting discourses (womanhood versus entrepreneurship), cultural norms and power structures. To reconcile such differences, the interviewees used two main types of identity work: 'doing gender' (that is, supporting the status quo of gender differences) and 'redoing gender' (that is, 'challenging gender differences') (García and Welter, 2011: 394). For some, entrepreneurship was a strategic tool used to assist in this 'work'.

In a related study, Orser et al. (2013: 248) explored the nature of being female and entrepreneurial. Respondents' narratives described how women were required to reconcile opposing identities, as they experienced both negative and positive outcomes from 'being female':

> Advantages included the ability to share and connect with other women and an ability to build relationships and learn through others' experiences. Being female also helped to foster relationships with potential customers, as 'female' was associated with being trustworthy and being able to 'walk the talk' . . . 'negative' included perceptions about difficult relationships with male suppliers or partners; old boys' networks; limited access to capital; lack of female role models; and self-limiting perceptions about growth (e.g., 'limits my ability to obtain financing through conventional methods', 'locker room mentality', 'lack of trust in women', 'feeling like an 'outsider', 'no sounding board').

In summary, one's entrepreneurial identity is a complex product of personal, sociocultural and economic influences (Down and Warren, 2008; Essers and Benschop, 2009; Werner, 2008). Gender plays a significant role in how individuals construct their entrepreneurial identity; and how women, as entrepreneurs, carry out enterprising activities. Female entrepreneurs have described multiple, sometimes affirming, sometimes negative, and frequently conflicting aspects of their entrepreneurial identity. Shaped by normative expectations, entrepreneurial identity shifts in time and space.

## Feminism and entrepreneurial identity

Early scholars who introduced feminist critique into the entrepreneurship literature (Fischer et al., 1993; Lee-Gosselin and Grise, 1990; Stevenson, 1990; Mirchandani, 1999; Bird and Brush, 2002; Ahl, 2004, 2006) encouraged researchers to examine the 'feminine' within the entrepreneurial content, and to undertake work that legitimizes the experiences of female entrepreneurs. A number of themes have followed, including a critique of the masculine discourse and sexist stereotypes associated with successful entrepreneurship, masculine power structures and systems, and evidence of systemic barriers to venture creation and enterprise growth. Studies also describe gender as an implicit and integral process and structure rather than merely a biological attribute. For example, Bird and Brush (2002) argue that gender is inherent within venture creation processes and enterprise structures. They suggest five dimensions that differentiate between the masculine and feminine, including conceptions of reality, time, action and interaction, power and ethics. Whereas the feminine construct of reality, for example, is reflective, iterative and ambivalent, masculine notions emphasize control and analysis. Whereas feminine values are responsive to others, conciliatory and open to negotiation, masculine values are described as aggressive and controlling.

A complementary stream of inquiry is advanced by feminist ethicists who question how early management theory has portrayed governance structures. In response, Machold et al. (2008) present a governance model of venture creation based on feminine 'ethics of care', a model which emphasizes relationships rather than financial motives for enterprise creation. Governance is described as a web of relationships that create reciprocity, relationships that lend to empowerment and emancipation: individuals empower and nurture others, both within and outside the organization. At a macro level, economists Walker et al. (2004) reconcile tensions between feminist (cooperative) and traditional (competitive) market theories. Noting that feminists have historically criticized competition, where competition is perceived as sexist and having detrimental consequences for women, Walker et al. (2004) recast commercial exchange processes. They argue that rather than being antagonistic (competitive), markets are socially driven. Rather than being divergent, markets are inherently cooperative: commercial competition is a symbiotic and interdependent force. At a fundamental level, competition and cooperation are two necessary components of social organization (Walker et al., 2004: 249): 'Once cooperation regarding the rules of the game exists, the game of competition will foster social wellbeing (and economic prosperity).' The authors conclude that the market is not inherently competitive and anti-feminist, as many feminist scholars have advanced.

To explore such collaborative and competitive relationships, Orser et al. (2013) described organizational structures employed by self-defined feminist entrepreneurs. Feminist values were expressed through the language of engagement, such as egalitarian, enabling and community-building. Organizational structures and working environments were described as informal, familial and non-hierarchical.

An overarching theme that emerged when describing relationships with external stakeholders (clients, suppliers and competitors) was cooperative, using words such as 'collaborative', 'fair', 'friendly', 'win–win', 'open' and 'honest'. Some described themselves as entrepreneurial missionaries, who perceived their role as affecting social change through entrepreneurial actions.

These findings are consistent with Fauchart and Gruber's (2011) research which explored founder identities and entrepreneurial decision-making in the European sporting goods sector. In a mixed-gender study of entrepreneurs, they observed three distinct dimensions of meanings or 'pure identity types': Darwinians, communitarians and missionary. The missionary identity is similar to the feminist entrepreneurial identity described by Orser et al. (2013) and Orser and Elliott (2015). While founders in the Fauchart and Gruber study did not self-identify as feminists (and furthermore, no gender influences or biological sex attributes were reported), both the missionary cohort and Orser et al.'s 'feminist' entrepreneurial cohorts articulated that their ventures affect social change: the founders were 'doing entrepreneurship' to 'pursue their political visions and advance particular causes, generally of a social or environmental nature' (Fauchart and Gruber, 2011: 944). Missionary entrepreneurs were making business decisions that were values-based and 'exemplary', to inspire others to use socially responsible practices. Their decisions were predicated on meanings such as: 'advancing a cause', 'being responsible for contributing to a better world' and 'demonstrating that alternative practices are feasible' (ibid.: 942). This body of literature leads us to the research question: how is feminist entrepreneurial identity expressed through founder decision-making?

## Methods

### Research approach

Fifteen self-identified 'feminist entrepreneurs' were recruited through three Canadian Women's Enterprise Centres to participate in this study. All responded to a call for participation with the following definition of feminist entrepreneur: 'female entrepreneurs who own and operate firms targeting female clients, with a double bottom line, one that includes helping women overcome subordination (e.g., for, by, and with women enterprises)'. The sample included entrepreneurs in the private (n = 12) and not-for-profit (n = 3) sectors, across a variety of sectors. Consistent with the profile of Canadian small and medium-sized enterprises, all but one enterprise (a diamond extraction operation) employed fewer than five employees.[2] See Orser et al. (2013) for more details about the recruitment approach and sampling methods. The sample profile is presented in Table 6.1.

### Data collection and analysis

Business owners participated in a telephone interview following a semi-structured interview protocol. All interviews were recorded and transcribed. Verbatim

**Table 6.1** Sample profile of feminist entrepreneurs

| Participant | Sector profile | Target market | Size and structure | Financing |
|---|---|---|---|---|
| C1 | Manufacturing (MFG)/retail clothing | Female hockey players | 1 owner/operator | Self-financed |
| C2 | Mining/exploration: all female board members | Investors; resource-based companies | 3 staff; ≈50 contractors | Public share offering(s) |
| C3 | MFG/retail clothing | Women in trades | 'Tight' structure: 2 directors/investors; offshore production | Self and one equity partner |
| C4 | Professional network | Women in business | 'Lean and mean' founder + 1 staff + 6 associates + 3 chapters | Self |
| C5 | Career/life coaching | Women in business | Australia, United Kingdom, Canada; very flat, entrepreneurial structure | Self |
| C6 | MFG/retail clothing | Professional women | Flat, collaboration, consensus | Self |
| C7 | Consultant | Women in developing countries | Sole proprietor; periodically contracts with associates | Self |
| C8 | Real estate: leased office space for start-ups | Start-up female entrepreneurs | 8 sharing office space: 'collaborative individualism' | Self |
| C9 | Social networking | Female professional mothers; 30–40 years | 3000 direct members; 6 part-time contact staff | Owner and partner |
| C10 | Education and training: beauty and aesthetics retail | Female students at school | 7 locations | Self (debt); franchise opportunities |
| C11 | Social networking | Women professionals | Founder + 10 staff; national advisory boards | Self |
| C12 | Professional service | Female entrepreneurs | Sole proprietor, contractors as required | Self |
| C13 | Industry association | Women in information, communications, technology | 6 office staff, volunteers, active board (35 members) | Membership fees, sponsorships |
| C14 | Financial services | Women business owners | Non-profit: 7 to 8 founders | Foundation: investment of approx. $4 billion |
| C15 | Financial services | Women-owned firms with revenues of at least $3 million | 1 person, 1 partner, contractors and associates (as required) | 2 partners: $5 million, all female investors with minimum of $2,000 each for 5 years |

transcripts were analyzed with the aid of a data analysis tool, NVivo8. Following an interpretive, inductive methodology (Miles and Huberman, 1994; Glaser and Strauss, 2006), data were coded according to emergent themes and validated by members of the research team. Participant websites were also reviewed; this provided additional information about the organization's mission, vision, products and/or services, marketing, branding, and so on. The summary results of the analyses are presented and discussed below.

## Results

To gain an understanding of how feminist entrepreneurial identity (FEI) was expressed through founder decision-making, participants were asked a series of open-ended questions about potential gender influences in venture creation. These included questions about their perceptions of 'self' as a feminist and an entrepreneur, their feminist values, and how (if at all) their feminist values influenced decision-making. Four major themes emerged. Feminist entrepreneurial identity was expressed through founder decisions about acquisition of resources, market positioning, governance structures and relationships.[3]

### Feminist values and feminist entrepreneurial identity

To explore the participants' identity as feminist entrepreneurs and how feminist values were enacted through entrepreneurship, participants were first asked if they would describe themselves as a 'feminist' and how their feminist values (if at all) had influenced their entrepreneurial decisions. As reported in Orser et al. (2013: 248), 'Responses were overwhelmingly affirmative, indicating a clear sense of feminist identity and feminist values. This was not surprising given the sample criteria as self-identified 'feminists'. The primary themes that emerged were a strong belief in equality, reducing barriers and limits to women's advancement (making change), empowering and supporting others, and following meritocratic principles for success. Identity as feminist entrepreneurs (FEs) was further expressed through their general approach to venture creation, as feminist entrepreneurs 'in action'. These values are clearly articulated as FEs described their motives: to serve women's needs ('I am the market'), 'build community with women like me', 'do more with my life', 'enable other women' and seize upon a unique opportunity to make a difference. The FEs expressed their desire to make social, personal and/or political change; and to empower, support or collaborate with other women and girls. For a more detailed discussion, see Orser et al. (2013).

### Resource acquisition

FEI was articulated in decisions about the acquisition of human and financial (start-up) resources and in securing market intelligence and advice. With respect to the recruitment of employees and contractors, feminist values were evidenced in selection criteria. FEs described hiring like-minded feminists who shared their values.

In addition, most emphasized the importance of following meritocratic principles in recruitment and selection: hiring the best person for the job. They also spoke about creating an inclusive workplace climate and continually trying to support and empower women within the enterprise. As one participant explained:

> It's what we do. We *breathe those values* because that's our mission. So, in this case, my business is directly focused on feminist values, the right of women to be paid for work of equal value, the right to advancement, all those things key to feminist ideology.

One respondent explicitly sought to support women who were 'financially struggling'. Two sought to hire men who ascribed to feminist values. However, as one FE explained, it was important to 'screen out' those who 'masquerade' as feminists:

> I'm not interested in two types of men who are not feminists. One is those who say that they are [a feminist] and *pretend* that they are, and the others who are just outright clear that they're not . . . I think that the ones who pretend that they are, are more dangerous than the ones who are outright that they're not because at least you know where they're coming from and you know where you stand.

In terms of acquiring financial resources for start-up and enterprise growth, respondents described their decisions in terms of their feminist values. All but one enterprise was self-financed. Identifying like-minded, feminist investors to finance growth was a priority, but seen to take considerable time and energy. As one participant observed on the difficulty of finding the right investor: 'there are a lot of different stripes of feminists . . . it's not a homogeneous group'. Another respondent who operated in the mining (extraction) sector had successfully raised equity capital, but not without significant challenges. In this non-traditional market, the very act of creating the enterprise was an expression of her feminist identity. Capital was secured almost entirely from female investors. Women populated the board of directors:

> After 10 years, a few of us who are largely A-type personalities, women who have been successful but always sort of been in the shadows of men, decided we're going to start our own company *for us*. So, one of my co-partners is a lawyer, (was a securities lawyer – she doesn't currently practice because she's involved in public companies) . . . and our board of directors is all women. So we decided that it was time to create a company where we owned the lion's share of the stock and it was based on *our* structure and *our* model.

With respect to the acquisition of expert knowledge, only two enterprises reported having a board of directors or advisors. Again, members were selected based on feminist values, expertise, and affiliation with other members and actors in the sector.

Another critical resource for FEs to acquire is reputational capital. 'While difficult to measure, reputation is one of the most valuable, intangible assets an enterprise possesses. '*Reputation* is a set of beliefs and evaluation about the enterprise held by an external group of stakeholders such as investors, clients and suppliers' (Orser and Elliott, 2015: 69). A positive reputation is associated with competitive advantage: improved access to customers, financing, key markets, cost advantages and favorable pricing. To build reputation, the FEs sought strategic alliances with respected, like-minded organizations. They expressed their FEI through decision-making that was consistent with their values and entrepreneurial motives: partnership agreements were predicated on having a shared feminist vision (making change for women and girls), and feminist values (operating in a manner which was collaborative, cooperative, demonstrating mutual respect and empowerment). For example, within this sample group, Mompreneurs, a networking and communication firm, partnered with Parents Canada to promote a shared vision of parenthood. Women in Communications and Technology (WCT) partnered with Catalyst (an influential non-profit organization that promotes inclusive workplaces for women), Status of Women Canada and the Canadian Board Diversity Council. Moxie Trades, a clothing manufacturer targeting women in the trades (for example, pink work boots), forged strategic relationships with organizations that support women in the trades (for example, Canadian Association of Women in Construction, Canadian Construction Women).

Decisions around the acquisition of additional resources to fuel enterprise growth were judiciously aligned with FEI. Growth and exit strategies reflected conscious attempts to build or sustain communities of like-minded individuals. This was not dependent on firm size or sector. For example, two founders of service-based enterprises pursued internationalization strategies which reproduced feminist identities by establishing relationships with feminist owners and operators abroad. They were selective and opportunistic in finding the right franchisee or partner: those who shared their individual and corporate feminist identity. Similarly, the founders of two service-based firms described how they deployed a values-based network strategy for growth, a strategy that enabled the enterprises to remain 'flat and flexible', 'collaborative' and 'constructive'. One founder established a network of six chapters, with chapter leaders who shared the founder's feminist vision. The second established coaching businesses in Australia and the United Kingdom (UK), articulating the decision for a 'very flat, very entrepreneurial' structure. This founder followed a 'train the trainer' approach whereby new coaches learned the founder's corporate philosophy and principles before being sent abroad as 'entrepreneurial missionaries'. This ensured quality control and consistency of (feminist) philosophy and mission. The founder described the mission as: 'my passion, my focus, is really to give women the tools to succeed in business as quickly as possible'.

## Market positioning

For many, the founder's feminist entrepreneurial identity (FEI) was reproduced through the organization's brand and market positioning. Being a feminist organization was the enterprise's key value proposition, embedded in the firm's branding strategy. Two examples follow. The Women's Executive Network (WXN) positions itself as a feminist, for-profit firm that empowers and supports women's leadership. The WXN web page articulates the WXN brand, differentiating it from other women's networking organizations. The founder pursued an internationalization strategy predicated on her own FEI. As the web page describes:

> At WXN, we inspire smart women to lead. WXN creates and delivers innovative network-ing, mentoring, professional and personal development to inform, inspire, connect and recognise our community of more than 22,000 smart women, their male counterparts and organisations. WXN enables our Partners and Corporate Members to become and to be recognised as employers of choice and leaders in the advancement of women. Founded in 1997, WXN is Canada's leading organisation dedicated to the advancement and recogni-tion of women in management, executive, professional and board roles. In 2008, WXN launched in Ireland, followed by London, UK in 2015, creating an international commu-nity of female leaders. (Women's Executive Network, 2016)

During the study period, the WXN was sold. The news release emphasized that the new owner shared the founder's values and commitment to a feminist cause: 'as a life-long advocate for diversity and a female CEO [chief executive officer] champi-oning HR [human resources] excellence in male-dominated industries (manufac-turing and automotive), Sherri is no stranger to adversity' (Jeffry, 2016).

In the case of Moxie Trades, a manufacturer of women's work wear, the founder's commitment to support girls and women is expressed through the company's brand: the logo, the firm's messaging, activities highlighted on the website, and the content of the owner's blog posts. Her own story is featured, where the founder expresses her struggles in a male-dominated field, personal attachment to her product, and how she wants others to 'find their moxie'. The organization's brand is an expression of her FEI: buying work boots is positioned as being more than just products, as customers buy into self-determination. As stated on the firm's website:

> The Moxie Trades story is about making the best products with the best brand with the best customer service. Not only do we sell work boots but also we share moxie with women everywhere. Moxie Trades is not about the work boots, it's about the women who wear them. Moxie is the ability to face fear with spirit and courage. Find Your MOXIE . . . We Dare YOU!

## Strategic compromises

As founders negotiated some of their key strategic decisions, several expressed dis-sonance in how they prefer to operate as FEs, and how they feel that they are forced to operate in order to achieve their mission and/or attain acceptable margins, to ensure that the enterprise is financially viable. They felt compelled to compromise. For instance, two FEs found supplier solutions that were not 'ideal' in terms of their feminist values and identity. When working with Chinese factory owners, one FE spoke about the need to adjust her expectations regarding equality in the workplace. Another mentioned having to deal with male buyers who have a 'locker room men-tality' and chauvinist attitudes. Compromises were also described in the operations of a nascent women's healthcare centre. The founder's vision for a women-focused centre was mobilized by recruiting an advisory council of like-minded, influential women leaders and patients. The founder and council legitimized the initiative through acquisition of a large lead donation from a respected, feminist philanthropist. However, having established the centre, operations were turned over to the larger hospital administration; and this was disappointing for many members (Orser and Elliott, 2015). Similarly, García and Welter (2011) describe how dealing with macho suppliers, for example, serves to 'produce gender' and reinforce gendered stereotypes rather than 'reproduce gender' in new ways that address and challenge women's subordination.

## Governance structures

Orser et al. (2013) report on how feminist entrepreneurs express their feminist values and ethics through governance structures. When asked, 'How would you describe the organizational and management structure of your business?', participants described structures that are 'flexible', have 'open communication', 'collaborative' (with equal participation of members of the team), 'informal' and 'non-hierarchical (flat) structure and relationships' (ibid.: 251). The descriptors aligned with their feminist values of equality, empowerment, mutual respect and democracy.

## Relationships

Similar alignment was evident when participants spoke about their relationships with employees, suppliers, customers and competitors Orser et al. (2013). Infused with words like 'collaborative', 'win–win', 'cooperative', 'friendly', 'open communications', 'constructive' and 'respectful', their narratives suggest that FEs are consistently producing and reproducing their FEI through their social interactions with others, as they forge relationships; both internal and external. These meaning-making activities were consistently aligned with their values. See Table 6.2 for a summary of these findings from Orser et al. (2013) that have been highlighted above.[4]

## Discussion

This study documents how feminist entrepreneurial identity (FEI) is expressed through strategic decisions associated with the acquisition of resources, market positioning, governance and relationship building. Many, but not all, decisions aligned with founders' feminist identities, and most respondents were able to conduct business in ways that were consistent with feminist values. Strategic decision-making enabled FEs to 'redo' gender by challenging the normative prescriptions of 'womanhood'. Resource acquisition strategies enabled FEs to grow their enterprises by establishing alliances with like-minded women, having a preference to hire feminists and partner with feminists and feminist organizations, attracting investment

**Table 6.2** Feminist entrepreneurial identity and values

| Case | Feminist identity | Motives | Structure and governance | Relationships: internal | Relationships: external |
|---|---|---|---|---|---|
| C1 | 'If I see an imbalance somewhere, about something not being fair and equal, I'm very verbal and I speak out.' | Could not find equipment for daughter: 'My passion is to support females in sports' | Collaborative; fluid; community oriented | Good rapport | Cooperative, flexible |
| C2 | 'I think we're all feminists but not in the feminist, crazy feminist mode ... I think the best person to get the job should get the job.' | 'We decided that it was time to create a company where we owned the lion's share of the stock. ... it was based on our structure and our model.' | All-female board of directors | Lots of communication | Cooperative; easy-going |
| C3 | 'I absolutely feel that [women] are under-utilized and not respected in business as much as they could be.' | 'I look to be the one stop destination for women's work wear and really promote women in the trades' | 'Lean', 2 directors, advisors as needed | Cooperative, friendly, honest; feels like home | Cooperative, friendly, honest |
| C4 | 'For some women they need more support in having an equal chance and we do go about things differently and so I think it's trying to build stronger woman.' | 'Offering women a community, a community where they could connect.' | Lean | Respectful, supportive | Team approach; build alliances |
| C5 | 'People should do what they're good at and what they're naturally suited to, regardless of gender; I just firmly believed that there were no limits for women.' | '[I'm] very passionate about getting women to succeed in businesses, not giving their power away.' | Flat and flexible structure; participative | Creative, entrepreneurial | Alliances, honest, open communication |
| C6 | 'I think that women and men should be treated equally. And that I believe in merit based promotions.' | 'It is really about empowering women, looking good and feeling good in the bodies we've been given' | Flat organization; collaborative | Familial, informal but professional | Win–win, share info, cooperative |

**Table 6.2** (continued)

| Case | Feminist identity | Motives | Structure and governance | Relationships: internal | Relationships: external |
|---|---|---|---|---|---|
| C7 | 'A feminist basically is a person who believes in equality of rights for men and women.' | 'Unless women … had real equality in very practical ways that nations could not change' | Small; 2 employees | | Persistent, polite |
| C8 | Post-structural feminist: 'collaborative individualism', 'I'm open to where feminism is going and I'm not sure. So I'm not imposing any type of structure.' | 'So the vision and purpose of my business is very much community development on entrepreneurship and collaborative individualism in communities.' | Collaborative individualism | Personal, collaborative | Collaborative, sharing |
| C9 | 'Mild feminist', 'there's still a lot of work that needs to be done to have women equal …I definitely want to support the initiatives of women and I still want to see a lot of change happen.' | 'Our mission, we say, is very simple. It's just to connect and inspire women.' | Community-building; loose, flexible structure | Informal, home-based | Win–win, work together, nurture relationship over time |
| C10 | Stated she was not a feminist but agreed with feminist principles defined by the interviewer: 'In business, I'm equal. In personal relationships I become a female, I want to be respected as one.' | 'I mean I am always, number one, wanting to improve the quality of life of women.' | Small company, professional | Professional | Professional, fair, give the best advice |
| C11 | 'I think a feminist is basically someone who believes in equality. It's a woman who believes that men and women should be treated equally.' | 'My vision was to create a community for female professionals across the public, private and non-profit sectors.' | Lean and entrepreneurial; small management team | Communication, teamwork, sharing, collaborative | Friendly, share best practices, learning |

| | | | | |
|---|---|---|---|---|
| C12 | Agreed with feminist principles defined by the interviewer: 'I don't like the term' | 'To provide a voice for small and micro enterprises and many of those were women.' | Small consulting firm | Family environment | Only work with people I like; kindred spirits |
| C13 | Liberal feminist but prefers the term humanist: 'I prefer humanist ... where there are specific issues, there's a very important role for feminism, because it is an ongoing issue for women to have the opportunities that they need ... want ... and frankly, deserve to have.' | 'Our mission is the advancement of women in the communications industry and I mean career advancement.' | Diversity of board leadership; non-hierarchical | Relaxed, non-hierarchical, pleasant | Positive, respectful, constructive, not demanding, focus on results |
| C14 | 'I think a feminist is someone who promotes women's opportunity ... I promote everybody's opportunity.' | 'There was a disconnect, a gap in the communication between entrepreneurs and investors.' | Small staff | Collaborative, win–win, exploration | Collaborative, win–win |
| C15 | 'It means to recognize the full potential of being a woman and we want to be women.' | 'We want to be the premiere private equity company that helps successful female entrepreneurs go to their next level of significant growth.' | Small company | Clear, hard-working bring out the best | Clear, hard-working bring out the best |

from like-minded feminists, and seeking guidance and advice, market intelligence, and referrals through assembly on boards of directors and councils of advisors. Many advisors shared feminist values. Market positioning was enhanced through feminist branding, brands predicated on commitment to empower consumers, members and other women and girls.[5]

Several FEs articulated the need to compromise their feminist aspirations in order to deal with masculine ideologies and male-dominated power structures (for example, suppliers, manufacturers, senior administrators). The need to 'redo' gender identity in order to grow their enterprise was evidenced in both non-traditional sectors (for example, mining, construction, manufacturing) and female-dominated sectors (healthcare, education). These observations are consistent with those reported by Ahl and Marlow (2012): in order to be 'credible actors' in the entrepreneurial domain, women construct social identities that reflect dominant masculinized norms (as cited in Eriksson-Zetterqvist, 2002). A delicate balancing act, the process of discarding and reclaiming feminine identity in order to adhere to masculine norms, is described by an FE in the diamond extraction (mining) sector:

> Many of the women that we work with, the [female] entrepreneurs, don't self-define as women. As a matter of fact, they've had so many years in the technical fields that being a woman was not an issue for them. It could be a detriment; sometimes they were excluded from things.

By minimizing their feminine identity, these FEs attempted to make change by working harder and being successful. They recognized, however, that their impact may be limited only to those male colleagues who were open-minded:

> OK, I see the way things are, some of them I'm going to be able to change and some of them I'm not. For many of our women, the way that they chose to change things is by working harder and being more successful. I think that many times, they don't even think about it. They just do it. They won't allow themselves to think about it during the process . . . you push through.

Many of the FEs had become extremely adept at reconciling different identities (for example, entrepreneur, miner, woman, mother, wife, friend, board member). Pratt and Foreman (2000) suggest that negotiating multiple identities can, for some, be manageable and enabling. Consciously retaining multiple identities allows individuals to draw on a range of self-referential frames in order to respond to a variety of situations. Conversely, multiple identities can produce psychological distress, conflict and overload. Pratt and Foreman (2000) describe how multiple identities relate to each other, and how this helps to explain whether individuals experience positive or negative outcomes. For example, organizational conditions (such as the support of powerful stakeholders) influence the intensity, legitimacy of and tension among identities. This was evidenced in the current study. Influential boards of advisors were seen to enhance the entrepreneur's legitimacy with other decision-

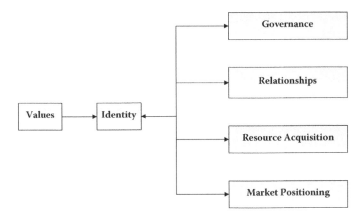

**Figure 6.1**   Feminist Entrepreneurial Identity

makers, such as prospective investors. Warren (2004) also observed the important role of women's networks in constructing and legitimizing (nascent) female business owners' identities.

The current study findings complement meaning-making activities associated with the 'missionary identity' entrepreneur, as described by Fauchart and Gruber (2011). Both the missionary and feminist entrepreneurial identity types were shaped by the founders' intent to make social and/or political change through venture creation, via strategic decision-making.[6] Fauchart and Gruber (2011) do not report on gender, nor consider the normative prescriptions of entrepreneurship as masculine or male. They do, however, acknowledge barriers in 'redoing' dominant notions (and practices) of capitalism, such as conspicuous consumption and environmental disrespect. As such, we observed multiple points of affiliation between the two studies.

Figure 6.1 integrates the current findings with published observations about the interrelationships among feminist values, feminist entrepreneurial identity and entrepreneurial decision-making (Orser et al., 2013; Orser and Elliott, 2015). This process model depicts, graphically, how feminist entrepreneurial identity is socially constructed through entrepreneurial decision-making, in an ongoing, reflexive manner. The arrows are bi-directional, between 'identity' and the four types of decision-making processes. These signify the ongoing interplay between FEI that is enacted through decision-making and FEI that is continually reproduced, as FEs reflect on the outcomes of these decisions and social interactions. While a diagram does not do justice to the complexity and 'social embeddedness' of the venture creation process – enacted in contexts that are gendered, economic, historical and cultural –it is useful in collating insights from our larger research program, and hence for framing future research propositions about the feminist identity construction process.

Feminist entrepreneurs articulated values such as a belief in equality, reducing barriers and limits to women's advancement, making social and political change for women and girls, empowering and supporting others, and following meritocratic principles for success. FEs expressed the opportunity to imprint such values as they create and co-create their ventures. Imprinting was reflected through governance structures, stakeholder relationships, resource acquisition and market positioning. FEs described how their enterprises were non-hierarchical, flexible and collaborative. Decentralized, networked structures were utilized and advisory boards were primarily composed of females and/or like-minded individuals. Internal relationships with employees were described as cooperative and familial. External relationships with customers, suppliers and competitors were described as cooperative and win-win partnerships. See Table 6.2 and Orser et al. (2013) for further details.

Through their interactions, the FEs continually engaged in identity work, aligning their values and attempting to resolve tensions surrounding decisions which did not fit perceptions of 'self'. Hence, the model illustrates how decisions are interrelated, shifting back and forth. The FEs described how they consciously reflected on their entrepreneurial identities and ways to ensure that decisions were consistent with their sense of 'self'. Several FEs described difficult compromises they made to acquire resources needed to fuel enterprise growth. FEs were also continually renegotiating their FEIs within the context of conflicting discourses around womanhood and entrepreneurship; actions that were often situated in masculine hierarchy, cultural norms and power structures.

## Implications

The findings have implications for a number of stakeholders in the entrepreneurial ecosystem, including mainstream and female-focused small business support agencies and women's economic empowerment organizations. For example, the extent to which small business training and support programs embrace and/or discourage feminist entrepreneurial endeavors is not yet clear. Given that small business program mandates typically prioritize revenue growth and employment creation, curriculum may conflict with feminist entrepreneurs' identity framework and ambitions (intentions such as affecting change for women and girls). Research is required to learn more about the lived experiences of entrepreneurial feminists, including: the incidence and efficacy of feminist governance practices; the socioeconomic impact of market positioning, including 'female-owned' and 'feminist' branding; the strengths and limitations of feminist relationships and networking strategies; protectionist and compromising behaviors; other perceived benefits and risks (such as backlash) associated with feminist entrepreneurship; and founders' enterprise support needs. Theory development might focus on explanations about the similarities and differences between 'feminine' (Eddlestone and Powell, 2008) and 'feminist' entrepreneurial identity. The conceptual model serves to frame the examination of related questions, such as:

- How do FEs negotiate conflicting gendered identities in their strategic decision-making about governance, relationships, resource acquisition and market positioning? What are the costs and benefits of such compromises?
- How are feminist identity compromises different (or the same as) those experienced by missionary, social or other entrepreneurs in their decision-making?
- How can the fiscal and social impacts of entrepreneurial feminism be measured?
- To what extent is feminist entrepreneurial identity and decision-making (around governance, strategic relationships, resource acquisition and market positioning) reflected in (and supported by) mainstream and/or female-focused small business support services, programs, policy, curriculum and training?
- In what ways do and can small business support programs assist FEs in employing entrepreneurship as a strategic tool to create a more democratized and legitimate market space for all entrepreneurs?

## Study limitations

Investigating feminist entrepreneurs 'doing identity work' offers the opportunity to examine further the intersection between gender, identity and entrepreneurial activity. However, the limitations of the study are notable. First, the sample does not represent the larger population of female business owners. Second, the potential bias of retrospective data is acknowledged. Third, cross-sectional data did not enable the research team to examine the ways in which gender and feminist entrepreneurial identity change in time, place and context.

## Conclusions

Building on identity and feminist theory, this study examined the association among feminist values, feminist entrepreneurial identity and decision-making. Empirical observations were based on 15 semi-structured interviews, an interpretive analysis was conducted and several themes emerged: resource acquisition through alliances and networking with like-minded partners (feminists), market positioning through feminist branding, and strategic compromises to reconcile business objectives and feminist values. Building on previously reported work (Orser et al., 2013), a conceptual model was developed which highlighted the research findings. This chapter provides new insights into the gendered nature of the venture creation process, and specifically the association among feminist entrepreneurial identity and founder decision-making. The work further refines an emerging praxis: entrepreneurial feminism (Orser and Elliott, 2015). In so doing, it extends the understanding of how female entrepreneurs negotiate meaning and express feminist values through entrepreneurial decision-making and action.

Notes

1   Given that identity construction is an inherently social endeavor, we do not make distinctions between different types of identity 'work': individual, role or social identity. Similarly, we do not make distinctions between individual or organizational levels of analysis.

2   Respondents granted permission for publication of identifying information, as per the University of Ottawa Research Ethics Board protocol.

3   Following Fauchart and Gruber (2011) the first two influences are strategic (acquisition of resources, market positioning), decisions that have important 'imprinting' effects on an emerging enterprise. Both were of particular interest in the expression of FEI.

4   Table 6.2 includes two columns on the left (feminist identity and entrepreneurial motives) which constitute inter-related meaning-making structures for FEI. As the FEs pursue entrepreneurial action, they express FEI through strategic decisions around governance, relationships, resource acquisition and market positioning.

5   Feminist branding appears as a subset of entrepreneurial empowerment marketing. A large-scale example is Walmart's 'Women-Owned' initiative. Partnering with women's organizations (for example, WEConnect International, Women's Business Enterprise National Council), Walmart has positioned the logo project as an 'ongoing commitment to empowering women around the world and helping women-owned businesses succeed and grow' (Walmart, 2015).

6   The missionary type was among the minority of Fauchart and Gruber's sample: 'pure' missionary entrepreneurs represented 9 of 49 respondents.

# References

Ahl, H. (2004), *The Scientific Reproduction of Gender Inequality*, Copenhagen: Copenhagen Business School Press.

Ahl, H. (2006), 'Why research on women needs new directions', *Entrepreneurship Theory and Practice*, 30(5), 595–623.

Ahl, H. and S. Marlow (2012), 'Exploring the dynamics of gender, feminism and entrepreneurship: advance debate to escape a dead end?', *Organization*, 19(5), 543–562.

Bird, B. and C. Brush (2002), 'A gendered perspective on organizational creation', *Entrepreneurship Theory and Practice*, 26(3), 41–65.

Bourne, K.A. (2007), 'Encountering one another: feminist relationships in organizational research', *Organization Management Journal Teaching and Learning*, 4(2), 120–133.

Bruni, A., S. Gheradi, and B. Poggi (2004), 'Entrepreneur-mentality, gender and the study of women entrepreneurs', *Journal of Organizational Change Management*, 17(3), 256–268.

Burke, P. (2006), 'Identity change', *Social Psychology Quarterly*, 69(1), 81–96.

Cardon, M., C. Zietsma, P., Saparito, B. Matherne and C. Davis (2005), 'A tale of passion: new insights into entrepreneurship from a parenthood metaphor', *Journal of Business Venturing*, 20(1), 23–45.

de Bruin, A., C. Brush and F. Welter (2006), 'Advancing a framework for coherent research on women's entrepreneurship', *Entrepreneurship Theory and Practice*, 31(3), 323–339.

Deaux, K. and B. Major (1987), 'Putting gender into context: an interactive model of gender-behavior', *Psychological Review*, 94(3), 369–389.

Down, S. and L. Warren (2008), 'Constructing narratives of enterprise: clichés and entrepreneurial identity', *International Journal of Entrepreneurial Behaviour and Research*, 14(1), 4–23.

Eddleston, K.A. and G.N. Powell (2008), 'The role of gender identity in explaining sex differences in business owners' career satisfier preferences', *Journal of Business Venturing*, 23(2), 244–256.

Eriksson-Zetterqvist, U. (2002), 'Construction of gender in corporations', in B. Czarniawska and H. Hopfl (eds), *Casting the Other*, London: Routledge, pp. 89–103.

Essers, C. and Y. Benschop (2009), 'Muslim businesswomen doing boundary work: the negotiation of Islam, gender and ethnicity within entrepreneurial contexts', *Human Relations*, 62(3), 403–423.

Fauchart, E. and M. Gruber (2011), 'Darwinians, communitarians, and missionaries: the role of founder identity in entrepreneurship', *Academy of Management Journal*, 54(5), 935–957.

Fenwick, T. and S. Hutton (2000), 'Women crafting new work: the learning of women entrepreneurs', Proceedings, 41st Adult Education Research Conference, University of British Columbia, Vancouver, June.

Fischer, E., A.R. Reuber and L. Dyke (1993), 'A theoretical overview and extension of research on sex, gender, and entrepreneurship', *Journal of Business Venturing*, 8(2), 151–168.

Frye, M. (1983), *The Politics of Reality: Essays in Feminist Theory*, Freedom, CA: Crossing Press.

García, M.D. and F. Welter (2011), 'Gender identities and practices: Interpreting women entrepreneurs' narratives', *International Small Business Journal*, 31(4), 384–404.

Gattiker, U.E. and L. Larwood (1986), 'Subjective career success: a study of managers and support personnel', *Journal of Business and Psychology*, 1(2), 78–94.

Glaser, B. and A. Strauss (2006), *The Discovery of Grounded Theory: Strategies for Qualitative Research*, New Brunswick, NJ: Aldine Transaction.

Henry, C., L. Foss and H. Ahl (2015), 'Gender and entrepreneurship research: a review of methodologies approaches', *International Small Business Journal*, 34(3), 217–241.

Jeffry, P. (2016), 'WXN and CBDC acquired by new CEO and Top 100 award winner Sherri Stevens', Press release, January.

Lee-Gosselin, H. and J. Grise (1990), 'Are women owner-managers challenging our entrepreneurship? An in-depth survey', *Journal of Business Ethics*, 9(4/5), 423–433.

Limerick, B. and J. O'Leary (2006), 'Re-inventing or recycling? Examples of feminist qualitative research informing the management field', *Qualitative Research in Organizations and Management: An International Journal*, 1(2), 98–112.

Machold, S., P. Ahmed and S. Farquhar (2008), 'Corporate governance and ethics: a feminist perspective', *Journal of Business Ethics*, 81(3), 665–678.

Marlow, S., C. Henry and S. Carter (2009), 'Exploring the impact of gender upon women's business ownership', *International Small Business Journal*, 27(2), 139–148.

Miles, M.B. and A.M. Huberman (1994), *Qualitative Data Analysis: An Expanded Sourcebook*, Thousand Oaks, CA: SAGE Publications.

Mirchandani, K. (1999), 'Feminist insight on gendered work: new directions in research on women and entrepreneurship, *Gender, Work and Organization*, 6(4), 224–235.

Nabi, G.R. (2001), 'The relationship between HRM, social support and subjective career success among men and women', *International Journal of Manpower*, 22(5), 457–474.

Nadin, S. (2007), 'Entrepreneurial identity in the care sector: navigating the contradictions', *Women in Management Review*, 22(6), 456–467.

Orser, B. and C. Elliott (2015). *Feminine Capital: Unlocking the Power of Women Entrepreneurs*, Palo Alto, CA: Stanford University Press.

Orser, B., C. Elliott and J.D. Leck (2013), 'Entrepreneurial feminists: perspectives about opportunity recognition and governance', *Journal of Business Ethics*, 115(2), 241–257.

Orser, B. and J. Leck (2010), 'Physician as feminist entrepreneur: the case study of the Shirley E. Greenberg Women's Health Centre', in C.G. Brush, E.J. Gatewood, A.M. de Bruin and C. Henry (eds), *Women's Entrepreneurship and Growth Influences: An International Perspective*, Cheltenham, UK and Northampton, MA, USA: Edward Elgar Publishing, pp. 284–300.

Pratt, M. and P. Foreman (2000), 'Classifying managerial responses to multiple organizational identities', *Academy of Management Review*, 25(1), 18–42.

Priola, V. (2004), 'Gender and feminine identities: women as managers in a UK academic institution', *Women in Management Review*, 19(8), 421–430.

Ridgeway, C. (2006), 'Linking social structure and interpersonal behaviour: a theoretical perspective on cultural schemas and social relations', *Social Psychology Quarterly*, 69(1), 5–16.

Stevenson, L. (1990), 'Some methodological problems associated with researching women entrepreneurs', *Journal of Business Ethics*, 9(4/5), 439–446.

Verheul, I., L.M. Uhlaner and A.R. Thurik, (2005), 'Business accomplishments, gender and entrepreneurial self-image', *Journal of Business Venturing*, 20(4), 483–518.

Vygotsky, L.S. (1978). *Mind in Society: The Development of Higher Psychological Processes*, Cambridge, MA: Harvard University Press.

Walker, D., J.W. Dauterive, E. Schultz and W. Block (2004), 'The feminist competition/cooperation dichotomy', *Journal of Business Ethics*, 55(3), 243–254.

Walmart (2015). 'Walmart launches "Women Owned" logo in-store & online', accessed 15 February 2015 at http://corporate.walmart.com/_news_/news-archive/2015/03/11/walmart-launches-women-owned-logo-in-store-online.

Warren, L. (2004), 'Negotiating entrepreneurial identity: communities of practice and changing discourses', *International Journal of Entrepreneurship and Innovation*, 5(2), 25–35.

Weedon, C. (1987), *Feminist Practice and Poststructuralist Theory*, Oxford: Basil Blackwell.

Welch, C.L., D.E. Welch and L. Hewerdine (2008), 'Gender and export behaviour: evidence from women-owned enterprises', *Journal of Business Ethics*, 83(1), 113–126.

Werner, A. (2008), 'The influence of Christian identity of SME owner-managers' conceptualisations of business practice', *Journal of Business Ethics*, 82(2), 449–462.

Women's Executive Network (WXN) (2016), 'About', https://www.wxnetwork.com/about/about-wxn/, accessed 10 February 2016.

Yohn, S.M. (2006), 'Crippled capitalists: the inscription of economic dependence and the challenge of female entrepreneurship in nineteenth-century America', *Feminist Economics*, 12(1/2), 85–109.

# 7 Identity and identity work in constructing the woman entrepreneur

*Richard T. Harrison and Claire M. Leitch*

## Introduction

Although the construct of identity has gained common currency in contemporary social science it is only relatively recently that it has come to the attention of scholars working in entrepreneurship. Much of this research has been empirical, employing a number of concepts (among them: role identity theory, social identity theory, structural identity theory, narrative and discourse analysis) to explore its role and impact (Hoang and Gimeno, 2010; Obschonka et al., 2012; Krueger, 2007; Cohen and Musson, 2000; Down and Reveley, 2004; Binari, 2012; Anderson and Warren, 2011; Boje and Smith, 2010; Down, 2006; Fauchart and Gruber, 2011; Oliver and Vough, 2012; Watson, 2009a; Miller and Le-Breton Miller, 2011). Specifically, identity research in entrepreneurship has focused on personal identity as one's sense of self, with a growing recognition of the 'looking-glass' relation between self-identity and a variety of social identities (Watson, 2009a; Anderson and Warren, 2001). It also focuses on identity as in some sense the fixed reference point around which individuals engage in entrepreneurial activities and roles, and on identity as a covariant of outcomes and processes of interest. This chapter is, in part, a response to a call for entrepreneurial identity research (Leitch and Harrison, 2016) that recognizes the need for more research on organizational context (studies of the process of identity formation in a wider range of entrepreneurial and small and medium-sized enterprise contexts, including discussion of identity and the family business; Harrison and Leitch, 2016); with a focus on the nature of identity work in entrepreneurship and the processes by which identities are constructed and negotiated over time as a tension between individual identity and identity as an entrepreneur.

'Identity' itself is a complex construct with multiple definitions (Abdelal et al., 2001), and has for the most part been researched from either a social identity theory (SIT) perspective (Tajfel, 1981) or a (role) identity theory (IT) perspective (Stryker and Serpe, 1982). Our understanding of identity in this chapter recognizes that SIT and IT have more commonalities than differences in the analysis of the multifaceted nature of identities in terms of their bases, processes and outcomes (Stets and Burke, 2000; Burke and Stets, 2009). Given this, identity can be defined for our purposes as 'a dynamic social product of the interaction of the capacities for memory, consciousness and organised construal with the physical and societal structures and influence processes which constitute the social context . . . identity resides in psychological processes but is manifested through thought, action and affect' (Breakwell, 2010: 63). This reflects Erikson's (1968: 22) argument that in identity 'we deal with a process "located" *in the core of the individual* and yet also *in the core of his* [sic] *communal culture* . . . identity formation employs a process of simultaneous reflection and observation'. It also acknowledges more recent processual arguments that the identity phenomenon comprises the three processes of identity formation, identity activation and resultant behavior (Bothma et al., 2015). As such, identities provide a meaning-making anchor: choices (decisions, outcomes) are identity-based and identity-congruent (Oyserman et al., 2012). Identities are, therefore, 'the traits and characteristics, social relations, roles, and social groups that define who one is . . . Identities are orienting, they provide a meaning-making lens and focus one's attention on some but not other features of the immediate context' (Oyserman et al., 2012: 69).

The enactment of an entrepreneurial identity is a complex process of identity work (Watson, 2009b). Identity, which is concerned with an individual's attitudes, beliefs and behaviors, provides entrepreneurs with a source of meaning from which to operate. However, many entrepreneurs, and especially women entrepreneurs, fail to see themselves as such, given that the gendering of the dominant entrepreneurship discourse assumes a male entrepreneurial identity (Bird and Brush, 2002; Bruni et al., 2004; Hamilton, 2013a). Current and traditional notions of entrepreneurship 'sustain the dominant myth and ideology of Western mentality: that the male (white) is first among equals' (Ogbor, 2000: 629). In essence it is 'more masculine than feminine, more heroic than cowardly' (Collins and Moore, 1964: 5). As masculinity is the normative, this presents a challenge for women entrepreneurs engaged in identity work, who 'strive to shape a relatively coherent and distinctive notion of personal self identity' (Watson, 2009a: 257) through dialogue between the inner self and an external discourse reflecting the social domain (Kenny, 2010; Sveningsson and Alvesson, 2003). Recently, critiques of entrepreneurial identity have highlighted the gender-blind assumptions that underpin it (Marlow and McAdam, 2012, 2015; Ahl and Marlow, 2012; Bruni et al., 2004). This work has revealed the masculine bias and related stereotypical behaviors and attitudes associated with entrepreneurial identity work in which women are considered 'other' (Kelan, 2009).

In this chapter we adopt a feminist perspective to address the following question: what is the nature of the identity work undertaken by women in the processes of identity formation, identity activation and resultant behavior in an entrepreneurial context? We do so in the context of an ethnographic case study of a female entrepreneur involved in the start-up and growth of her family's business. This extends research on identity work in entrepreneurship that has started to question the androcentrism inherent in current notions of the entrepreneurial identity (Marlow and McAdam, 2015; Díaz García and Welter, 2013). In so doing, we argue that there is scope to more fully enrich our theoretical understanding of identity and identity formation, their relationship to entrepreneurial processes, practices and activities,

and specifically to the communicative practices that shape gender identity formation (Duveen and Lloyd, 1990). This entails three shifts of emphasis. First, we focus
on identity as a social as well as a personal construct (Fearon, 1999; Watson, 2009a).
Second, we draw attention to the importance of considering identity as dynamic
and fluid rather than as a (relatively) fixed and unchanging feature. Third, on the
basis of this, we concentrate on the process through which entrepreneurial identities are formed and shaped. Specifically, we argue that only by understanding the
dynamics of identity formation is it possible to relate identity to entrepreneurial
outcomes. By exploring how a female entrepreneur performs identity work within
different entrepreneurial contexts we provide increased insights into the historical,
social and cultural influences on identity work (Hamilton, 2013a; Bruni et al., 2005).
We also demonstrate how identity is co-constituted over time and in relation to
others, highlighting that is inextricable from context. By taking a feminist perspective on the identity work performed by the female entrepreneur we shed light on
how she shapes her identity, and how it is shaped to fit with an entrepreneurial
representation.

The chapter is structured as follows. We begin by summarizing the key elements
of contemporary understandings of identity in entrepreneurship, including
recent discussions on gender and identity. We then discuss our ethnographic,
longitudinal research design and data analysis protocols. On the basis of this we
provide a summary of the findings and critically reflect on the implications of
our analysis for a feminist understanding of gender relations, identity work and
entrepreneurial action. The contributions of the chapter are methodological, conceptual and empirical. Methodologically we demonstrate how an ethnographic
approach can allow us to make a contribution to the still relatively sparse literature of empirical studies addressing identity construction on the personal level in
depth (Svenningsson and Alvesson, 2003). Conceptually, as entrepreneurship is
gendered masculine (Ahl, 2004, 2006) and tends to be viewed as the default option,
this research provides a gendered perspective on identity work (Bruni et al., 2005).
Empirically, we provide greater insights into how gender has shaped a female
entrepreneur's experiences and ambitions within the context of a family business
in its start-up phase.

## Identity

### Identity theory

The search for identity is a central symptom of individualism (Ybema et al., 2009:
299). Identity is not something which we can objectify as an observable entity, but
that which we can construct or articulate in an ongoing interaction with our social
environment: 'that work of art which we want to mould out of the friable stuff of life
is called "identity"' (Bauman, 2000: 82). In discussions of identity there is a tension
between the image of harmony, logic and consistency, and everyday experience. If
identity is a negotiation between self and society, between what is within us and
what lies outside, it is at the same time both that which is perceived by others and

that which is projected by ourselves (Ybema et al., 2009). However, as Bauman (2000) points out, this appears to be fixed and solid only when seen from outside, by others. From the perspective of one's own biographical, lived experience identity remains fragile, fluid and vulnerable. Given this, in contemporary management and organization theory identity is increasingly being seen as friable, fluid, ephemeral and fragile (Bauman, 2000), and the research focus is shifting from identity per se to the processes of identity formation (Ybema et al., 2009; Clegg and Baumeler, 2010; Coupland and Brown, 2012).

Much contemporary research on identity and identity work, particularly in the European tradition, is informed by the metaphor of social construction (Ainsworth and Grant, 2012). This focuses on processes and considers not only the 'what' but also the 'how' of identity and identity work. In addition, it is predicated on the argument that discourse is central to the social construction of identity (Clarke et al., 2012; Ybema et al., 2012; Beech et al., 2012; Mallett and Wapshott, 2012; McInnes and Corlett, 2012). For Watson (2008), conventional research into identity has followed a two-step process in which a discourse is identified (for example, of leadership, of entrepreneurship, of professionalism) and individuals are examined to determine the extent to which they have taken on a particular identity (that is, of a leader, an entrepreneur or a professional). Against this, he argues that social identities are central to the discourses which people reference in their identity work (Figure 7.1).

Accordingly, within the various discourses of, for instance, enterprise, management and leadership, there are one or more social identities of the 'entrepreneur', 'manager' and 'leader'. In other words, 'elements of discourse are personified in the form of "social-identities" in a way which makes them meaningful, accessible and appealing or unappealing to the individual, and in a way that the abstractions of a "discourse" could not' (Watson, 2008: 129). Given that in liquid modernity there are multiplicities of diverse, competing and contradictory discursive pressures on

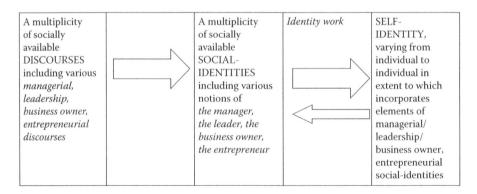

**Source:**   Adapted from Watson (2008: 128).

**Figure 7.1**   The relation between discourses and self-identities

every individual, engagement in identity work is unavoidable. While individuals themselves can have input into these social identities (represented by the small arrow in Figure 7.1), what is important as the basis for our analysis is the recognition that the multiplicity of discourses and social identities are incorporated to varying extents in the development of unique self-identities. This provides the starting point for the research reported in this chapter: 'the crux of the matter, for the researcher, is this: the extent to which people embrace particular social identities or "personas" as elements of their self-identity is a matter for empirical investigation' (Watson, 2008: 129).

## Identity and entrepreneurship

Entrepreneurial identity is a similarly complex construct with multidisciplinary roots and an associated range of conceptual meanings and theoretical roles (Powell and Baker, 2013; Leitch and Harrison, 2016). As our representation of the internalization and incorporation of socially held behavioral expectations, it reflects the past (what used to be true of one), and influences both the way we feel, think and behave in the present (what is true of one now) and what we seek in the future (the person one expects, wishes, feels obligated or fears to become) (Oyserman et al., 2012). It also represents a frame of reference for reading social situations, behaviors and actions, signifying who we are in relation to others, and how we differ from them. If, as Falck et al. (2009) suggest, an individual's sense of identity is influenced by considerations of social desirability, and entrepreneurial roles 'are a set of socially held behavioural expectations attached to the positions external to an individual' (Murnieks and Mosakowski, 2007: 2), then entrepreneurial activities are infused with meaning as a result of the expression of an individual's identity, and identities both drive and are driven by entrepreneurial actions. However, entrepreneurs do not construct their identities alone: identity bridges the individual and the social and creates a medium through which the entrepreneurial self and the social interact (Ybema et al., 2009; Watson, 2009b). As firm creation is both an individual (or team) and an inherently social activity, and organizations are social constructions, the bridging construct of identity is increasingly being applied to exploring and explaining entrepreneurs' attempts to understand who they are and are not, and what they do and do not, at all stages in the entrepreneurial process.

Most contemporary research on identity in entrepreneurship sees it as real, objective and measurable. The emphasis is primarily on identity as an external representation, and the analytical frameworks employed concentrate on establishing the co-variance between it and other phenomena of entrepreneurial interest (Leitch and Harrison, 2016). This is very much a research program grounded in the principles and practices of modernity, in which attempts are made to investigate, measure, analyze, record and classify particular phenomena (Leitch and Harrison, 2016). However, the construction of a single entrepreneurial identity, whether desirable or not, is difficult due to the agentic nature of the entrepreneurial process and absence of normative institutionalized exemplars (Marlow and McAdam, 2015; Down, 2006), the shifting conceptualizations of the archetypical entrepreneur in popular discourse (Watson, 2013a) and the evident heterogeneity of entrepreneurial identities (Fauchart and Gruber, 2011; Cardon et al., 2009; Alsos et al., 2016).

## Women entrepreneurs and identity

For some actors an important aspect of identity work is the desire for affirmation as a legitimate member of a particular grouping (Butler, 2004), in this case as an entrepreneur: the creation of a sense of belongingness reinforces self-confirmation (Hogg, 2006). However, Hamilton (2013a: 90) warns that 'we are not free to author our own identities; we draw on those available to us in order to creatively configure a sense of self'. Accordingly, feminists have argued that for women entrepreneurs this can be particularly challenging, especially if they want to achieve visibility and entrepreneurial legitimacy (Marlow and McAdam, 2015; De Clercq and Voronov, 2009; Stead, 2017). Historically the entrepreneurship literature has assumed that the process of founding and growing a venture results from the efforts of a lone, male entrepreneur, resulting in the traditional normative gendered stereotyping of entrepreneurs of 'think entrepreneur, think male', and as a result ignores entrepreneurship as the enactment of feminist values (Orser et al., 2013; Ogbor, 2000; Wilson and Tagg, 2010). Despite this, there is dispute regarding the gender-blind assumptions informing the analysis of entrepreneurial identity. On the one hand, for some, the ideal entrepreneur reflects the male prototype, drawing on masculine assumptions as generic, which means that normative constructions of femaleness and femininity are not necessarily aligned with contemporary understandings (Marlow and McAdam, 2015; Ahl and Marlow, 2012). On the other hand, a growing body of work studying women entrepreneurs cautions that the feminist argument that the field is gender-blind is no longer valid (Hamilton, 2013b). Indeed, it could be argued that focusing on the study of women entrepreneurs from a perspective of difference from men (the dominant perspective), is gender-blind in itself as it mitigates against examining the male norm (Sunderland, 2004; Harrison et al., 2015).

Part of the critique of gender as difference represented as gender-as-variable research is the perpetuation of oppositional binaries, which assumes homogeneity of the sexes, as well as a tendency towards essentialism (Leitch et al., 2017; Harrison and Mason, 2007). This results from the distinctions that Oakley (1972) advanced between sex as a biological category (female and male) and gender as a social construction (feminine and masculine), and the subsequent mapping of socially ascribed characteristics of femininity and masculinity to a particular sex so that masculine attributes are associated with the male and accorded greater respect, legitimacy and authority (Bowden and Mummery, 2009). Such a hierarchical gender binary ignores the co-constitution of both male and female aspects of gender in the construction of an entrepreneurial identity. In disregarding the dynamism and fluidity of identity work such a perspective also continues the notion of a decontextualized static and stable identity. However, identity work is complicated, constantly shifting and negotiated with others, being constitutive of rather than external to identity: 'The inner self is not an autonomously owned space to which we can attach preferred identities but rather, is embedded within culture and context' (Marlow and McAdam, 2015: 793; Butler, 1993). In other words, constructing and reconstructing identity occurs in everyday lives and settings. In the research reported in this chapter we pose the following research question: how and to what extent is female entrepreneurial identity shaped by historical life-events and their contemporary embeddedness in and experience of social situations and networks?

## Methodology

Fundamental to the research reported in this chapter are three transitions in perspective in entrepreneurial identity research (Leitch and Harrison, 2016): first, there is a move from the static analysis of identity per se to the process of identity construction, in which identity work as the means by which this emerges is important; second, there is a resultant shift from social identity to the concept of self-identity; and third, in entrepreneurship, as in organization studies more generally, there is growing interest in the situational nature of identity construction, which has not yet been empirically and systematically investigated (Soekijad and Skovgard Smith, 2012). As such, this research responds to Hjorth et al.'s (2008) call for work which goes beyond the uncreative and decontextualized research currently dominant in entrepreneurship (see Welter, 2011; Wright et al., 2014), and sees individuals as creative and emergent beings who continuously exchange with others to shape their identities and life-orientations (Watson, 2013a). Given that 'identity issues call for considerable depth and richness' (Svenningsson and Alvesson, 2003: 1170), a single case study research design (Watson, 2008, 2009b; Perren and Ram, 2004; Svenningsson and Alvesson, 2003) using ethnographic techniques was adopted which allowed insights, experiences, meanings and interpretations in a particular context to be uncovered.

### Ethnographic case study research

Despite growing interest in management (Cunliffe, 2010; Van Mannen, 1988), to date there has been relatively little use of ethnographic methods in entrepreneurship (Watson, 2013b). These are particularly relevant for research explicitly focusing on identifying and articulating the entrepreneurial process (Dana and Dana, 2005; Moroz and Hindle, 2012). Specifically, if entrepreneurial action – in this instance, identity work and the process of identity construction – is viewed as a key feature of contemporary social organization with its own institutional logic, then an ethnographic approach, as a distinctive type of research, helps to provide an illuminating perspective on these issues (Watson, 2012).

There is an emerging research agenda focused on exploring identity work and formation as a fluid, complex, multifaceted and context-specific process in which both the external (representation of self) and internal (biographical, lived experience) perspectives are important. Given that gender is a social construction, our choice of an interpretivist ethnographic research design and methodology was informed by three specific considerations (Svenningssson and Alvesson, 2003; Watson, 2008).

First, the research focus is on identity work as a process of emergence (Chia and Holt, 2006) rather than on the static representation of identity. Second, self-identity is socially constructed and, thus, is not meaningful in isolation from the social world of other people (Jenkins, 1996; Oyserman et al., 2012). That means that the identity work individuals engage in is not primarily or exclusively an internal, self-oriented process. Rather, through talk and action the inwardly directed process of internal self-reflection and the outwardly oriented process of external engagement with various social identities are integrated (Watson, 2008: 130). Third, although there are some empirical studies of the role of context in entrepreneurial identity formation, in particular (Down and Reveley, 2009; Miller and Le Breton-Miller, 2011), there remains little formal investigation of the situational nature of identity construction by individuals facing change, where the process of identity work depends on the situation they are in and on the interests that are at stake in those specific concrete situations (Soekijad and Skovgard Smith, 2012).

Coupled with a longitudinal research design, observational research provides a valuable opportunity for the study of identity in progress, avoiding the dangers of relying on retrospective, (re)constructed accounts and providing a context for understanding and interpreting interview-based material (Mallett and Wapshott, 2012). We adopted a case study approach (Perren and Ram, 2004) informed by hermeneutic and phenomenological perspectives (Cope, 2005; Laakkonen, 2012; Hindle, 2004; Neergaard and Parm Ulhøi, 2007) to allow for a focus on process and context which are central to the interpretation of identity. We follow Hilliard (1993) in seeing the case study as a research design that is appropriate for addressing particular types of research objectives where the prime interest is on the temporal unfolding of variables within individual subjects through the collection of direct observational qualitative data. In applying this we follow Gibbert and Ruigrok (2010) on strategies to ensure rigor in case study research, which focus primarily on the detailed reporting of the concrete research actions taken so that the reader may appreciate the logic of the specific case study (Leitch et al., 2010).

## Research context

Our research is nested within a more extensive, longitudinal case study investigation into the process of leader and leadership development in entrepreneurial ventures, all of which were focused on opportunity recognition, exploitation and venture growth (Shane and Venkataraman, 2000; Morris et al., 2015). We followed leaders from 22 companies drawn from several cohorts of a leadership development program (Leitch et al., 2012).[1] Mary, the subject of this case study, was one of these owners. When she started the venture with her husband (Sam) and father-in-law (James) she was 54 years old and had no prior entrepreneurial experience, having previously worked in a number of shopfloor and office roles in large companies in the textile and consumer electronics assembly industries. However, when James indicated that he wished to establish an engineering business in a sector in which he had over 30 years' experience, and Sam over 25 years, she was persuaded to join the venture. Although Mary acknowledges that she knew nothing about founding a business, having provided the majority of the start-up capital she became a director alongside James and Sam. James, as father and founder, was initially managing director, ostensibly with responsibility for the overall direction and management of the business. Sam was production manager, and on his father's retirement became managing director. At the outset, Mary was focused on managing the administrative functions, though gradually took on the leadership role, albeit not formally acknowledged.

## Data collection

The authors, together with a researcher[2] trained in ethnographic field research methods, collected data over approximately an 18-month period using a combination of overt observation, conversations, interviews and documentary materials, and regularly compared field notes and experiences for consistency (see Appendix). This is consistent with the distinctive nature of ethnographic research, which is predicated on a commitment to methodological holism (Gellner and Hirsch, 2001) in which researchers 'observe closely the actions, meanings, artefacts and outcomes that constitute the field' (Watson and Watson, 2012: 685). Given that anything in the research context is potentially relevant, it is the combination of material from diverse sources that forms the 'ethnographic record' (Kuper, 1994: 17), which is the basis for deepening our understanding of the aspect of modern life under consideration (Watson and Watson, 2012).

Given the volume of material we are obviously not in a position to provide a comprehensive analysis of everything this might tell us about the formation of entrepreneurial identity. As is common in ethnographic research, we have to exercise selectivity as researchers in the choice of data to present and the manner in which it is presented. Our approach to this has been to use the longitudinal single case study – drawing in particular on the interviews and conversations with Mary, informed by the relevant portions of the field notes and observational data – to shine a light on entrepreneurial identity construction.

The interviews were unstructured and open-ended and no specific reference was made to identity. Our intention was to open the possibility of 'gaining an insight into the experiences, concerns, interests, beliefs, values, knowledge and ways of seeing, thinking and acting' of the participant (Schostak, 2006: 10). As such, the focus is on the interview as an interactive process where both the interviewer and interviewee are co-constructing meaning and interpreting this process (Cassel, 2005; Denzin, 2001). In this respect the approach differs from that of the conventional qualitative interviewer, for whom the semi-structured interview is designed as a purposive exploration of the phenomenon of interest. All interviews were recorded and transcribed verbatim and field observations from each session were also written up to provide a text for analysis. In line with assurances given to participants, their names and business identities have been changed to ensure anonymity.

## Data analysis

The analysis reported here relates specifically to data pertaining to Mary and her business. Data analysis has been informed by recent discussions of interpretivist research in entrepreneurship (Leitch et al., 2010; Leitch and Hill, 2015), and followed the protocols of the grounded theory framework (Strauss and Corbin, 1998; Glaser and Strauss, 1967). Specifically, this uses three basic elements: concepts/codes (basic units of analysis), categories (more abstract than concepts) and propositions/themes (relationships among categories). Coding was carried out in three stages: first, open coding, the identification of relevant concepts/codes; second, axial coding, the refinement of these concepts into categories; and third, selective coding, the process of relating one category to another to generate themes.

At the open coding stage, familiarity was gained through close reading and re-reading of the text that supported early coding of the transcriptions. Data were broken down into codes by asking simple questions, such as 'Who?', 'What?', 'When?', 'Where?', 'Why?' and 'How?' These codes were then compared and similar occurrences – that is, duplication – were placed under the same concept/code, to provide a list of unique codes for further analysis. Axial coding was conducted to refine, reclassify and group each concept/code into categories. Finally, selective coding occurred which consisted of making connections between the different categories to develop theoretical interpretations. Throughout the analysis, constant comparison was made between existing data and emerging categories until data saturation was obtained. In the present study, the case analysis of the emergence of Mary's identity, this was not achieved at the end of the data collection process for the leadership development program and, therefore, it was decided to carry out the further interviews as specified above after its completion.

While 'pure' grounded theory sees conceptual sense-making, that is, theory emerging from the data (Glaser, 1999), our approach was to work iteratively, switching back and forth between the inductive and the deductive (Watson, 2012). Thus, the research process involved ongoing iteration across the data collection, analysis and interpretation phases. Nevertheless, relying on the coding protocols of grounded theory allowed the data to be organized and structured 'according to the issues and topics identified by participants as being important for the phenomenon of interest' (Leitch and Hill, 2015: 6). In essence, themes were 'derived from the concepts and categories which social actors use to interpret and understand their worlds' (Jones, 1985: 25).

## Findings: the construction of entrepreneurial identity

After open coding of Mary's data, 51 discrete concepts/codes were identified. Through axial coding undertaken by two of the researchers these were combined into six categories, which were checked for coherence and consistency by a third member of the project research team (Leitch et al., 2010) (Table 7.1). In this section

**Table 7.1**  Inductive analysis and data coding: the case of Mary

| Open coding (concepts/codes) | Axial coding (categories) |
| --- | --- |
| Knowledge and expertise<br>Lack of knowledge<br>Experience<br>Acquisition of knowledge<br>Job role and skills | Knowledge, expertise and experience |
| Confidence<br>Naivety<br>Self-awareness<br>Self-confidence<br>Initiative<br>Adaptability<br>Influencing<br>Differentiating characteristics<br>Managing change<br>Fear<br>Formative years<br>Personal attributes<br>Self-reflective<br>Gender<br>Delegation<br>Self-efficacy | Personal attributes |
| Learning dimensions<br>Training<br>Leadership development<br>Peer learning<br>Learning orientation | Learning |
| Funding<br>Investor relations<br>Recession and economic climate<br>Competitors<br>Customer benefits<br>Commercial awareness<br>Overview of business<br>Change<br>Survival of business | Business |
| Serendipity<br>Owner manager<br>Succession planning<br>Business as child<br>Maternalistic nurturing<br>Family dynamics | Family business dynamics |

**Table 7.1**    (continued)

| Open coding (concepts/codes) | Axial coding (categories) |
| --- | --- |
| Leadership | Leadership |
| Developing awareness of being a business owner | |
| Relationship between leader and business | |
| Role and leadership | |
| Contingency of entrepreneurial leader role | |
| Legitimacy | |
| Partnership roles and mutual dependence | |
| Nature versus nurture (born not made) | |
| Formal title versus role played | |
| Discipline | |

we present a narrative drawing on each category – knowledge, expertise and experience; personal attributes; learning; business; family business dynamics and leadership – to demonstrate how Mary's identity has been constructed (Watson, 2012; Gartner, 2010).

This narrative is based on Mary's reflections on, and interpretations of, her evolving role in the business that allows the identification of dimensions of the construction of her identity. In presenting this story we continue to exert the selectivity central to the ethnographic research process and, accordingly, draw on all of the material available to us to provide a holistic account of Mary's identity construction (van Mannen, 1988; Cunliffe, 2010). We do so as a contribution to the still relatively sparse literature of empirical studies addressing in-depth identity construction on the personal level (Svenningsson and Alvesson, 2003). As the identities of individuals in contemporary organizational contexts are frequently fluid and fragmented, and that 'identity lacks sufficient substance and discreteness to be captured in questionnaires or single interviews and to be measured and counted' (Svenningsson and Alvesson, 2003: 1165), our aim was to produce a thick rich case account of identity construction.

## Knowledge, expertise and experience

Mary has been on a journey, from a position where she did not know what she was doing at the inception of the business, to one where she could describe herself with some degree of self-confidence as a business owner. She acknowledged that at the outset of the business the directors collectively faced a steep learning curve. While James had some management experience, he had no wider commercial and business development experience; and Sam's expertise was restricted to technical and operational aspects (indeed, initially he worked on the shopfloor). Mary very clearly articulated how she felt initially:

> I had no experience at all, I had absolutely no experience in business or bookkeeping or anything, I had spent my whole life on a shop-floor . . . [this was] a massive step . . . but because I put some money in, James made me a director of the company, which again was a huge, great big step and I felt as if I was totally out of my depth at that point, I didn't know what to do.

By the end of the research she was able to reflect on what had changed in her: 'Belief in myself. I think I can quite honestly hold my head up now and say I'm a business woman. I would never have done that before.'

As reflected in the shift embodied in these two quotations, we explore Mary's journey and discuss the nature of the identity work in which she engaged in this process of identity construction.

## Personal attributes

Mary's initial concern about her lack of knowledge, expertise and experience is associated with her personal attributes and, in particular, the negative dimensions of lack of confidence, fear and naivety. These, together with the more positive personal attributes – for example, initiative, adaptability and influencing skills – in turn underlie the commitment she has shown to learning. This is reflected in a rapid expansion in her technical knowledge of the business and in her broader understanding of its commercial dynamics and competitive context.

Within this there is an increase in her appreciation of the tensions and implications of being in a family business. A further manifestation of learning as an emergent category in this narrative is the importance of leadership and leadership development, which is also stimulated by both her negative and positive personal attributes as well as her developing knowledge of the business. Collectively these six categories interrelate to construct Mary's identity.

Given that Mary made it clear that establishing this business, becoming an director/ owner and playing a significant part in the day-to-day running of the enterprise was alien to her, it is clear that she perceived that she lacked relevant knowledge, experience and expertise. This is in the context of a wider absence of significant managerial and leadership experience in her co-founders. This meant that Mary did not have access within the business to the sort of coaching and mentoring expertise that would help her grow into the role of director/owner. The narrative of her identity construction, therefore, is set within the context of the absence of meaningful support. Mary is explicit about Sam and James's limitations, notwithstanding their knowledge of and experience in the production technology involved:

> James was the only one that had any management experience, he had no business experience, he still doesn't but he had a bit of management experience, so it was him and I that did the [initial shopfloor recruitment] interviews and we picked all the wrong people, you know, we just didn't have a clue, we sort of went on a wing and prayer.

> For the first year and a half I would say, Sam worked on the shopfloor, until his back was that bad that he couldn't do any more and he had to start on lighter duties.

Mary acknowledges that initially she was not comfortable in this new venture which is displayed in her frequent allusions to a lack of confidence, fear and concerns about her ability to effectively carry out her role: 'No, I was frightened. I'm still the same, it feels that I've been frightened all my life and I'm thinking: no, I'm going to do it now.'

Much of this fear and lack of confidence appears to be situational. In our first interview with Mary she reflected on her earlier shift from the shopfloor, working as a machinist in the textile industry, to being an engineer's assistant in electronics assembly: 'I loved that job, it was very interesting. So, I suppose that gave me a wee bit of confidence in myself that I was capable of doing an awful lot more than what I had done in the past.'

However, this confidence did not translate into the new venture. Mary did not identify herself as a director, owner or leader of the company; indeed, she did not even consider herself capable of being a competent book-keeper. From the outset the company experienced significant problems. Within the first year James made a costly error in materials ordering which almost put them out of business. To address this issue their new investors had to refinance to a larger extent than had been anticipated, and as a result their ownership share was raised to 50 percent.

Around this time also, James started to indicate that he would like to retire, as it became increasingly clear that the commitment required to launch and grow a successful business far exceeded his expectations. This was compounded by his poor managerial skills, particularly in supervising the shopfloor workforce. Together these brought about a crisis in Mary's mind: 'we thought, he's [James] the only one that's got any management experience here, what on earth are we going to do? . . . [so] we started looking into what training we needed to take the company forward if James left.'

## Learning

This suggests that Mary, to a much greater extent than Sam, was developing a strong sense of what was needed to be done to secure the future of the business. However, she made it clear that it was only on the suggestion of an external business development advisor that she decided to attend a development program targeted at leaders/owners of new and growing businesses. In other words, the opportunity for learning emerged more as an enforced response to circumstances than as a manifestation of a growing awareness of entrepreneurial identity. Indeed, Mary's initial reaction reflected both her lack of confidence and her non-articulation of an identity as a director, owner or leader: 'When [programme director] was here telling me about the course, I was very enthusiastic about it and then I got cold feet with the price of the course and I thought "am I worth spending that kind of money?"'.

This relates back to Mary's discovery that events in her formative years had shaped her self-awareness. In particular, she recalled a specific incident from her school years. She tells of how at the age of ten her teacher split the class into two groups:

> The grammar[3] group who were all her favourites and she wanted to teach them because she thought that they would go far and . . . the group where she couldn't be bothered with the pupils . . . So we were left at one side of the room with a book to read, you know, left to get on with it ourselves.

The ten-year-old Mary was not happy about this and asked to be moved into the grammar group, an aspiration that was dashed by her teacher: 'She went, you must be joking, she said you think I'm going to waste my time teaching you, she said you will never amount to anything in your life. And that has stuck with me forever.'

This illustrates the importance and impact of even quite early events in an individual's life history as antecedents to identity construction: while the negative consequences of this stigmatization continue to show in Mary's lack of confidence, as in her response to the program director, she recognizes that this drove her, and continues to drive her, to achieve. In the context of the current narrative her decision to participate in the development program was Mary's response to what she saw as another challenge: 'We had a bit of a discussion about it and we decided that yes, I should do it anyway . . . I need to do something to get me to the level I need to be at. It's something that needs to be done.'

For Mary this level was to become confident in making decisions. It is not that she did not make decisions, nor that they were not the correct ones, but that she was not always assured that they were right because, as she put it on the first day of the leadership program: 'I don't have business experience, I don't have role models to learn from, I've not been brought up in business, I've just been flung in – I need to know that I'm doing the right things.'

By the end of the first day on the program she had discovered that she was not the only person who did not have much confidence in their capabilities. More specifically, she began to appreciate that problem-solving and decision-making abilities do not come naturally to many people, including those she saw as successful business leaders. This prompted a realization that she has natural capabilities to do these. By the end of the program she was able to reflect more expansively on what she had learned:

> It was finding out that I wasn't a million miles away from where I needed to be, that I was instinctively doing the right things. Before that I had been very, very doubtful about whether I was doing things right or not . . . [Now] I know I've got something about me that a lot of people don't have. I don't even think its ambition, so I don't know what it is. I call it initiative, I've got a lot of initiative, I can go into a situation and I can see what needs to be done and I can get on with it . . . there's not an awful lot of people that have that.

For Mary this structured learning and development process played a central role in the construction of her identity. Not only did it stimulate her to re-evaluate incidents in her formative years and their impact on her sense of self, but it also provided a framework for conversations with her peers, coaches and program faculty, which led her to reconsider who she was. Reflecting on the program a year after its completion, she summarized this change as follows:

> I thought I would feel like an interloper when I went there, I was absolutely terrified . . . I can remember thinking before I went there they're going to see right through me, they're going to know that I am no good at anything and that there's no way that I am a business person and I shouldn't be there.

By the end of the course she had discovered that everybody else had the same kind of problems as herself, and as a result she reported that not only had her confidence been built, but that she really felt that she had a right to be there. In other words, she had arrived at a position where in answer to the question 'What do you consider yourself to be?' she could unequivocally answer, 'Definitely a business woman'.

## Business and family business dynamics

Her articulation of this is couched in her much more highly developed business and commercial awareness, as well as her recognition that she is increasingly displaying a number of key leadership behaviors. In terms of business awareness she attributes the survival of the business through the recession to have been based on the guidance she and Sam have provided: 'I think if anybody can get themselves through this [the recession], then they have got the right to call themselves a business person because it's taken some very, very hard decisions and some real, real tough measures to get us to this point.'

Mary has not incorporated a sense of being a leader into her emerging identity, notwithstanding the fact that she participated in a leadership development program, which she found to be of enormous benefit. Indeed, it is quite the opposite:

> I'm saying I don't see myself as a leader . . . maybe I've lost my definition of what a leader is . . . because the more I'm talking about it the more I'm thinking I probably make an awful lot of decisions and not force a lot of things to be done . . . [for example] if we're needing to cut costs and things like that, the initial ideas or the initial thing would be for me to say this is what the state of the company is and we need to do something about it.

In other words, whether in terms of viewing herself as a business owner or leader, Mary's constructed identity is partial, fragmentary, in a continuing state of evolution and emergent in the process of conversation, including those with the researchers. One particular incident in the development of the business crystallizes this. As noted above, Mary, Sam and James had brought new investors into the business to fund their planned expansion before the recession. Mary acknowledged that she learnt a lot from interacting with them. However, when James retired, the investors sought to move Mary and Sam into new, non-core operational roles and to bring someone else in to run the company. For Mary this was anathema, and she presents one of the clearest expressions of her emerging identity as a business owner, one which drew more on a nurturing familial interpretation than a conventional entrepreneurial one:

> This is our baby ... this is our child, this is for us to nurture and bring it up. I think if Sam had retired instead of James, I don't think the business would have survived, if I had retired and either of them had stayed I don't think the business would have survived. I think it needed what happened to happen.

This strengthened her resolve and sense of identity as a legitimate business owner. Although she did not, and still does not, have the designation of managing director (reflecting the primogeniture characteristic in the family business; Hamilton, 2013a), Mary acknowledges that in this instance it was she who drove the negotiations to exit the investors and restore full control of the business to the family.

## Leadership and identity

Mary's story of identity construction is of course an unfinished work-in-progress which continues beyond the research period reported on here. In presenting our narrative we have gained an insight into the experiences, concerns, interests, beliefs, values, knowledge and ways of seeing, thinking and acting of Mary which confirms that the process of identity construction is neither complete nor linear. From the inductive analysis a number of categories have been identified – knowledge, expertise and experience; personal attributes; learning; business; family business dynamics; and leadership – that impacted on Mary's construction of her identity. These are, of course, not presented as necessarily generalizable to the population of entrepreneurs/business owners at large but rather offer an indication of the insights to be gained from ethnographic-type studies such as that reported here. It is also clear from the narrative that these categories do not exist independently and do not discretely influence the process of identity construction. In the following section, therefore, key overarching themes that emerged from the final, selective coding stage of the analysis are presented.

## Discussion: the process of identity construction

From Mary's story three overarching themes about identity construction in general emerge, as well as two that are specifically related to gender. While these are at one level specific to a particular case, the selective coding process allows for the identification of themes that are of wider applicability to the analysis of the social process of interest. It is important to note that even though Mary was specifically asked if she felt being a woman impacted on her experiences of being either an entrepreneur or leader, she stated that she felt this was irrelevant. Nevertheless, in the analysis of the themes we draw attention to the role gender plays in the construction of Mary's identity as an entrepreneur. In doing this we are looking at the familiar differently, permitting us to make observations that might not align with prevailing constructions and conceptualizations of entrepreneurs (Jennings and Brush, 2013; Hurley, 1999).

## Identity representation: the self and the social

First, in discussing entrepreneurial identity there is a disjoint between the generic socially accepted view and the entrepreneur's self-image. For Mary this was clearly and consistently articulated throughout the entire research process. She expressed a view of entrepreneurs, business owners and leaders that was very much at odds with her self-perception, to the extent that for much of the time we interacted with her she saw them as 'other' and herself as outwith these sets. In DeRue and Ashford's (2010) terms, there is a clear distinction between espoused and ascribed leadership (or entrepreneurship): in their view, leadership identity is coconstructed in organizations when individuals claim and grant leader and follower identities in their social interactions. Through this claiming-granting process, individuals internalize an identity as leader or follower, and those identities become relationally recognized through reciprocal role adoption and collectively endorsed within the organizational context. Our research suggests a refinement to the apparent symmetry of this process and questions the de facto automatic or inevitable internalization of this identity. Mary increasingly played the role of the entrepreneurial leader in this venture, and was described by others in these terms – she was granted a leader/entrepreneur identity – but never herself claimed or espoused this as part of her own consciously internalized or articulated identity. This reflects a more general issue, that frequently a mismatch is evident between the categories researchers use to represent the lived experiences of the participants in their research, and those used by the participants themselves. In privileging the former over the latter in identity research in entrepreneurship there is a danger that as researchers we lead participants into the articulation of identity descriptors that are not in fact part of their own cognitive map. What is required, thus, is a deeper awareness of the 'native categories' (Chapman and Buckley, 2002; Harris, 2000), that is, the fundamental concepts that 'people use to identify and explain to themselves what is happening to them' (Green, 2009: 418). These native categories are sufficiently elemental to carry cultural weight and sufficiently familiar to be used constantly and intuitively. The issue here is that the native categories constructed by us in a research community do not necessarily mesh with those in the society or social group we seek to research; in other words, they have connotations, nuances and shades of meaning which are understood in one but not the other, and there are no obvious interlocutory or translation mechanisms. It is for this reason that we have sought to demonstrate the relevance of in-depth, ethnographic research to give voice to participants and to explicate identity construction in their own terms and categories.

## Identity construction as an unconscious process

Second, identity work emerges from our analysis as something implicit, a conclusion at odds with the emphasis in much of the contemporary literature that the construction of identity is deliberately, systematically and explicitly engaged in. At no point in the research did Mary give any indication that she was purposively seeking to construct a particular identity, and to the extent that she can be construed to be engaging in identity work through her professional and personal relationships, conversations and engagements, this is not with a view to the self-consciously aware creation of a particular identity. For future research on identity in entrepreneurship this implies that we need a more nuanced understanding of the dynamic interrelationships between the discourses of social identity and their appropriation of these by individuals to themselves. Current research, including that drawn on in this chapter, assumes that individuals consciously and deliberately identify and take on elements of desired, perhaps aspirational, social identities that they then use to represent themselves to the world. The evidence from our research suggests, however, that this process may not be deliberate, explicit and intentional. As a result we will need to rethink the manner in which self-identity is constructed by the individual and socially constructed by the wider community to which they belong.

## The influence of life history

Third, the development of entrepreneurial identity is driven at least in part by a desire for social legitimacy and acceptance, in an ongoing process of discourse between self and other. For Mary there is a strong connection between key events in her life history (early school, experience, work history, family relocation) and her desire to succeed in a business venture in which she had no confidence in her ability to lead. Through a series of conversations, including those with the leadership development program team and the research team, she progressively established herself in her own mind as a legitimate and accepted member of the entrepreneurial, owner-manager community, or in Gee's (2000) terms, affinity grouping. This is seen, for example, in her acceptance by the end of the research process that she would find it appropriate and unexceptional to join relevant business networks (for instance, Chamber of Commerce, Institute of Directors), something that was alien to her at the outset. For future entrepreneurial identity research this continuous process of discourse between self and other in identity construction raises a methodological challenge. The approach adopted in this chapter provides a depth of analysis not available from more traditional methods. Despite this, it also emphasizes the need to be aware that the presence of the researcher can influence what they observe or are told. If, as Watson and Watson (2012) argue, there is an identity work component to practically every conversation, we see that in the course of interviews and conversations the participants' notions of who they are will be rehearsed and developed in the dialogue of the interview.

The analysis of identity and identity construction we have presented in this chapter is consistent with Acker's (1990) model for the study of gendering, which identifies four sets of processes involved in the gendering of organizations: (1) divisions between women and men, as in the sexual division of labor and economic roles, are constructed; (2) symbols and imagery that represent, express, justify and maintain these distinctions are constructed; (3) processes of interaction in the workplace help to keep men in a dominant position; and (4) women and men adopt internal mental processes to locate themselves as individuals and lead them to identify and act in gender-appropriate ways. From a gender perspective a number of elements are striking about Mary's observations and revolve around two issues: first, her attaining credibility and legitimacy as both an entrepreneur and entrepreneurial leader; and second, her visibility and invisibility in the family-owned venture, which is within a male-dominated sector.

## Attaining and gaining credibility

While not explicitly articulating her need for credibility and acceptance as an entrepreneur, she explains, in the context of joining a leadership development program, that she felt like an interloper and not a business person. Clearly, a tension exists between her evaluation of her capabilities and experiences with her perceptions of those of her peers, in that she feels significantly different or 'other' from and not similar to the rest of the group, which she seems to view homogeneously (Snihur, 2016; Ibarra and Barbulescu, 2010). The particular cohort of the leadership development program of which Mary was a participant was male-dominated, indeed she was one of only two women who initially joined, and the only one to complete it. This is not necessarily unique as women leaders in entrepreneurial businesses are generally under-represented, marginalized, often isolated, lacking role models and with little opportunity to share their experiences (Leitch et al., forthcoming; Stead, 2017). As an 'intruder' into a male territory (Gherardi, 1996), Mary was different from the normative population of the program cohort of male business owners and leaders, thus making it difficult, initially at least, for normative suggestions of femininity and femaleness to fit (Marlow and McAdam, 2015). For women, their gendered characterization and associated gender biases, which tend to be pervasive, subtle, deep-rooted and covert, make it harder to feel a sense of belonging (Kandola, 2009).

Claiming entrepreneurial legitimacy with a desired reference group is made more challenging for Mary as it stems from a negative position of inadequacy and lack of confidence, instead of the more positive and deliberate attempt to stand out through conveying novelty (De Clercq and Voronov, 2009). Throughout Mary's story she constantly refers to 'not being good at anything'. The source of this stems from her experiences at school where she was not deemed to be sufficiently intelligent to join the top stream or group (once again being deemed 'other'), reinforced by subsequent events including the attitudes and behaviors of the investors. Even though Mary was a participant on a leadership development program she does not even consider herself to be a leader, which may reflect a domain-specific lack of confidence, attributable to a clash with the 'ideal worker' stereotype, a lack of supervisory support, and too few role models (Coffman and Neuenfeldt, 2014). However, as she progressed on the program and discovered that the problems she faced and the solutions she derived were not radically different from those of her peers, it is evident that Mary's identification with the group grew, which demonstrates nicely the self-reinforcing aspect of identity work. Attaining legitimacy not only requires contextualized recognition and approval for the self as a credible subject within a particular setting (Lounsbury and Glynn, 2001: 546), but also by self-confirmation leads to an increased sense of belonging (Hogg, 2006).

## Women in family businesses: the issue of invisibility

Our understanding of the ways in which women are presented and gain credibility in family businesses remains limited, arguably as a result of phenomenon of the 'invisible women', which can be explained by the dominant patriarchal discourse and practice in entrepreneurship (Hamilton, 2013b; Patterson et al., 2012). Drawing on Mulholland's (1996a, 1996b) notion of 'entrepreneurial masculinities', Hamilton (2013a) demonstrates how patriarchal forces and women's domestic labor and feminine ideologies play a fundamental role in the development of particular masculinities. Women's invisibility is perpetuated due to the inherent patriarchal strategies and practices at play, so even though they play an active part in their venture's wealth creation they do not receive the recognition they deserve.

At the outset Mary's role in the business was as office manager, focused on the commercial aspects and managing the administrative functions; while James, as father and founder, was managing director, ostensibly with responsibility for the overall direction and management of the business; and Sam, as his son, was production manager, in charge of the shopfloor. The ways in which these titles were assigned did not accurately reflect the actual allocation of responsibilities and tasks, and as the findings highlight, increasingly Mary more explicitly demonstrated leadership capabilities and strategic oversight. While internally Mary's role was explicitly acknowledged by the workforce, the rewards generated by her were subsumed into Sam's rewards, via the title of managing director, which he assumed on his father's retirement. The title confers a certain status and is associated with particular behaviors and responsibilities, and thus, from an external perspective at least, Sam is assumed to be the owner-manager and lead entrepreneur. This potentially downplays the role carried out in the business by Mary and diminishes our understanding of the everyday entrepreneurial practice of women (Hamilton, 2013b). Even though, to all intents and purposes, Mary is the entrepreneurial leader of the business, which Sam himself acknowledges, the fact that he succeeded his father demonstrates the dominance of primogeniture, whereby the eldest son, irrespective of his skills and capabilities, becomes the business's natural successor (Hoy and Sharma, 2006).

## Summary

The adoption of an ethnographic approach allowed us to highlight the fluidity of identity construction arising from, contributing to and being shaped, either consciously or unconsciously, by social practices at different levels (the family, the business and society more generally). Our analysis reveals that the construction of an entrepreneurial identity is dynamic, fluid, and constantly negotiated and renegotiated within different and constantly changing relationships, expectations and scenarios. In short, it demonstrates that entrepreneurial identity construction arises from and is related to entrepreneurial practice. The application of a gender lens draws attention to the pervasiveness and subtlety of deeply engrained historical, socio-economic and cultural ideas and practices and their impact in shaping a female entrepreneur's experiences and ambitions.

At the outset we represented identity formation in Watson's (2008) terms as a process of socially available discourses framing a range of available social identities that are appropriated through identity work to form self-identity (Figure 7.1). Based on our analysis, and incorporating some elements of work identity theory (Bothma et al., 2015), we extend this model as the basis for further research on gender and identity in entrepreneurship (Figure 7.2). First, when considering individual identity, more research is needed into the foci for identity formation (Watson's 'discourses'). Our research has pointed to the importance of life history in this, but these foci can be thought of more generally to include: life spheres (the prominent cultural, political, religious, financial or economic spheres in which

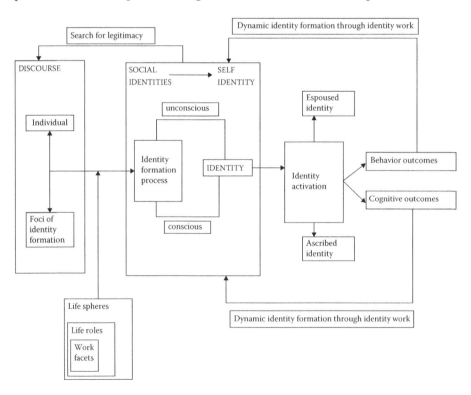

**Figure 7.2**   A process model of entrepreneurial identity construction

individuals function, draw significant discourses and discussions as they negotiate self and social identities); life roles (including career, work, home and family, community, leisure, study); and work facets (the specific aspects of the work context that individuals choose to identify with) (Bothma et al., 2015). All three aspects are inescapably gendered, and future research on the formation of women's entrepreneurial identity could usefully examine the way in which life spheres impact on life roles and thence shape work facets in the construction of identity. Second, there is scope for additional research on the identity formation process out of which identity arises (Watson's 'social identities' and 'self-identity' nexus). Specifically, our research has highlighted the extent to which this process is unconscious: prior research has for the most part assumed agentic intentionality in the search for legitimacy, and the unconscious, but no less important, role of life spheres, life roles and work facets has been relatively neglected. Given the dominant masculinist discourse of entrepreneurship, the extent to which women are shaped by rather than shaping these discourses remains an important focus for research. Third, and going beyond Watson's (2008) model, identities are not just about who we are, but also about what we do. The malleability, context-sensitivity and dynamic construction of identity (Oyserman et al., 2012) – the identity activation process – whether identity is espoused by the self or ascribed by others, is associated with behavioral and cognitive outcomes which in turn feed back into the identity formation process. Our research has shown that the link between identity formation and activation and (entrepreneurial) outcomes is not clear-cut: unpacking and understanding this relationship is a major challenge for the wider understanding of women's entrepreneurial identity.

## Conclusion

Our approach in this chapter has been to locate the interplay between identity, identity work and gender in the social domain: 'Theorizing gender exclusively at the level of the subject risks letting social relations disappear ... allowing gender to be seen as located primarily in the individual ... Gender is not only the psychic ordering of biological difference, it is the social ordering of that difference' (Marshall, 1994: 112). In so doing we eschew essentialist notions of identity and view identity construction as an ongoing process that is dynamic and fluid, not stable or fixed. We follow Bradley (2007: 90) in believing that employment and family relationships are important locations of the social ordering of gender, not least when they are bound up in issues of ownership and leadership in the family business. Accordingly, we bring a feminist perspective to interrogate the data in terms of both entrepreneurship more broadly and family business more specifically. Entrepreneurship, specifically business ownership, we see as a manifestation of the gendered segregation of work (Hakim, 2000) and reflected in the continued existence of 'gendered niches' (Crompton, 1997) which reflect beliefs that women are more suited for some activities, men for others: androcentrism and the domination of masculine norms perpetuate the idea that business ownership itself is 'male'; but even within the ownership of a business the gendered niches occupied by women are commonly of lower status ('office manager') and reward, with accompanying challenges for identity.

The search for identity in the construction of the woman entrepreneur involves challenging the prevailing discourse of masculinity and 'fit work' as represented in the discourse of entrepreneurship. In so doing, as Mary's case demonstrates, it requires confronting the symbols and stereotypes of maleness as reflected in attitudes and patterns of behavior. In this, stepping outside the workplace, for example by participating in a leadership development program, can act as an 'identity work crucible', helping the woman entrepreneur overcome negative workplace-based interactions. Thus, it becomes possible to transcend the internalization and acceptance of traditional views of gender-appropriateness and begin the process of shaping and accepting an entrepreneurial identity.

Notes

1   All participants were founders, owners or chief executive officers of growth-oriented ventures engaged in a nine-month executive education program focused on personal leadership assessment and development and business development and growth. Participants were required to pay at least 50 percent of the costs of the program (the remainder coming from the regional economic development agency). The authors of this chapter were not involved in the development and delivery of the program, but did undertake an assessment of its effectiveness (Leitch et al., 2009).

2   We would like to thank Dr Christel McMullan for her contribution to the data collection for this project.

3   At this time in the United Kingdom there was a process of educational selection at the age of 11: the grammar school stream, representing about 30 percent of the age cohort, followed an academic curriculum designed to prepare them for university entrance; the remainder followed a more vocational programme aimed at preparing them for direct entry to the labor market.

# References

Abdelal R., Y.M. Herrara, A.I. Johnston and T. Martin (2001), 'Treating identity as a variable: measuring the content, intensity and contestation of identity', accessed December 27, 2015 at http://www.people.fas/harvard.edu/~johnston/identity.pdf.

Acker, J. (1990), 'Hierarchies, jobs and bodies: a theory of gendered organizations', *Gender and Society*, 4, 139–158.

Ahl, H. (2004), *The Scientific Reproduction of Gender Inequality*, Abingdon: Marston Book Services.

Ahl, H. (2006), 'Why research on women entrepreneurs needs new directions', *Entrepreneurship Theory and Practice*, 30, 596–621.

Ahl, H. and S. Marlow (2012), 'Exploring the dynamics of gender, feminism and entrepreneurship: advancing debate to escape a dead end?', *Organization*, 19, 543–562.

Ainsworth, S. and D. Grant (2012), 'Revitalising scholarship in identity studies', *Scandinavian Journal of Management*, 28, 60–62.

Alsos, G., T. Clausen, U. Hytti and S. Solvoll (2016), 'Entrepreneurs' social identity and the preference of causal and effectual behaviours in start-up processes', *Entrepreneurship and Regional*, 28 (3/4), 234–258.

Anderson, A.R. and L. Warren (2011), 'The entrepreneur as hero and jester: enacting the entrepreneurial discourse', *International Small Business Journal*, 29, 589–609.

Bauman, Z. (2000), 'Liquid Modernity', Cambridge: Polity Press.

Beech, N., C. Gilmore, E. Cochrane and G. Greig (2012), 'Identity work as a response to tensions: a re-narration in opera rehearsals', *Scandinavian Journal of Management*, 28, 39–47.

Binari, M. (2012), 'The emotional embeddedness of corporate entrepreneurship: the case of envy', *Entrepreneurship Theory and Practice*, 36, 141–170.

Bird, B. and C.G. Brush (2002), 'A gendered perspective on organizational creation', *Entrepreneurship Theory and Practice*, 26, 41–65.

Boje, D. and R. Smith (2010), 'Re-storying and visualising the changing entrepreneurial identities of Bill Gates and Richard Branson', *Culture and Organization*, 16, 307–331.

Bothma, F.C., S. Lloyd and S. Khapova (2015), 'Work identity: clarifying the concept', in P.G.W. Jansen and G. Roodt (eds), *Conceptualising and Measuring Work Identity*, Dordrecht: Springer, pp. 23–51.

Bowden, J. and P. Mummery (2009), *Understanding Feminism*, New York: Accumen Press.

Bradley, H. (2007), *Gender*, Cambridge: Polity Press.

Breakwell, G.M. (2010), 'Resisting representations and identity processes', *Papers on Social Representations* 19, 6.1–6.11, http://www.psych.lse.ac.uk/psr/PSR2010/19_06Breakwell.pdf, accessed May 28, 2016.

Bruni, A., S. Gherardi and B. Poggio (2004), 'Doing gender, doing entrepreneurship: an ethnographic account of intertwined practices', *Gender, Work and Organisation*, 11, 406–429.

Bruni, A., S. Gherardi and B. Poggio (2005), *Gender and Entrepreneurship: An Ethnographic Approach*, London: Routledge.

Burke, P.J. and J.E. Stets (2009), *Identity Theory*, Oxford: Oxford University Press.

Butler, J. (1993), *Bodies that Matter*, New York: Routledge

Butler, J. (2004), *Undoing Gender*, London: Routledge.

Cardon, M.S., J. Wincent, J. Singh and M. Drnovsek (2009), 'The nature and experience of entrepreneurial passion', *Academy of Management Review*, 34, 511–532.

Cassell, C. (2005), 'Creating the interviewer: identity work in the management research process', *Qualitative Research*, 5, 167–179.

Chapman, M. and P. Buckley (2002), 'The use of native categories in management research', *British Journal of Management*, 8, 283–299.

Chia, R. and R. Holt (2006), 'Strategy as practical coping: a Heideggerian perspective', *Organization Studies*, 27, 635–655.

Clarke, C., D. Knights and C. Jarvis (2012), 'A labor of love? Academics in business schools', *Scandinavian Journal of Management*, 28, 5–15.

Clegg, S. and C. Baumeler (2010), 'Essai: From iron cages to liquid modernity in organization analysis', *Organization Studies*, 31, 1713–1733.

Coffman, J. and B. Neuenfeldt (2014), *Everyday Moments of Truth: Frontline Managers are Key to Women's Career Aspirations*, New York: Bain & Company.

Cohen, L. and G. Musson (2000), 'Entrepreneurial identities: reflections from two case studies', *Organization*, 7, 31–48.

Collins, O.F. and D.G. Moore (1964), *The Enterprising Man*, East Lansing, MI: Michigan State University.

Cope, J. (2005), 'Researching entrepreneurship through phenomenological inquiry', *International Small Business Journal*, 23, 159–183.

Coupland, C. and A.D. Brown (2012), 'Identities in action: processes and outcomes', *Scandinavian Journal of Management*, 28, 1–4.

Crompton, R. (1997), *Women's Work in Modern Britain*, Oxford, Oxford University Press.

Cunliffe, A. (2010), 'Retelling tales from the field: in search of organizational ethnography 20 years on', *Organizational Research Methods*, 13, 224–239.

Dana, L.P. and T.E. Dana (2005), 'Expanding the scope of methodologies used in entrepreneurship research', *International Journal of Entrepreneurship and Small Business*, 2, 79–88.

De Clercq, D. and M. Voronov (2009), 'Toward a practice perspective of entrepreneurship: entrepreneurial legitimacy as habitus', *International Small Business Journal*, 7, 395–419.

Denzin, N.K. (2001), 'The reflexive interview and a performative social science', *Qualitative Research*, 1, 23–46.

DeRue, D.S. and S.J. Ashford (2010), 'Who will lead and who will follow: a social process of identity construction in organizations', *Academy of Management Review*, 35, 627–647.

Díaz García, C. and F. Welter (2013), 'Gender identities and practices: interpreting women entrepreneurs' narratives', *International Small Business Journal*, 31, 384–403.

Down, S. (2006), *Narratives of Enterprise: Crafting Entrepreneurial Identity in a Small Firm*, Cheltenham, UK and Northampton, MA, USA: Edward Elgar Publishing.

Down, S. and J. Reveley (2004), 'Generational encounters and social formation of entrepreneurial identity: "young guns" and "old farts"', *Organization*, 11, 233–250.

Down, S. and J. Reveley (2009), 'Between narration and interaction: situating first-line supervisor identity work', *Human Relations*, 62, 379–401.

Duveen, G. and B. Lloyd (1990), *Social Representations and the Development of Knowledge*, Cambridge: Cambridge University Press.

Erikson, E.H. (1968), *Identity, Youth and Crisis*, New York: W.W. Norton.

Falck, O., S. Heblich and E. Ludemann (2009), 'Identity and entrepreneurship', CESIFO Working Paper No. 2661 (Category 4: Labour Markets – May).

Fauchart, E. and M. Gruber (2011), 'Darwinians, communitarians, and missionaries: the role of founder identity in entrepreneurship', *Academy of Management Journal*, 54, 935–957.

Fearon, J.D. (1999), 'What is identity (as we now use the word)?', www.stanford.edu/~jfearon/papers/iden1V2, accessed August 23, 2012.

Gartner, W.B. (2010), *ENTER: Entrepreneurial Narrative Theory Ethnomethdology and Reflexivity*, Clemson, SC: Clemson University Digital Press.

Gee, P.J. (2000), 'Identity as an analytic lens for research education', *Review of Research in Education* (2000–2001)2, 99–125.

Gellner, D.N. and E. Hirsch (eds) (2001), *Inside Organizations: Anthropologists at Work*, Oxford: Berg.

Gherardhi, S. (1996), 'Gendered organizational cultures: narratives of women travellers in a male-world', *Gender, Work and Organizations*, 3, 187–201.

Gibbert, M. and W. Ruigrok (2010), 'The "what" and "how" of case study rigor: three strategies based on published research', *Organizational Research Methods*, 13, 710–737.

Glaser, B. (1999), 'The future of grounded theory', *Qualitative Health Research*, 9, 836–845.

Glaser, B. and A. Strauss (1967), *The Discovery of Grounded Theory: Strategies for Qualitative Research*, Chicago, IL: Aldine.

Green, W.S (2009), 'Religion and society in America', in J. Neusner (ed.), *World Religions in America*, 4th edn, Louisville, KN: Westminster John Know Press, pp. 413–422.

Hakim, C. (2000), *Work-Lifestyle Choices in the 21st Century: Preference Theory*, Oxford: Oxford University Press.

Hamilton, E. (2013a), *Entrepreneurship across Generations: Narrative, Gender and Learning in Family Business*, Cheltenham, UK and Northampton, MA, USA: Edward Elgar Publishing.

Hamilton, E. (2013b), 'The discourse of entrepreneurial masculinities (and femininities)', *Entrepreneurship and Regional Development*, 25, 90–99.

Harris, S. (2000), 'Reconciling positive and interpretative international management research: a native category approach', *International Business Review*, 9, 755–770.

Harrison, R.T. and C.M. Leitch (2016), 'The process of identity construction in family entrepreneurship: a discursive psychology perspective', in A. Fayolle, G. Dossena, C. Bettinelli and K. Randerson (eds), *Family Entrepreneurship: Rethinking the Research Agenda*, Abingdon: Routledge, pp. 118–133.

Harrison, R.T., C.M. Leitch and M. McAdam (2015), 'Breaking glass: toward a gendered analysis of entrepreneurial leadership', *Journal of Small Business Management*, 53, 693–713.

Harrison, R.T. and C. Mason (2007), 'Does gender matter? Women business angels and the supply of entrepreneurial finance', *Entrepreneurship Theory and Practice*, 31, 445–472.

Hilliard, R.B. (1993), 'Single-case methodology in psychology in psychotherapy process and outcome research', *Journal of Consulting and Clinical Psychology*, 61, 373–380.

Hindle, K. (2004), 'Choosing qualitative methods for entrepreneurial cognition: a canonical development approach', *Entrepreneurship Theory and Practice*, 28, 575–607.

Hjorth, D., C. Jones and W. Gartner (2008), 'Introduction to "Recreating/recontextualising in entrepreneurship"', *Scandinavian Journal of Management*, 24, 81–84.

Hoang, H. and J. Gimeno (2010), 'Becoming a founder: how founder role identity affects entrepreneurial transitions and persistence in founding', *Journal of Business Venturing*, 25, 41–53.

Hogg, M.A. (2006), 'Social identity theory', in P.J. Burke (ed.), *Contemporary Social Psychological Theories*, Palo Alto, CA: Stanford University Press, pp. 111–136.

Hoy, F. and P. Sharma (2006), 'Navigating the family business education maze', in P.Z. Poutziouris, K.Y. Smyrnious and S.B. Klein (eds), *Handbook of Research in Family Business*, Cheltenham, UK and Northampton, MA, USA: Edward Elgar Publishing, pp. 11–24.

Hurley, A.E. (1999), 'Incorporating feminist theories into sociological theories of entrepreneurship', *Women in Management Review*, 14, 54–62.

Ibarra, H. and R. Barbulescu (2010), 'Identity as narrative: prevalence, effectiveness and consequences of narrative identity work in macro work role transitions', *Academy of Management Review*, 35, 135–154.

Jenkins, R. (1996), *Social Identity*, London: Routledge.

Jennings, J. and C. Brush (2013), 'Research on women entrepreneurs: challenges to (and from?) the broader entrepreneurship literature?', *Academy of Management Annals*, 7, 663–715.

Jones, S. (1985), 'The analysis of depth interviews', in R. Walker (ed.), *Applied Qualitative Research*, Aldershot: Gower, pp. 56–70.

Kandola, B. (2009), *The Value of Difference: Eliminating Bias in Organizations*, London: Pearn Kandola.

Kelan, E. (2009), *Performing Gender at Work*, Basingstoke: Palgrave Macmillan.

Kenny, K. (2010), 'Beyond ourselves: passion and the dark side of identification in an ethical organization', *Human Relations*, 63, 857–875.

Krueger, N. (2007), 'What lies beneath? The experiential essence of entrepreneurial thinking', *Entrepreneurship Theory and Practice*, January, 123–138.

Kuper, A. (1994), *The Chosen Primate: Human Nature Cultural Diversity*, Cambridge, MA: Harvard University Press.

Laakkonen, A. (2012), *Construction of the Entrepreneurial Identity in the Family Business Context: A Cross-Cultural Study*, Jyväskylä Studies in Business and Economics 108, Jyväskylä, Finland: University Library of Jyväskylä.

Leitch, C.M. and R.T. Harrison (2016), Editorial: 'Identity, identity formation and identity work in entrepreneurship: conceptual developments and empirical applications', *Entrepreneurship and Regional Development*, 28 (3/4), 177–190.

Leitch, C.M. and F.M. Hill (2015), 'The efficacy of the qualitative variant of the critical incident technique (CIT) in entrepreneurship research', in H. Neergaard and C. Leitch (eds), *Handbook of Qualitative Research Techniques and Analysis in Entrepreneurship*, Cheltenham, UK and Northampton, MA, USA: Edward Elgar Publishing, pp. 224–250.

Leitch, C.M., F.M. Hill and R.T. Harrison (2010), 'The philosophy and practice of interpretivist research in entrepreneurship: quality, validation and trust', *Organizational Research Methods*, 13, 67–84.

Leitch, C.M., M. McAdam and R.T. Harrison (2017), 'Identity work and the development of leadership in an entrepreneurial context: does gender matter?', in T. Nelson, C. Henry and K. Lewis (eds), *The Routledge Companion to Global Female Entrepreneurship*, London: Routledge, pp. 235–252.

Leitch, C.M., C. McMullan and R.T. Harrison (2009), 'Leadership development in SMEs: An action learning approach', *Action Learning: Research and Practice on Action Learning and SMEs*, 6 (3), 243–264.

Leitch, C.M., C. McMullan and R.T. Harrison (2012), 'The development of entrepreneurial leadership: the role of human, social and institutional capital', *British Journal of Management*, 24, 347–366.

Lounsbury, M. and M.A. Glynn (2001), 'Cultural entrepreneurship: stories, legitimacy and acquisition of resources', *Strategic Management Journal*, 22, 545–564.

Mallett, O. and R. Wapshott (2012), 'Mediating ambiguity: narrative identity and knowledge workers', *Scandinavian Journal of Management*, 28, 16‒26.

Marlow, S. and M. McAdam (2012), 'Analyzing the influence of gender upon high-technology venturing within the context of business incubation', *Entrepreneurship Theory and Practice*, 36 (4), 655‒676.

Marlow, S. and M. McAdam (2015), 'Incubation or induction? Gendered identity work in the context of technology business incubation', *Entrepreneurship Theory and Practice*, 39 (4), 791‒816.

Marshall, B. (1994), *Engendering Modernity: Feminism, Social Theory and Social Change*, Cambridge: Polity.

McInnes, P. and S. Corlett (2012), 'Conversational identity work in everyday interaction', *Scandinavian Journal of Management*, 28, 27‒38.

Miller, D. and I. Le-Breton Miller (2011), 'Governance, social identity and entrepreneurial orientation in closely held public companies', *Entrepreneurship Theory and Practice*, 35, 1051‒1076.

Moroz, P.W. and K. Hindle (2012), 'Entrepreneurship as a process: toward harmonizing multiple perspectives', *Entrepreneurship Theory and Practice*, 36 (4), 781‒818.

Morris M.H., X. Neumeyer and D.F. Kuratko (2015), 'A portfolio perspective on entrepreneurship and economic development', *Small Business Economics*, 45, 713‒728.

Mulholland, K. (1996a), 'Gender and property relations within entrepreneurial wealthy families', *Gender, Work and Organziation*, 3, 78‒102.

Mulholland, K. (1996b), 'Entrepreneurialism, masculinities and the self-made man', in D.L. Collinson and J. Hearn (eds), *Men as Managers, Managers as Men: Critical Perspectives on Men, Masculinities and Managements*, London: SAGE Publications, pp. 123‒149.

Murnieks, C.Y. and E.M. Mosakowski (2007), 'Who am I? Looking inside the entrepreneurial identity', *Frontiers of Entrepreneurship Research*, available at SSRN (http://ssrn.com/abstract=1064901), downloaded May 9, 2012.

Neergaard, H. and J. Parm Ulhøi (2007), 'Introduction: Methodological variety in entrepreneurship research', in H. Neergaard and J. Parm Ulhøi (eds), *Handbook of Qualitative Research in Entrepreneurship*, Cheltenham, UK and Northampton, MA, USA: Edward Elgar Publishing, pp. 1‒14.

Oakley, A. (1972), *Sex, Gender and Society*, London: Temple Smith.

Obschonka, M., G. Maximilian, R.K. Silbereisen and U. Cantor (2012), 'Social identity and the transition to entrepreneurship: the role of group identification with workplace peers', *Journal of Vocational Behaviour*, 80, 137‒147.

Ogbor, J. (2000), 'Mythicizing and reification in entrepreneurship discourse: ideology critique of entrepreneurial studies', *Journal of Management Studies*, 35, 605‒630.

Oliver, D. and H.C. Vough (2012), 'Practicing identity: the emergence of organisational identity in start-up firms', paper presented at the 2012 Academy of Management Annual Meeting, Boston, MA.

Orser, B.J., C. Elliott and J.D. Leck (2013), 'Entrepreneurial feminists: perspectives about opportunity recognition and governance', *Journal of Business Ethics*, 115 (2), 241‒257.

Oyserman D., K. Elmore and G. Smith (2012), 'Self, self-concept and identity', in M.R. Leary and J.P. Tangney (eds), *Handbook of Self and Identity*, New York: Guilford Press, pp. 69‒104.

Patterson, N., S. Mavin and J. Turner (2012), 'Envisioning female entrepreneur: leaders anew from a gender perspective, *Gender in Management: An International Journal*, 27, 395‒416.

Perren, L. and M. Ram (2004), 'Case study method in small business and entrepreneurial research', *International Small Business Journal*, 22, 83‒101.

Powell, E.E. and T. Baker (2013), 'It's what you make of it: founder identity and enacting strategic responses to adversity', *Academy of Management Journal*, 57 (5), 1406‒1433.

Schostak, J. (2006), *Interviewing and Representation in Qualitative Research*, Maidenhead: Open University Press.

Shane, S. and S. Venkataraman (2000), 'The promise of entrepreneurship as a field of research', *Academy of Management Review*, 25, 217‒226.

Snihur, Y. (2016), 'Developing optimal distinctiveness: organizational identity processes in new ventures engaged in business model innovation', *Entrepreneurship and Regional Development*, 28 (3/4), 259–285.

Soekijad, M. and I. Skovgard Smith (2012), 'Situational identity at work: how professionals strategically construct and use identity', paper presented at the 2012 Academy of Management Annual Conference, Boston, MA.

Stead, V. (2017), 'Belonging and women entrepreneurs; women's navigation of gendered assumptions', *International Small Business Journal*, 35 (1), 61–77.

Stets, J.E. and P.J. Burke (2000), 'Identity theory and social identity theory', *Social Psychology Quarterly*, 63, 224–237.

Strauss, A. and J. Corbin (1998), *Basics of Qualitative Research: Techniques and Procedures for Developing Grounded Theory*, Thousand Oaks, CA: SAGE Publications.

Stryker, S. and R.T. Serpe (1982), 'Commitment, identity salience and role behavior', in W. Ickes and E.S. Knowles (eds), *Personality, Roles and Social Behavior*, New York: Springer, pp. 199–218.

Sunderland, J. (2004), *Gendered Discourses*, Basingstoke: Palgrave Macmillan.

Sveninngsson, S. and M. Alvesson (2003), 'Managing managerial identities: organizational fragmentation, discourse and identity struggle', *Human Relations*, 56, 1163–1193.

Tajfel, H. (1981), *Human Groups and Social Categories: Studies in Social Psychology*, Cambridge: Cambridge University Press.

Van Mannen, J. (1988), *Tales from the Field*, Chicago, IL: University of Chicago Press.

Watson, T.J. (2008), 'Managing identity: identity work, personal circumstances and structural circumstances', *Organization*, 15, 121–143.

Watson, T.J. (2009a), 'Entrepreneurial action identity work and the use of multiple discursive resources: the case of a rapidly changing family business', *International Small Business Journal*, 27, 251–274.

Watson, T.J. (2009b), 'Narrative, life story and manager identity: a case study in autobiographical identity work', *Human Relations*, 62, 425–452.

Watson, T. (2012), 'Making organisational ethnography', *Journal of Organizational Ethnography*, 1, 15–22.

Watson, T. (2013a), 'Entrepreneurial action and the Euro-American social science tradition: pragmatism, realism and looking beyond "the entrepreneur"', *Entrepreneurship and Regional Development*, 25 (1/2), 16–33.

Watson, T. (2013b), 'Entrepreneurship in action: bringing together the individual, organisational and institutional dimensions of entrepreneurial action', *Entrepreneurship and Regional Development*, 25 (5/6), 404–422.

Watson, T. and D. Watson (2012), 'Narratives in society, organizations and individual identities: an ethnographic study of pubs, identity work and the pursuit of "the real"', *Human Relations*, 65, 683–704.

Welter, F. (2011), 'Contextualising entrepreneurship: conceptual challenges and ways forward', *Entrepreneurship Theory and Practice*, 35 (1), 165–184.

Wilson, F. and S. Tagg (2010), 'Social constructionism and personal constructionism: getting the business owner's view on the role of sex and gender', *International Journal of Gender and Entrepreneurship*, 2, 68–82.

Wright M., J.J. Chrisman, J.H. Chua and L.P. Steier (2014), 'Family enterprise and context', *Entrepreneurship Theory and Practice*, 38 (6), 1247–1260.

Ybema, S., T. Keenoy, C. Oswick, A. Beverungen, N. Ellis and I. Sabelis (2009), 'Articulating identities', *Human Relations*, 62, 299–322.

Ybema, S., M. Vroemisse and A. van Marrewijk (2012), 'Constructing identity by deconstructing differences: building partnerships cross cultural and hierarchical divides', *Scandinavian Journal of Management*, 28, 48–59.

# Appendix

**Table 7A.1**  Data collection process

| Activity | Location | Content and purpose |
|---|---|---|
| Overt observation of sessions on the leadership development program | 7 two-day residential sessions | Observation of participants' involvement in the program, attitudes to leadership, self-awareness and identity as leaders |
| Action learning sets | 7 half-day in-company sessions | Observation of participant interaction and discussion in company-located small group (4–5) action learning sets |
| Participant 1:1 semi-structured interviews (n = 22) | At end of each two-day session | Focus on their personal and professional/business progress as the program progressed |
| Informal discussions with participants (22), facilitators (3), presenters (6), program manager (1) | Throughout the program | For context and triangulation of observational and interview data |
| Documents and papers | Relating to the background of participants and their companies, and to program design and development | Context-setting, and a guide to interview questions |
| Unstructured open-ended interviews (2) with Mary | At Mary's company, six months and 12 months after completion of the leadership development program | Reflections on her experience of the program, exploration of her life history (Marlow and McAdam, 2012) |
| Semi-structured interviews with Mary's co-employees (4) and family members (2) | At company premises | Contextualizing Mary's leadership development as seen by those she works closely with |

Outcomes:
130 hours of participant observation across 14 program and action learning sessions.
28 conversations with program delivery staff.
Almost 200 pages of field notes and observations.
28 face-to-face interviews (lasting 30 minutes to 3 hours) with Mary, her program cohort and members of her family and business.

# PART III

Confidence

# 8    Context, cognition and female entrepreneurial intentions: it is all about perceived behavioral control

*Malin Brännback, Shahrokh Nikou, Alan L. Carsrud and Diana Hechavarria*

## Introduction: a brief theoretical review of intentions

The most frequently used theoretical model for studying intentions, and especially entrepreneurial intentions is based on the 'theory of planned behavior' (TPB) (Ajzen, 1991). This model in turn was derived from the 'theory of reasoned action' (TRA) (Fishbein and Ajzen, 1975). While the TPB has proven robust in numerous studies and contexts, even when researchers took considerable liberties with altering the variables (Brännback et al., 2007; Krueger et al., 2000), there has been considerable critique with respect to assumed volitional control in particular (Bagozzi and Warshaw, 1990; Brännback et al., 2007). The original model, the TRA, assumed that the intentions to act were under volitional control of the actor. As a response to this critique, the TPB was introduced. This model included perceived behavioral control (PBC) to accommodate for situations where the intender was potentially limited in carrying out the intention. PCB is a measure of perceived ease or difficulty of performing the intended behavior. That is, a measure of the actual control over the behavioral intention a person has to carry out the behavior when the opportunity arises. Bagozzi and Warshaw (1990) were not content with the TPB either, and argued that the TPB only applied to partially volitional behavior, and that before the actual behavior occurred the intention was only a series of attempts or trials. Hence their introduction of the 'theory of trying' (TT).

The concept of perceived behavioral control (PBC) in turn was strongly influenced by Bandura's concept of self-efficacy (Bandura, 1986). While the concepts are clearly related, according to Ajzen (2002) they are distinct. Perceived self-efficacy is a person's subjective belief (not an objective measure) over their capability to carry out a task. It is a subjective belief of control over behavior, but not over the outcome:

> Perceived behavioral control simply denotes subjective degree of control over performance of the behavior itself. The distinction here is the same as that between efficacy expectation (that is, the perceived ability to perform a behavior) and outcome expectation (that is, the perceived likelihood that performing the behavior will produce a given outcome (Ajzen, 2002: 668).

169

Ajzen continues to point out that the term really should be 'perceived control over performance of behavior'.

If these two constructs are separate, we should be able to find empirical support for this. The study we report on below is part of a larger set of studies where we included a variety of cognitive factors impacting entrepreneurial intentions. Here we are specifically concerned with self-efficacy and perceived behavioral control. The scales we used for self-efficacy were from Chen et al. (2001) and Liñán and Chen (2009) for perceived behavioral control. At face value the scales seem almost identical. The latter includes the word 'control' among the items, and our fear was whether respondents would be sensitive to this. Our concern was that we tend to use scales and measures that are similar for measuring quite different things. To be blunt: do we know what we are measuring? It seems that we do. The results show that there are no convergent validity or reliability issues. In entrepreneurship research 'self-efficacy' and 'perceived behavioral control' are sometimes used as synonyms and interchangeably and sometimes as distinct constructs. We treated them as separate constructs, and discovered something interesting.

## Context and the cognitions and female entrepreneurial intentions

The importance of context in understanding the success and failure of any business is not new, but this understanding remains incomplete. Context is not only a careful description of a social setting, but spans everything from spatial to institutional and even temporal settings. For example, we know from the field of strategy that critical success factors are firm-specific (context) factors enabling a firm to create a competitive advantage in a market (context) which they are serving. Interestingly, the role of context in entrepreneurship research has frequently been neglected (Gartner, 1985; Welter, 2011). But there are instances when context – within entrepreneurship – becomes everything, and a valid excuse to define and describe that specific type of entrepreneurship as special, and all phenomena within that particular area as not general. Therefore, it sometimes seems as if the requirement of generalizability has to be disregarded, or at least treated differently (Brännback and Carsrud, 2016). Such an area would be biotechnology, distinguished as a special case of technology entrepreneurship. Take, for example, two reports written for the Finnish National Technology Agency (TEKES) in 2001 and 2005, and a book chapter in 2008. These were titled 'Finnish Pharma Cluster –Vision 2010' (Brännback et al., 2001) 'Pharma development in Finland today and 2015' (Brännback et al., 2004), and 'Strategy and strategic thinking in biotechnology entrepreneurship' (Carsrud et al., 2008). Another area is obviously female entrepreneurship, where 'female' is not just to signify gender but also to state differences from male entrepreneurship. Thus, gender can and should also be seen as a 'gender context' that exists in other contexts (Welter, 2011). To us, social activities occur in multiple contexts, where gender is one such context.

Obviously, we argue that context influences the cognitions and behaviors of both male and female entrepreneurs, not only in the start-up process but also in subsequent decisions to grow the venture. Context offers deeper insights into how individuals interact with situations, and how situations influence individuals, which allows us to explain seemingly anomalous results (Johns, 2006). Contextual factors set boundaries for theoretical generalizations, thus indicating how we can improve the theory lens by contextualizing entrepreneurship theory (Whetten, 1989). Accordingly, cognitive embeddedness informs us on the 'ways in which the structured regularities of mental processes limit the exercise of economic reasoning' among founders (Zukin and DiMaggio, 1990: 15–16). Yet, research on the impact of context on entrepreneurial cognitions and behaviors remains in its infancy (Welter, 2011). Our greatest concern is over the usual assumption that the impact of context is the same for both men and women, hence gender as such is not recognized as a context in itself but merely reduced to a control variable. However, there are, as we know, notable examples in women's entrepreneurship research that identify contextual factors unique to the female founder experience (Brush et al., 2009) and in ethnic entrepreneurs (Kloosterman et al., 1999). This line of research offers useful theoretical perspectives by proposing multilayered embeddedness concepts which recognize the diverse institutional and socio-spatial contexts in which human agency is embedded.

The reason why context is often ignored is that context is difficult to describe and explain. As we have shown above, many researchers assume that context is equal in its impact for all involved (female and male). Clearly, to assume that the effects of society are the same for women as for men, even at a superficial level, is naive. We have seen studies on entrepreneurial passion which assumed that all the entrepreneurs were male, and their investors were male. The context of passion for male entrepreneurs most likely is very different both physiologically and cognitively from the context for female entrepreneurs. Perception of an investment opportunity will differ based on the gender of the investors as well. Thus, different contexts could have differential impacts of passion on investment decisions of investors (Brännback and Carsrud, 2016).

One of the more subtle reasons that context is often ignored is because the empirical research in entrepreneurship uses statistical analysis and quantitative modeling. While there are certainly valid reasons for this, it does make it hard, if not impossible, to translate a complex context into a set of easily measured variables to plug into some structured equation models. Therefore, researchers take the easy way out by controlling for simple demographic factors such as age, firm size, industry, income level and marital status. Gender is not always considered as a factor to control for, but it ought to be. Rarely do you see discussions about religious beliefs impacting cognitions and behaviors, but obviously they do. It would help in understanding context to include a short section describing the known context, and then in the discussion section to take in the implications of context on the results.

We argue that we need to be researching the impact of context on the entrepreneurial cognitions of men and women rather than assuming that they are unimportant, irrelevant, or the same for both genders (Brännback and Carsrud, 2016). As we will show here, there are differences in how males and females perceive behavioral control, and we suggest that part of the explanation for this can be found in contexts and, obviously, cognition – and that it is indeed gendered too. As Welter (2011: 173) rightly argues, 'a first challenge in contextualizing entrepreneurship is to make entrepreneurship theory more context sensitive, that is, to contextualize theory'. Frequently, context is taken for granted, and its impact is underappreciated or it is controlled away (Johns, 2006). All said, we propose the following hypotheses.

One important context which we expect to have an impact on entrepreneurial behavior is family business background. Much anecdotal evidence suggests that this impact can be positive and negative. In this study we assume the effect to be positive. But we also assume that the impact will be gendered; hence the following hypotheses:

*H1: Family business background has a direct positive effect on female entrepreneurial intentions.*

*H1a: Family business background has a direct positive effect on male entrepreneurial intentions.*

*H2: Perceived behavioral control mediates the relationships between family business background and entrepreneurial intentions for females.*

*H2a: Perceived behavioral control mediates the relationships between family business background and entrepreneurial intentions for males.*

*H3: Self-efficacy mediates the relationships between family business background and entrepreneurial intentions for females.*

*H3a: Self-efficacy mediates the relationships between family business background and entrepreneurial intentions for males.*

Rarely do we see context studied with respect to how context impacts self-efficacy, perceived behavioral control, social norms, intentions and, much less, the actual entrepreneurial behaviors of either males or females. Some researchers assume social norms are contextual factors. Worse yet, they often assume that norms have equal impact on males and females.

But anyone conversant with social norms knows that there are different norms for the two genders. For example, in most cultures first-born males inherit the family firm, while girls are expected to marry and have children rather than run the family firm (even anno 2016). Likewise, personal attitudes towards entrepreneurship are not evenly distributed aming males and females, but most researchers ignore this reality. Others view environmental factors as context, which on the surface may seem to impact equally on each gender, but women are often the ones who have to deal with those factors such as gathering firewood or water if in a subsistence existence (Brännback and Carsrud, 2016).

*H4: Social norms have a direct positive effect on female entrepreneurial intentions.*

*H4a: Social norms have a direct positive effect on male entrepreneurial intentions.*

*H5: Perceived behavioral control mediates the relationships between social norms and entrepreneurial intentions for females.*

*H5a: Perceived behavioral control mediates the relationships between social norms and entrepreneurial intentions for males.*

*H6: Self-efficacy mediates the relationships between social norms and entrepreneurial intentions for females.*

*H6a: Self-efficacy mediates the relationships between social norms and entrepreneurial intentions for males.*

*H7: Personal attitude towards entrepreneurship has a direct positive effect on female entrepreneurial intentions.*

*H7a: Personal attitude towards entrepreneurship has a direct positive effect on male entrepreneurial intentions.*

*H8: Perceived behavioral control mediates the relationships between personal attitude towards and entrepreneurial intentions for females.*

*H8a: Perceived behavioral control mediates the relationships between personal attitude towards and entrepreneurial intentions for males.*

*H9: Self-efficacy mediates the relationships between personal attitude towards and entrepreneurial intentions for females.*

*H9a: Self-efficacy mediates the relationships between personal attitude towards and entrepreneurial intentions for males.*

Finally, we wanted to distinguish between self-efficacy (SE) and perceived behavioral control (PBC).

*H10: Perceived behavioral control has a direct positive effect on female entrepreneurial intentions.*

*H10a: Perceived behavioral control has a direct positive effect on male entrepreneurial intentions.*

*H11: Self-efficacy has a direct positive effect on female entrepreneurial intentions.*

*H11a: Self-efficacy has a direct positive effect on male entrepreneurial intentions.*

For this study we once again used the dominant model of entrepreneurial intentions – the theory of planned behavior – as the theoretical basis (Figure 8.1).

## Methods and data

### Data collection and instrument

In order to have a comprehensive list of measures and to ensure the reliability of the measurement, extensive relevant studies from top-ranked entrepreneurship journals were selected and thorough reviews were performed. In this research, the sets of survey items for each of the latent constructs are chosen from previously validated measurement items (Table 8.1). Some of the survey items are slightly modified to fit the specific context of this research. For instance, to examine the impact of the family business background and measure its impacts to become an entrepreneur, we employ established measures from Mathews and Moser (1995), Schröder et al. (2011) and Zellweger et al. (2011) which have the initial focus on the impact of the family business background across different cultures and gender behaviors.

In order to examine the moderating role of self-efficacy and perceived behavioral control on the intention to become an entrepreneur, we used the survey items developed by Chen et al. (2001) and Wilson et al. (2007) and for PBC (Liñán and Chen, 2009). Moreover, the other scales are established in previous research (e.g., Kautonen et al., 2010; Liao and Welsch, 2005). All items were measured using seven-point Likert scale from 'strongly agree' to 'strongly disagree', or 'unpleasant' to 'pleasant'.

A self-explanatory survey questionnaire was employed and we used a pen and paper-based questionnaire as an instrument to collect data. In addition to the general questions, a number of background (demographic information) questions were asked in relation to the respondents' experience working in a business (firm) owned by a member of family. Compeau et al. (2012) and Lu et al. (2010) state that college students are the young generation who are most likely to be active in developing new business ideas. So, a convenience sampling approach was employed to collect data. We argue that a convenient sample making use of the students for data collection is an appropriate approach when one intends to understand the behavioral intentions towards a given phenomenon (for example, entrepreneurial intention). During 2011–2014 data were collected on various measures.

Subjects were 2282 students participating in a study on the cognitive factors impacting entrepreneurial intentions. They represented urban universities in Canada, Chile, China, Finland, Germany, Spain, Turkey and the United States of America.

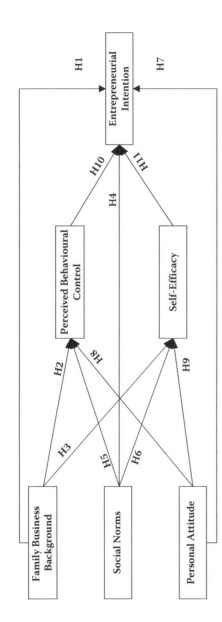

**Figure 8.1** The conceptual model and hypotheses

**Table 8.1**   Question items used in the study

| Construct | Item/measure<br>Seven-point Likert scale, ranging from 1 = 'strongly disagree' to 7 = 'strongly agree', or 1 = 'unpleasant' to 7 = 'pleasant'. | Measure source |
|---|---|---|
| Family business background | Does a member of your family own (greater than 5 per-cent) and operate a business?<br>Have you worked in a business owned by a member of your family?<br>When you graduate, do you intend to work for the family business? | Mathews and Moser (1995), Schröder et al. (2011), Zellweger et al. (2011) |
| Perceived behavioral control | To start a firm and keep it working would be easy for me.<br>I am prepared to start a viable firm.<br>I can control the creation process of a new firm.<br>I know the necessary practical details to start a firm.<br>I know how to develop an entrepreneurial project.<br>If I tried to start a firm, I would have a high probability of succeeding. | Liñán and Chen (2009) |
| Social norms | My family would see it as very positive if I would start my own business.<br>My friends would see it as very positive if I would start my own business. | Kautonen et al. (2010) |
| Self-efficacy | I will be able to achieve most of the goals that I have set for myself.<br>When facing difficult tasks, I am certain that I will accomplish them.<br>In general, I think that I can obtain outcomes that are important to me.<br>I believe I can succeed at most any endeavor to which I set my mind.<br>I will be able to successfully overcome many challenges.<br>I am confident that I can perform effectively on many different tasks.<br>Compared to other people, I can do most tasks very well.<br>Even when things are tough, I can perform quite well. | Chen et al. (2001), Wilson et al. (2007) |
| Personal attitude | Being an entrepreneur implies more advantages than disadvantages to me.<br>A career as entrepreneur is attractive for me.<br>I had the opportunity and resources, I'd like to start a firm.<br>Being an entrepreneur would entail great satisfactions for me.<br>Among various options, I would rather be an entrepreneur. | Liñán and Chen (2009) |
| Entrepreneurial intentions | I am ready to do anything to be an entrepreneur.<br>My professional goal is to become an entrepreneur. | Liñán and Chen (2009) |

**Table 8.1**   (continued)

| Construct | Item/measure<br>Seven-point Likert scale, ranging from 1 = 'strongly disagree' to 7 = 'strongly agree', or 1 = 'unpleasant' to 7 = 'pleasant'. | Measure source |
|---|---|---|
| | I will make every effort to start and run my own firm.<br>I am determined to create a firm in the future.<br>I have very seriously thought of starting a firm.<br>I have the firm intention to start a firm some day. | |

We received 2038 complete questionnaires – 797 females (39.1 percent) and 1241 males (60.9 percent) – which included several well-established and validated scales including those on self-efficacy, social norms, perceived behavioral control, family business background, personal attitudes towards entrepreneurship, and entrepreneurial intentions. We specifically wanted to understand the role of context of family business background and social norms on entrepreneurial intentions. We used personal attitude to assess personally perceived desirability.

The respondent average age was 25 years old. More than 31 percent of the respondents (N = 635) had a job in addition to going to school; 136 respondents (6.7 percent) operated their own businesses at the time of the survey, and 748 (36.7 percent) indicated that they had worked in a business owned by a member of their family. Of female respondents, 404 (~50 percent) mentioned that a member of their family owned or operated a business. Interestingly, when asked whether they had ever worked in a business owned by a family member, only 276 (36 percent) replied in the affirmative. Moreover, when asked to indicate if their intention after graduation was to become an entrepreneur, 316 (40 percent) responded in the affirmative. This shows that having the experience of working in a family business positively influenced their intention to become an entrepreneur after graduation.

## Reliability and validity

Exploratory and confirmatory factor analyses were executed to confirm the measurement validity, and the results show that our measurements are valid (see Table 8.2). An exploratory factor analysis (EFA) using the Promax rotation was employed in order to build the factor structures. After several iterations of the EFA, the final output resulted in six factors (see Figure 8.1). We computed a curved estimation test for all the relationships in the model and found that all relationships are sufficiently linear. This test is necessary in order to make sure that we can use the covariance-based SEM analysis such as one used, for example, in AMOS. Due to having more than one independent variable predicating the dependent variable, we also performed a multicolinearity test to see whether our data are affected by

**Table 8.2**  Descriptive statistics, convergent validity, internal consistency and reliability

| Construct | Items | Factor loadings | Mean | Std. dev | AVE[a] | SCR[b] | $R^2$ | Cronbach's α |
|---|---|---|---|---|---|---|---|---|
| Family business | FB5 | 0.53 | 3.49 | 1.51 | 0.542 | 0.752 | 0.28 | 0.723 |
| | FB5B | 0.83 | 3.37 | 1.48 | | | 0.69 | |
| | FB5C | 0.47 | 3.38 | 1.49 | | | 0.22 | |
| Social norms | SN66 | 0.89 | 5.01 | 1.69 | 0.775 | 0.873 | 0.81 | 0.871 |
| | SN67 | 0.86 | 5.23 | 1.53 | | | 0.74 | |
| Perceived behavioral control | PBC30 | 0.69 | 3.76 | 1.48 | 0.564 | 0.855 | 0.47 | 0.886 |
| | PBC31 | 0.76 | 3.53 | 1.63 | | | 0.65 | |
| | PBC32 | 0.81 | 3.92 | 1.54 | | | 0.69 | |
| | PBC33 | 0.83 | 3.57 | 1.62 | | | 0.58 | |
| | PBC34 | 0.76 | 3.73 | 1.61 | | | 0.58 | |
| | PBC35 | 0.64 | 4.22 | 1.55 | | | 0.41 | |
| Self-efficacy | S-EFC88 | 0.70 | 5.40 | 1.21 | 0.585 | 0.918 | 0.49 | 0.924 |
| | S-EFC89 | 0.77 | 5.29 | 1.2 | | | 0.60 | |
| | S-EFC90 | 0.80 | 5.57 | 1.14 | | | 0.63 | |
| | S-EFC91 | 0.78 | 5.46 | 1.26 | | | 0.61 | |
| | S-EFC92 | 0.82 | 5.52 | 1.15 | | | 0.67 | |
| | S-EFC93 | 0.81 | 5.55 | 1.18 | | | 0.65 | |
| | S-EFC94 | 0.70 | 5.27 | 1.23 | | | 0.49 | |
| | S-EFC95 | 0.73 | 5.34 | 1.8 | | | 0.53 | |
| Personal attitude | PA25 | 0.66 | 4.95 | 1.56 | 0.660 | 0.906 | 0.43 | 0.905 |
| | PA26 | 0.82 | 5.15 | 1.62 | | | 0.67 | |
| | PA27 | 0.81 | 5.24 | 1.71 | | | 0.66 | |
| | PA28 | 0.86 | 5.18 | 1.60 | | | 0.74 | |
| | PA29 | 0.90 | 4.77 | 1.78 | | | 0.79 | |
| Entrepreneurial intentions | EIN36 | 0.73 | 3.49 | 1.75 | 0.741 | 0.945 | 0.53 | 0.942 |
| | EIN37 | 0.84 | 3.96 | 1.92 | | | 0.71 | |
| | EIN38 | 0.84 | 4.30 | 1.96 | | | 0.70 | |
| | EIN39 | 0.93 | 4.21 | 1.93 | | | 0.88 | |
| | EIN40 | 0.88 | 4.16 | 2.01 | | | 0.78 | |
| | EIN41 | 0.64 | 4.36 | 2.03 | | | 0.84 | |

**Notes:**
[a] Average variance extracted.
[b] Scale composite reliability.

multicollinearity. The results show no evidence of multicollinearity. Moreover, in order to test the path relationships from being affected by common method bias (CMB), we executed a common method bias test through the common latent factor (CLF). The CMB test did not show any paths being affected by a common method bias.

IBM AMOS 21 and IBM SPSS 21 software were used to test the reliability and validity of the measurement model. To examine the reliability of the data, we first computed the Cronbach's alpha test. The recommended threshold for Cronbach's alpha ($\alpha$) requires a reliability of 0.6 or higher; in the current measurement model the Cronbach's alpha values are all above the recommended values, indicating that the measures all have acceptable reliability with respect to their respective constructs; see Table 8.2.

In the next step we executed the convergent validity and discriminant validity tests to examine how the establishment of the latent constructs performed within the conceptual model and the data. Convergent validity indicates the extent to which each measurement item loads within the corresponding construct. The convergent validity test shows that the constructs are not affected by this issue. The psychometric properties of the measures are tested through the average variance extracted (AVE) index (Fornell and Larcker, 1981) and the composite reliability (CR) index (Bagozzi and Edwards, 1998). Both indices are above the recommended values of 0.50 and 0.70, respectively, and thus we did not find any issues regarding to these tests; see Table 8.3. The values for R-squared, the measure of how close the data are associated with the regression line, are shown in Table 8.2. The R-squared values show the percentage of the response variables variations, which are explained by a linear regression line. Moreover, discriminant validity indicates the extent to which items within a construct are distinct from other items of those other constructs in the model. Previous scholars stated that the square roots of the AVE of the construct should be greater than the correlation estimates with the other constructs (Bagozzi and Edwards, 1998; Campbell and Fiske, 1959; Fornell and Larcker, 1981). The results show that the square root of AVEs of all constructs are greater than those of other constructs. Therefore, all correlation values have met the recommended threshold values (see Table 8.3).

**Table 8.3**  Inter-construct correlations and AVE

|  | CR | AVE | S-Norms | Efficacy | Intentions | PBC | Attitude | F-Business |
|---|---|---|---|---|---|---|---|---|
| Social norms | 0.873 | 0.775 | 0.880 | | | | | |
| Self-efficacy | 0.918 | 0.585 | 0.354 | 0.765 | | | | |
| Entrepreneurial intentions | 0.945 | 0.741 | 0.542 | 0.326 | 0.861 | | | |
| Perceived Behavioral control | 0.885 | 0.564 | 0.397 | 0.379 | 0.646 | 0.751 | | |
| Personal attitude | 0.906 | 0.660 | 0.545 | 0.369 | 0.783 | 0.542 | 0.812 | |
| Family business background | 0.752 | 0.542 | 0.064 | 0.130 | 0.142 | 0.216 | 0.166 | 0.634 |

**Table 8.4**    Model fit indices

| Model fit indices | GFI | AGFI | CFI | NFI | TLI | RMSEA |
|---|---|---|---|---|---|---|
| Cut-off value | >0.90 | >0.80 | >0.90 | >0.80 | >0.90 | <0.080 |
| Obtained value | >0.94 | >0.92 | >0.96 | >0.95 | >0.96 | <0.026 |

## Results and implications

We used the structural equation modelling (SEM) technique to test the research conceptual model as well as the postulated hypotheses. The results show that we have obtained a good model fit, $\chi^2$ (1104) = 4287.145 and CMIN/DF = 3.883. The entrepreneurial intentions is explained by a variance of 69 percent, self-efficacy is explained by variance of 19 percent, and PCB is explained by variance of 42 percent. The model fit indices show acceptable values and satisfy the cut-off values, and thus our research model presents a good fit with the data (see Table 8.4).

### Hypotheses testing

The model for the male respondents differs from the female model. Figure 8.2 shows the conceptual model for females and Figure 8.3 for males. Results show that PBC and SE mediate the relationship between the family business, social norms and personal attitude to entrepreneurial intentions. However, in the female group SE did not mediate the relationship between the family business and entrepreneurial intention, thus H3 is not supported. For the male group this path H3a ($\beta$ = 0.10, p < 0.005) is fully mediated by SE. However, with respect to social norms and personal attitude towards entrepreneurship we found that both factors have a positive and direct effect on entrepreneurial intentions among female respondents (social norms H4: $\beta$ = 0.12, p < 0.001; personal attitude towards entrepreneurship H7: $\beta$ = 0.54, p < 0.001) as well as male respondents (social norms H4a: $\beta$ = 0.12, p < 0.001; personal attitude towards entrepreneurship H7a: $\beta$ = 0.58, p < 0.001). Thus these hypotheses are accepted in the model. Results also show that perceived behavioral control mediates the relationship between social norms and entrepreneurial intentions for both female and male respondents (H5: $\beta$ = 0.18, p < 0.001; and H5a: $\beta$ = 0.14, p < 0.001).

We expected to find a positive relationship between the family business background and entrepreneurial intention, as we argued that this is an important contextual factor. However, the analysis findings do not support this assumption, thus both H1 and H1a are rejected in the model. However, we found a mediating effect of perceived behavioral control between the family business background and entrepreneurial intentions for both females and males, thus H2 ($\beta$ = 0.15, p < 0.001) and H2a ($\beta$ = 0.14, p < 0.001) are supported in the model.

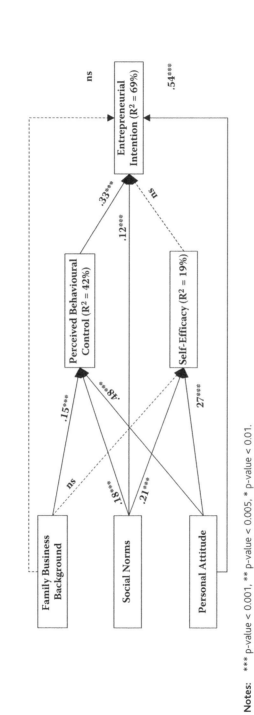

**Notes:** *** p-value < 0.001, ** p-value < 0.005, * p-value < 0.01.

**Figure 8.2** Female respondents

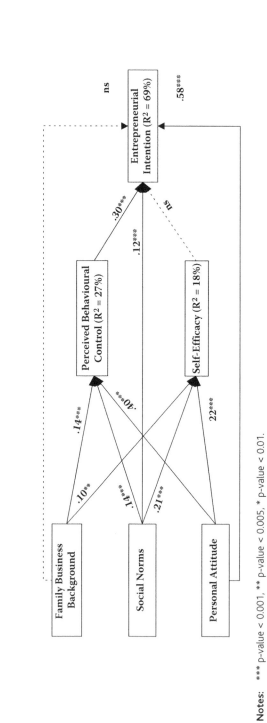

**Notes:** *** p-value < 0.001, ** p-value < 0.005, * p-value < 0.01.

**Figure 8.3**  Male respondents

Similarly, we found support for H6 ($\beta$ = 0.21, p < 0.001) and H6a ($\beta$ = 0.21, p < 0.001), where we assumed that self-efficacy mediates the relationships between the social norms and entrepreneurial intentions. Again, there was no difference between genders. The results show that there is a positive relationship between the perceived behavioral control and entrepreneurial intentions for female H10 ($\beta$ = 0.33, p < 0.001) and male H10 ($\beta$ = 0.30, p < 0.001), but the results do not support H11 and H11, where we postulated that there is a direct positive relationship between the self-efficacy and entrepreneurial intentions.

Thus, we assumed gendered differences to a much larger extent than we actually found. However, we did find that self-efficacy did not mediate the relationship between family business background and entrepreneurial intentions among women. This hinted towards a potential distinctiveness between self-efficacy and perceived behavioral control, as suggested by Ajzen (2002).

Given the theoretical foundation and given the results shown in Figures 8.2 and 8.3, we conducted one additional analysis. We tested whether PCB alone mediates entrepreneurial intentions when self-efficacy is considered as an independent variable as well. This test was conducted in the female group, and the results are shown in Figure 8.4.

Results support the significant mediating role of PBC on entrepreneurial intentions. While social norms and personal attitude towards entrepreneurship have a significant direct impact on intentions, SE and family business background do not have a direct positive relationship with entrepreneurial intentions. The model accounts for 42 percent of the variance in PBC, and 69 percent of the variance in entrepreneurial intentions. By this alteration, we may find an explanation as to why family business background has no significant relationship with SE as assumed in H3. This assumption may also hold true for the respondents' intentions to become an entrepreneur in the future. In other words, for women, the lack of experience of working in an environment which is owned by a member of a family does directly influence the SE of a person, and thereby impacts the entrepreneurial intentions. However, working in a family business positively impacts both SE and PBC among males.

## Conclusion

The really interesting thing here is that family business does not impact the subjective belief of women of whether they think they will become entrepreneurs (Figure 8.2), but does indeed impact whether they think they will actually succeed in doing so. From Figure 8.4 we then find that all four factors – family business, social norms, personal attitudes and self-efficacy – create a sense of understanding that it is 'do-able' and that the outcome is real. As we know from theory, self-efficacy is merely a subjective belief in one's capacity. This belief may be true, or just a fantasy. Women seem to take their intentions far more seriously. Unless they believe in

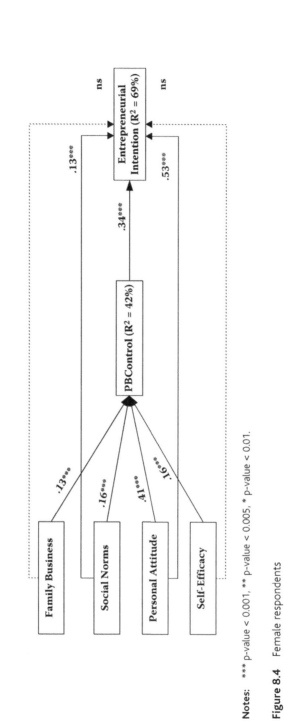

**Notes:** *** p-value < 0.001, ** p-value < 0.005, * p-value < 0.01.

**Figure 8.4** Female respondents

what they intend to do, and that they believe they will succeed in what they set out to do, they will most likely not engage in the task. In Figure 8.2 we see that self-efficacy does not influence entrepreneurial intentions, and family business has no influence on self-efficacy. Intending to create a venture seems to be a real thing for women. Ajzen also argued that PBC was a better predictor of subsequent activity. Our study clearly shows that perceived behavioral control and self-efficacy are distinct concepts, and we also find that their impact is gendered.

Finally, we feel we must acknowledge that women are generally older than men when creating their own ventures. While our data contain responses from eight countries, we have yet to analyze thoroughly how the responses differ across these countries, as we have some indication that the variation is substantial. We find initial indications that the factors driving entrepreneurial intentions are very different across countries; in some countries there are clear differences between genders; and in a few countries there are no differences whatsoever. Much to our surprise, Chile appears to be a country where men and women are alike. In fact, our initial analysis suggests that in no country are men and women alike. Our study also shows that while we think we know everything about entrepreneurial intentions, there is still a need for further studies. However, at this point we would strongly suggest the use of novel research methods and to strongly challenge the TBP model with respect to dependent and dependent variables. What is driving what? Do we have the right research design? Do we have the right measures? Are we asking the right questions?

## References

Ajzen, I. (1991), 'The theory of planned behavior', *Organizational Behavior and Human Decision Processes*, 50(2), 179–211.

Ajzen, I. (2002). 'Perceived behavioral control, self-efficacy, locus of control and the theory of planned behavior', *Journal of Applied Social Psychology*, 32(4), 665–683.

Bagozzi, R. and P. Warshaw (1990), 'Trying to consume', *Journal of Consumer Research*, 17(2), 127–140.

Bagozzi, R. P. and E.A. Edwards (1998),'Goal setting and goal pursuit in the regulation of body weight', *Psychology and Health*, 13(4), 593–621.

Bandura, A. (1986), 'The explanatory and predictive scope of self-efficacy theory', *Journal of Social and Clinical Psychology*, 4(3), 359–373.

Brännback, M. and A.L. Carsrud (2016), 'Understanding entrepreneurial cognitions through the lenses of context', in F. Welter and W. Gartner (eds), *Future Studies of Context in Entrepreneurship*, Cheltenham, UK and Northampton, MA, USA: Edward Elgar Publishing Ltd, 16–27.

Brännback M., A.L. Carsrud, N. Krueger and J. Elfving (2007), '"Trying" to be an entrepreneur', Babson College Entrepreneurship Research Conference, Madrid, Spain.

Brännback, Malin, Pekka Hyvönen, Hannu Raunio, Maija Renko and Riitta Sutinen (2001), 'Finnish Pharma Cluster – Vision 2010', TEKES Technology Review 112/2001.

Brännback, Malin, Markku Jalkanen, Kalevi Kurkela and Esa Soppi (2004), 'Securing pharma development in Finland today and in 2015', TEKES Technology Review 163/2004.

Brush, C., A. de Bruin and F. Welter (2009), 'A gender-aware framework for women's entrepreneurship', *International Journal of Gender and Entrepreneurship*, 1(1), 8–24.

Campbell, D.T. and D.W. Fiske (1959), 'Convergent and discriminant validation by the multitrait-multimethod matrix', *Psychological Bulletin*, 56(2), 81–105.

Carsrud, Alan, Malin Brännback and Maija Renko (2008), 'Strategy and strategic thinking in biotechnology entrepreneurship', in Holger Patzelt and Thomas Brenner (eds), *Handbook of Bioentrepreneurship*, Heidelberg: Springer Verlag, pp. 83–99.

Chen, G., S.M. Gully and D. Eden (2001), 'Validation of a new general self-efficacy scale', *Organizational Research Methods*, 4(1), 62–83.

Compeau, D., B. Marcolin., H. Kelley and C. Higgins (2012), 'Research commentary-generalizability of information systems research using student subjects-a reflection on our practices and recommendations for future research', *Information Systems Research*, 23 (4), 1093–1109.

Fishbein, M. and I. Ajzen (1975), 'Belief, attitude, intention and behavior: An introduction to theory and research', Reading, MA: Addison-Wesley.

Fornell, C. and D.F. Larcker (1981), 'Evaluating structural equation models with unobservable variables and measurement error', *Journal of Marketing Research*, 18(1), 39–50.

Gartner, W. B. (1985), 'A conceptual framework for describing the phenomenon of new venture creation', *Academy of Management Review*, 10(4), 696–706.

Johns, G. (2006), 'The essential impact of context on organizational behaviour', *Academy of Management Review*, 31(2), 386-408.

Kautonen, T., S., Luoto and E.T. Tornikoski (2010), 'Influence of work history on entrepreneurial intentions in 'prime age' and 'third age': A preliminary study', *International Small Business Journal*, 28(6), 583–601.

Kloosterman, R., J. van der Leun and J. Rath (1999), 'Mixed embeddedness: (in)formal economic activities and immigrant businesses in the Netherlands', *International Journal of Urban and Regional Research*, 23(2), 253–277.

Krueger, N., M. Reilly and A. Carsrud (2000), 'Competing models of entrepreneurial intentions', *Journal of Business Venturing*, 15(5), 411-432.

Liao, J. and H. Welsch (2005), 'Roles of social capital in venture creation: Key dimensions and research implications', *Journal of Small Business Management*, 43(4), 345–362.

Liñán, F. and Y.W. Chen (2009), 'Development and cross-cultural application of a specific instrument to measure entrepreneurial intentions', *Entrepreneurship Theory and Practice*, 33(3), 593–617.

Lu, H.P., J.C.C. Lin., K.L. Hsiao and L.T. Cheng (2010), 'Information sharing behavior on blogs in Taiwan: Effects of interactivities and gender differences' *Journal of Information Science*, 36(3), 401–416.

Mathews, C. H. and S.B. Moser (1995), 'Family background and gender: Implications for interest in small firm ownership', *Entrepreneurship & Regional Development*, 7(4), 365-378.

Schröder, E., E. Schmitt-Rodermund and N. Arnaud (2011), 'Career choice intentions of adolescents with a family business background', *Family Business Review*, 24(4), 305–321.

Welter, Friederike (2011), 'Contextualizing entrepreneurship: conceptual challenges and ways forward', *Entrepreneurship Theory and Practice*, 35(1), 165-183.

Whetten, D.A. (2009), 'An examination of the interface between context and theory applied to the study of Chinese organizations', *Management and Organization Review*, 5(1), 29–55.

Wilson, F., J. Kickul and D. Marlino (2007), 'Gender, entrepreneurial self-efficacy, and entrepreneurial career intentions: implications for entrepreneurship education', *Entrepreneurship Theory and Practice*, 31(3), 387–406.

Zellweger, T., P. Sieger and F. Halter (2011), 'Should I stay or should I go? Career choice intentions of students with family business background', *Journal of Business Venturing*, 26(5), 521–536.

Zukin, S. and P. DiMaggio (1990), 'Introduction', in S. Zukin and P. DiMaggio (eds), *Structures of Capital: The Social Organization of the Economy*, Cambridge: Cambridge University Press, pp. 1–36.

# 9 Motherhood as a springboard for women's entrepreneurial action

*Magdalena Markowska*

## Introduction

Motherhood is a life-changing experience for a woman. Some women experience the transition into motherhood as smooth and enriching, while for others it is a challenging or even traumatic experience (that is, post-partum depression) (Jamison Griebenow, 2006; Muzik et al., 2009). Becoming a mother closely impacts a woman's identity and often has consequences for her career (Feldman and Bolino, 2000; LaRossa and LaRossa, 1981). The changing perception of self coincides with the adoption of a mother's identity and is reflected in changing life goals and values (Luckman, 2015). After becoming a mother, a woman is likely to focus more on balancing her family and work life (Walker and Webster, 2007; Mainiero and Sullivan, 2005), and to develop several skills and competencies, including creativity and innovativeness, problem-solving, managing resources, communication and leadership (Ellison, 2005; Grzelakowski, 2005). Simply put, motherhood provides a woman with a broad array of new – positive and/or negative – experiences, and human capital that could potentially be used to identify and pursue new career opportunities.

Given the changes to life goals and values, mothers often see an entrepreneurial career – a career involving all relevant experiences related to the individual's creation of a new economic activity that forms a unique pattern over her lifespan (Markowska, forthcoming) – as an attractive option (Parker, 2010). For example, a 2013 study in the United Kingdom (UK) reported that close to 90 percent of British mothers would like to start their own venture and become a mumpreneur (Morrison, 2013). Regardless of whether a woman is pushed or pulled into entrepreneurship, a mumpreneur is a mother who decides to start her venture and develops an identity of a mother entrepreneur. Becoming a mumpreneur allows a woman to create new economic value, often related to the mother's role or child-raising, to combine the identity of a mother with the identity of an entrepreneur, and to balance her family and work (Richomme-Huet et al., 2013).

Yet, despite increased interest in the phenomenon of mumpreneurship, a deep understanding of what drives mothers to engage in entrepreneurship is still missing. For example, while extant research has focused on analyzing the institutional and socio-economic factors influencing mothers' decisions on whether or not to engage in entrepreneurship – such as the need for a second income or the flexibility of working time (Duberley and Carrigan, 2013; Ekinsmyth, 2011, 2013) – the personal factors, such as entrepreneurial self-efficacy, have not received much attention. More specifically, self-efficacy – a perceived belief about one's own capacity to perform a task successfully – is vital for entrepreneurial action (Chen et al., 1998; Zhao et al., 2005). Researchers, however, assert that women are less confident and less self-efficacious than men (Chen et al., 1998), showing a lower willingness to start a business (Kourilsky and Walstad, 1998), and driven by different motivations (Carter and Brush, 2004; Manolova et al., 2008). Paradoxically, although women, especially young ones, are said to have lower initial intentions and lower confidence in engaging in entrepreneurship, more and more women across the globe are embarking on an entrepreneurial path (De Bruin et al., 2006; García and Welter, 2013; Shelton, 2006). For example, in Sweden in 2010, female entrepreneurs represented 34 percent of the overall entrepreneurial population; 58 percent of these were mumpreneurs. The number of female entrepreneurs in the UK increased by 9.6 percent between 2011 and 2013, three times more than among men during the same period (Morrison, 2013). Also, Schindehutte et al. (2003), analyzing United States women entrepreneurs, argue that the majority of them are married and most have children.

Therefore, given the evidence of the rising number of mumpreneurs, two questions gain particular urgency: (1) Why are women prone to developing into entrepreneurs after becoming mothers? (2) Can motherhood be considered a springboard for women's entrepreneurial action? In an attempt to answer these two questions, I use Albert Bandura's social cognitive theory to develop an argument and propose that the experience of motherhood is likely to act as a springboard that provides a boost for women's self-confidence in general, and entrepreneurial self-efficacy in particular, as well as contributing to increased interest in entrepreneurial action. More specifically, I argue that motherhood has potential to be a practice and a resource and a source of very strong maternal identity; taking care of and raising children provides women with vast and relevant experience that in many ways resembles entrepreneurial experience, giving women the necessary encouragement and feedback regarding their capabilities.

Consequently, the chapter makes three contributions. First, it proposes that motherhood is a resource, an identity and a practice. This is achieved by arguing that the experience of motherhood provides women with the necessary boost of self-efficacy and self-confidence, and consequently increases their interest and willingness to engage in entrepreneurship. Also, the adoption of the mother identity contributes to the perception of motherhood as a valuable resource for an entrepreneurial action. Second, while it is clear that the context of motherhood differs from that of starting and running a venture, the nature of many of the tasks is similar, and hence, mastery experience in one translates into higher perceived self-efficacy in the other. Finally, I suggest that women entrepreneurs should not be treated as a homogenous group. The mumpreneurs, and the remaining women entrepreneurs, are likely to be driven by different factors, have different motivations and (self-) beliefs, and have different needs. As such, the chapter contributes to both women's entrepreneurship and self-efficacy literature.

The remainder of the chapter is structured as follows. I begin by discussing entrepreneurial self-efficacy and its importance for entrepreneurial action. Next, I elaborate on the experience of motherhood and its impact on women's self-efficacy. In the following section, I present the core argument of the chapter, suggesting that motherhood is a resource, an identity and a practice, and acts as a springboard for women's entrepreneurial action; this is juxtaposed with discourses and findings from extant research. Finally, I discuss the implications of the ideas presented, and draw conclusions.

## The nexus of person and entrepreneurship

Intentionality, goals and foresight drive individuals' actions (Bandura, 1986; Frese and Sabini, 1985). More specifically, action is influenced by intentions that are formed in deep cognitive structures. Intentions are viewed as the strongest predictors of action, because they are formed from an individual's deep beliefs; that is, deeply held strong assumptions underpinning an individual's sense-making and decision-making (Krueger, 2007; Krueger and Brazeal, 1994).

Acting on beliefs about oneself, one's own values and desires helps an individual to express their individuality and give purpose to their life (Bandura, 1999). Perception of self – or self-identity – and beliefs about action control are key in this process (Bandura, 1986, 1999; Skinner et al., 1988). While self-identity directs which courses of action are deemed attractive, coinciding with the beliefs and values one holds (Bandura, 1999), the action control beliefs help make sense of whether an individual is capable and willing to engage in a particular action that they consider to lead to the desired goal (Skinner et al., 1988). In other words, how one perceives one's self influences what one wants to do with one's life, and how one perceives one's own efficacy influences whether one feels in control of performing the action successfully (Bandura, 1977, 1999).

For example, more and more individuals consider becoming an entrepreneur to be an attractive career move (Sullivan et al., 2007). While the decision to engage in an entrepreneurial career may be driven by pull factors (for example, an individual identifies an opportunity and engages in entrepreneurship to exploit it), push factors (which include a lack of other career or income options), a search for balance in family–work life, or a need for career stimulation and the possibility to learn and acquire new business skills and competencies (Brush, 1992; Hughes, 2003; Markowska, forthcoming; Schjoedt and Shaver, 2007); a belief in one's own efficacy is also required to perform well in this role. Simply put, if desired and dared, an entrepreneurial career offers the possibility to express oneself through entrepreneurship.

## Perceived self-efficacy in an entrepreneurial task

An entrepreneurial task involves making decisions about creating new economic value in the face of uncertainty (Davidsson, 2004; McMullen and Shepherd, 2006). The decisions are related to the entrepreneurship process, and include creating and/ or selecting an opportunity, deciding on the legal status of the venture, gathering resources, bringing stakeholders on board, and managing the venture – including time, people, finance, growth and exit strategies (Read and Sarasvathy, 2005). The entrepreneurial task is inherently complex and requires individuals to create strategies that help deal with these uncertainties and challenges.

Given the inherent uncertainty of the entrepreneurial process (identifying, evaluating and exploiting an entrepreneurial opportunity), individuals often make judgements about the entrepreneurial task at hand based on their perceived beliefs, namely, their own capacity to engage in the task and perform it successfully. Research shows that individuals with high self-belief who engage in an entrepreneurial action set more ambitious goals, develop better (business) plans, use feedback constructively and persist through setbacks (Bandura, 1989). In other words, high self-efficacy helps in managing complex behaviors which require numerous different skills (that is, self-regulatory self-efficacy), such as entrepreneurial tasks (Bandura, 1989).

Becoming efficacious in making these decisions is pivotal for entrepreneurial success. Prior research asserts that previous experience helps to increase self-efficacy levels. More specifically, in his social cognitive theory, Bandura (1986) identified four ways to form and adapt the perceptions held about one's own skill level and self-efficacy. These are: mastery experience, modelling behavior, social persuasion and psychological arousal (Bandura, 1977, 1982, 1997).

Enactive mastery, often conceptualized as learning by doing, refers to the acquisition of new skills through the direct experience of the task. According to Bandura (1977), engaging directly in the experience provides direct feedback on one's own capabilities and has the strongest impact on self-efficacy beliefs. While success (positive experiences) helps to strengthen the beliefs (including their stability and resilience), repeated failures lower them (Wood and Bandura, 1989). More specifically, Zhao et al. (2005) found that previous entrepreneurial experience contributes to development of stronger self-efficacy beliefs about entrepreneurship. Interestingly, the broader the experiences, the stronger the self-efficacy beliefs become (Krueger, 1993). Enactive mastery, however, is a gendered phenomenon, and research shows that women are less likely than men to have direct experience of entrepreneurship (Dempsey and Jennings, 2014).

Vicarious modelling, on the other hand, presumes that new skills and perceptions are acquired through indirect experience; that is to say, through the observation of others engaging in the task. For example, Davidsson and Honig (2003) found that being exposed to entrepreneurial family members results in individuals forming higher perceptions of their own capacity to deal with similar entrepreneurial tasks. Also, Zellweger et al. (2011) found that coming from a family business background had a positive effect on individuals' efficacy in pursuing an entrepreneurial career. Similarly, Greene et al. (2013) found that the example of mothers has a strong impact on the career decisions of their daughters. The impact of modelling on the strengthening of self-efficacy depends on the subject's similarity to the person being observed (the model); the more similar they are, the more impactful the behavior.

Social persuasion helps to strengthen self-efficacy beliefs as a result of being influenced by others. This provides additional external motivation and feedback that others believe in one's skills and capabilities (Bandura, 1977). However, the feedback needs to be realistic; otherwise the result is failure and a lowering of self-efficacy beliefs. Women are more likely to receive negative feedback about their performance, and as a result are not very likely to strengthen their self-efficacy through social persuasion (Dempsey and Jennings, 2014). Women are also more dependent on hearing feedback; often they need the approval of others to engage in action and to perform.

Finally, psychological states, including mood, are likely to influence how individuals think and feel about their capabilities and skills. As argued by Bandura (1986), it is not the kind and extent of emotions and moods, but rather how these emotions are interpreted, that influences whether self-efficacy beliefs will change or not. Research shows that women have neither a strong positive nor a strong negative affect with respect to entrepreneurship (Dempsey and Jennings, 2014). In other words, women are less emotional, and less afraid of the possibility of an entrepreneurial career.

Furthermore, differences in self-efficacy stem not only from the source (that is, how they were acquired), but also occur in terms of scope, level of specificity and strength (Bandura, 1977, 1986). The scope of self-efficacy describes the breadth of beliefs, from broad generic beliefs to the domain, or even task-specific. For example, individuals may feel very confident in general, but not very efficacious when engaging in entrepreneurship (Boyd and Vozikis, 1994). The level of specificity depends on the complexity of performance criteria, how detailed those are. Finally, the strength of self-efficacy beliefs influences whether individuals perceive them as strong or weak. This research area observes the most differences between men and women entrepreneurs. For instance, research has found that young women (predominantly MBA students) do not believe in their own capacities, especially those related to entrepreneurship; they focus on what they lack in terms of the requisite skills and abilities, and as a consequence, often limit or lower their career aspirations, even though objectively they possess the same capabilities as men (Wilson et al., 2007). Similarly, research comparing the pre-entrepreneurship skills and knowledge of women and men found that women reported a higher perceived lack of competencies and greater need for training than men, even though the evaluators assessed that the skills and competencies of women were higher than those of men (Jones and Tullous, 2002).

Consequently, although much is known about self-efficacy in general, we still do not know much about self-efficacy among mumpreneurs. In particular, the majority of research looking at gender differences uses samples of students or young adolescents, but research based on samples of women who are active entrepreneurs is lacking.

## Entrepreneurial self-efficacy and women

Entrepreneurial self-efficacy is a domain efficacy defined as an individual's confidence in their ability to successfully perform entrepreneurial roles and tasks (Chen et al., 1998; De Noble et al., 1999; McGee et al., 2009; Zhao et al., 2005). Researchers have attempted to operationalize the concept and agreed that entrepreneurial self-efficacy is a multidimensional construct (McGee et al., 2009). For example, in an attempt to understand perceived entrepreneurial self-efficacy among young people, Wilson et al. (2007) approached entrepreneurial self-efficacy in a more generic way. Their measures involved perceptions of being able to solve problems, managing money, being creative, getting people to agree with you, being a leader and making decisions. More generally, McGee et al. (2009) relate self-efficacy to the different phases of entrepreneurship, while Chen et al. (1998) and De Noble et al. (1999) focus more on self-efficacy related to entrepreneurial tasks. In none of the cases has it been analyzed in detail how the self-efficacy of men and women differs across the individual tasks or phases.

Research asserts that self-efficacy is a great predictor of behavior 'because it refers to cognitive evaluations of personal capabilities in reference to the specific task of entrepreneurship ... [being] both individual and contextual' (Chen et al., 1998: 312). However, research has also found that there is a difference in how men and women appraise their capabilities (Wilson et al., 2007). More specifically, women view their capabilities more critically, and consequently make a lower evaluation of their perceived level of self-efficacy. The reasons for such appraisal may be in the stereotypical masculine characteristics and behaviors ascribed to entrepreneurship: risk-taking, competitiveness, aggressiveness and economic rationality; the typical feminine characteristics are perceived as lacking, and do not conform to this norm (Ahl, 2007; Marlow and McAdam, 2013).

Perceiving lower levels of self-efficacy, young women form lower intentions to engage in entrepreneurship (Eddleston et al., 2006; Kickul et al., 2004). Bandura (1992) and Wilson et al. (2007) argue that to increase entrepreneurial self-efficacy, relevant mastery experiences are crucial. Women who have gained relevant mastery experience, even if in unrelated domains, are likely to start feeling more self-efficacious. Hence, newly acquired experience can lead to transformation of the low intentions into strong intentions and action. Consequently, this learning process – acquisition of relevant direct and indirect experience – is likely to be the reason for the rise of women's entrepreneurship.

# Motherhood as a springboard for entrepreneurial action

Motherhood has been situated at the center of women's entrepreneurship (Brush et al., 2009), with more and more researchers beginning to see the role identity of a mother as a possible resource, and motherhood not necessarily as a constraint or obstacle (Eddleston and Powell, 2012; Ekinsmyth, 2011, 2013; Leung, 2011). Women are able to use the normative gender role ascribed them to create entrepreneurial opportunities (Brush, 1992; DeTienne and Chandler, 2007), and design them to reflect their values and norms (Leung and Uy, 2010). Similarly, the experience of motherhood provides women with new experiences and allows them to grow new competencies which are likely to offer positive feedback to their perceived self-efficacy.

Motherhood is a life-changing experience for a woman, one that closely impacts her everyday practices, responsibilities, needs and desires, and her identity. Some women feel overwhelmed by the situation. In fact, becoming a mother often changes diametrically how women perceive their role as an individual. Often, after becoming a mother, a woman re-evaluates her life plans and values (Luckman, 2015). Even though the woman quickly needs to get into a mother's role and begin to nurture her baby, she needs time to establish for herself what kind of mother and what kind of woman she wants to be; what kind of mother's identity she will craft (Thornton, 2014).

Consequently, motherhood can be experienced differently. Some will experience it as an enriching, positive happening in their lives; others will see it as a burden and an obstacle or even threat to their life plans. Yet, women who consider motherhood a positive experience will treat it as a resource, an identity or a practice (see Figure 9.1). Experiencing motherhood as a resource allows women to acquire new skills and subsequently use them; even if motherhood may contribute to physical exhaustion, it adds to the perception of self as resourceful and capable, feeding back on the mother's confidence and self-efficacy. The gender identity and the mother's identity can also be considered a resource to rely on. Motherhood as an identity has the potential to fill the mother with a new meaning of who she is and what it means to her, but at times it may also limit the options that she would consider attractive. The new mother's identity comes with new values and new aspirations, and makes a woman re-evaluate her choices and her actions. Finally, motherhood as a practice reflects the everyday activities, the nurturing practices she uses to raise her child, to teach the child how to build relationships and thrive in society.

## Motherhood as a resource

Motherhood is being considered more and more as a resource (Ellison, 2005; Leung, 2011). In the past, motherhood often led women to stay at home, or for those vocationally active was considered as an obstacle to furthering their careers (Heilman, 2012; Heilman and Okimoto, 2008; Jean and Forbes, 2012). Such a

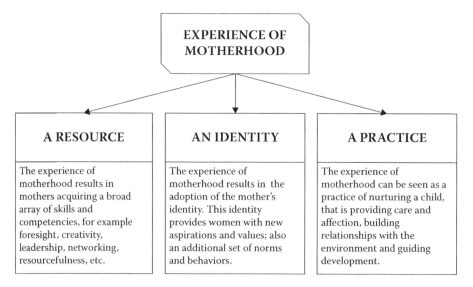

**Figure 9.1**   The dimensions of the experience of motherhood

view emphasized the assumed blurriness of a woman's brain during the time of pregnancy and maternity, which was considered rather detrimental to performance outcomes. Additionally, becoming a mother was often considered to decrease a woman's commitment to work, and subsequently women were made to pay the penalty for motherhood (Benard and Correll, 2010; Glauber, 2007).

Extant research on motherhood as a positive experience focuses on two different aspects: first, gender role identity as a resource (Leung, 2011); and second, the extraordinary neuroplasticity of the mother's brain, and her subsequent potential and capacity for learning (Ellison, 2005). While the gender identity stream focuses on the benefits of adopting an additional identity as a mother, the neuroscience neuroplasticity stream of research emphasizes the enhanced capacity of the brain, given the incredible neuroplasticity that is produced by the experience of motherhood. It is argued that this new capacity (human capital) translates into, and thus can be taken advantage of in, the different life dimensions (Kim et al., 2010; Pitts-Taylor, 2010).

It has been argued that motherhood can actually boost women's brainpower (through biological and social processes), provided that it is experienced with eagerness and enthusiasm (Thornton, 2014). In her essay, Thornton (2014: 273) argues that the 'mommy economicus' (the term she adopted from Bourdieu) is 'agile, flexible, and adept at directly leveraging the customary practices of motherhood – including caring for both her home and her children – for corporate profit and personal empowerment'. This means that the increased brain capacity becomes a valuable resource that can be used to create economic value, but also leads to changes in perceptions and beliefs about what a woman is capable of. Simply put, the changes in the brain resulting from the motherhood experience can lead to changes in self-efficacy beliefs.

More generally, the experience of motherhood as a resource provides women with a rich abundance of experiences and possibilities for competence and capability development. Raising a child requires from a mother the ability to multitask and to be creative. The latter refers to creativity in both solving resource constraints and coming up with new innovative and interesting ways to occupy their children (such as games, activities, and so on). In bringing up their children, women develop the capacity to arrive at new solutions, new combinations or new applications of different tools and resources. Similarly, working on budget, individuals learn how to access resources they do not currently possess, creating things from the materials at hand, and become resourceful when means are lacking. In addition, they also learn how to manage time and people, as well as to lead others: their children. Simply put, motherhood provides women with various resources, including both the more tangible ones (such as skills and competencies) and the intangible ones (for example, increased self-efficacy levels).

## Motherhood as identity

Motherhood is accompanied by changes in a woman's family and work life and in her sense of identity (Innamorati, Sarracino and Dazzi, 2010). Becoming a mother is important for most women, and the majority actively engage in crafting such an identity. This comes with a number of expectations regarding a woman's behavior, both internally and externally, which is driven by the social context. This is why many women often face contradictory or incongruent societal expectations about their roles as a woman, a mother and an individual when they construct their identity (Douglas and Michaels, 2004).

Although being a good mother is paramount to the majority of women, how women choose to enact their identity differs a lot, and depends on whether they have a choice or are forced by situational circumstances (that is, single mother, unexpected motherhood, and so on). For example, a 'choosing' mother decides whether she wants a career, children or both, based on what fits her best and what coincides with her values (Sandberg, 2013); the 'have it all' mother does not want to choose and engages in both (Ekinsmyth, 2013). There are of course also mothers who have no other choice than to engage in both work and the rearing of children. Among those mothers who have a choice, some women choose to reject the identity of a 'stay-at-home mother' in order not to be considered boring and uninteresting (Ekinsmyth, 2011). Many of those women take the first step into entrepreneurship and 'explicitly seek to merge creatively the "specialties of mothering with those of business practice" in order to accommodate and prioritize the former' (Ekinsmyth, 2011: 105). Simply put, women engage in crafting the identity of a mother that best fits their expectations, values and needs.

The women who choose the entrepreneurship path begin to craft their identity as a mumpreneur, combining entrepreneurship and family (Duberley and Carrigan,

2013; Ekinsmyth, 2013). Mother entrepreneurs combine and use two identities to craft the desired image of themselves, often building the idea and concept of their venture within their identity and values as a mother. Interestingly, being a mumpreneur offers women the possibility to combine the feminine characteristics common for a mother with those masculine ones which are considered essential for business, including independence, aggressiveness, risk-taking, autonomy and courage (Gupta et al., 2009). This means that motherhood as identity can help a woman to craft a desired image and identity, help her focus on the important values and needs, and subsequently shape her behavior as a mumpreneur. Hence, motherhood as identity is about self-identification and self-definition as a person.

## Motherhood as practice

Motherhood is about action and practice (Ellison, 2005). It is similar to entrepreneurship, because it is not about who you are and what characteristics you have, but rather about what you do (Gartner, 1988). Practicing nurturing a child offers women feedback on their capabilities and offers them the possibility to engage in action and to test different approaches. As argued by Ellison (2005), exposure to a new experience – here, motherhood – results in changes in behavior, and women becoming better at what they do. More specifically, she says: 'not only is the brain altered with new experiences but . . . positive, emotionally charged and challenging experience can improve and help preserve its functioning' (ibid.: 29). Engaging in the practice of nurturing a child provides women with experiences that can help them to grow and feel more efficacious.

Motherhood becomes an entrepreneurial practice. Ellison (2005) argues that motherhood bestows upon women an entrepreneurial drive and can help them to build new capacity. She argues that the direct experience of motherhood has stronger effects on motivation, risk-taking, skill acquisition and competencies such as creativity and/or multitasking than formal education. Motherhood seen from this perspective is about self-improvement, self-actualization and self-benefit. It is a practice.

## The resemblance between motherhood and entrepreneurship

There is a visible resemblance between the experience of motherhood and entrepreneurship. More specifically, both experiences are deeply connected to identity, both provide individuals with human capital (experience, knowledge and skills), and uncertainty is inherent in both. (See Table 9.1 for comparison of motherhood and entrepreneurship.)

Engaging in the mother's role both results in the crafting of a strong mothering identity and develops numerous competencies and skills. It also provides women with positive reinforcement and the conviction that if they are able to perform this role well and execute the role tasks successfully, they may also be capable of starting up and growing a company. As shown above, many of the skills required for raising

**Table 9.1**  The relevance of experiences acquired during motherhood for entrepreneurship

| Experience | Dimensions | Motherhood | Entrepreneurship |
|---|---|---|---|
| As a resource | Skills and competencies | Creativity in finding new games and ability to create and develop new games, toys, etc.; problem-solving; managing resources, including bootstrapping and budget for after-school activities; communication skills; ability to convince, etc. | Creativity in creating and/ or identifying new means– ends combinations; ability to develop new products/services; problem identification and solution – opportunity identi-fication; managing people and resources; bootstrapping; sales and communication skills, etc. |
| | Network | Creating network of mothers to help each other and make more effective use of time and resources – for example, pool-ing picking up and dropping off children from day care or school; bringing them to free-time activities, etc. | Creating or joining existing net-work to get access to informa-tion, customers and suppliers, to share resources. |
| | Identity | Mother's identity and even normative gender identity could be considered a source of new and/or additional values and guiding principles on how to nurture own child. | Mother's identity, normative gender identity or professional identity could be considered a source of new values and ideas for identifying problems and coming up with new solu-tions, including entrepreneurial opportunities. |
| As an identity | Identification process and adoption of identity | Typically, the mother's iden-tity is a very strong and posi-tive identity – could be seen as both role and social identity. Identification with the role usually occurs very rapidly. | Entrepreneurial identity can be singular or multiple; its sali-ence depends on the level of identification with the role and the salience of other identities, including the professional one. It could be both role and social identity. |
| | New values, aspirations | With the adoption of the iden-tity, new values and norms of behavior are likely to gain importance, such as flexible working time, time for family, etc. | With the adoption of the iden-tity, new values and norms of behavior are likely to gain importance, such as acting true to oneself, constantly looking for new opportunities to emerge and possibilities to exploit them. |

**Table 9.1**   (continued)

| Experience | Dimensions | Motherhood | Entrepreneurship |
|---|---|---|---|
| | Possible role conflict | Adopting a mother's identity may lead to a conflict with, for example, professional identity. Resolving the conflict is important for achieving perceived success. | Adopting an entrepreneur's identity may lead to a conflict with, for example, professional identity. Resolving the conflict is important for successful pursuit of the opportunity. |
| As a practice | Nurturing | To nurture means to take care of, to protect, to provide nutrition, to encourage, to love, to help develop. | To nurture means to take care of, to protect, to provide resources, to encourage, to develop a venture. |
| | Uncertainty | Raising a child involves uncertainty of how the child will respond, how the environment may respond. | Uncertainty is inherent when undertaking an entrepreneurial action. |
| | Relationship building | Learning to build relationships with others is pivotal for a healthy social life. Relationships help people learn across the world, to get access to and/or ideas about new possibilities, bond and communicate with others. | Relationships are important for entrepreneurial action: they help get access to information and resources, and help create lasting relationships with stakeholders, which may contribute to identifying new opportunities. |

a child – which include, but are not limited to, multitasking, creativity, managing and/or operating on a budget, scheduling, time management and problem solving – resemble the skills required when starting and running an entrepreneurial venture (McGee et al., 2009; Wilson et al., 2007).

Having developed various skills while bringing up a child and being exposed to various unexpected situations, mothers are more prepared to deal with and accept the uncertainty of an entrepreneurial action. They have learned that it is possible to acquire new competencies through direct experience. Often they have created new products, arrived at new solutions to problems encountered on the way, and had ideas about what else they could do to solve their own and others' problems. Many women create their own networks of mothers to help each other when needed by making better and more efficient use of time and resources. For example, it is common for mothers to share picking up and dropping off their children at school with other mothers to save time and increase their own flexibility.

## Mumpreneurship: a response to mothers' increased self-efficacy beliefs

The increasing levels of confidence and entrepreneurial self-efficacy in particular are likely to attract more women to entrepreneurship, providing them with feedback about their capability. As discussed above, the importance of self-efficacy stems from the direct relationship with the intention to engage in a behavior (Boyd and Vozikis, 1994; Wood and Bandura, 1989) and its impact on career decision-making (Lent and Hackett, 1987). High self-efficacy not only increases perseverance in the face of obstacles, but also encourages individuals to choose challenging activities and approach new situations as learning experiences (Bandura, 1986, 1997). Entering an entrepreneurial path may be one of the attractive and challenging activities.

Relevant mastery experiences are pivotal for increasing domain self-efficacy (Bandura, 1992). The experience of performing well as a mother and managing the many facets of the 'job' provides positive reinforcement and feedback for women's self-efficacy beliefs. Despite considerable physical exhaustion, being emotionally vested in raising their children, many women begin to believe that they are capable of doing this well and that they have the skills and competence to manage and accomplish multiple different tasks related to their dependants (Teti and Gelfand, 1991). Krueger (2007) argues that it is the conscious and emotionally charged practicing of new skills that helps to change perceptions and deeply held assumptions, as well as strengthening self-efficacy beliefs. So that even women who begin to doubt their ability to do anything right due to their exhaustion will realize their potential, once they recover. Furthermore, it is not only the self-efficacy beliefs, but also those regarding different means–ends combinations and access to resources (resourcefulness) which are improved. More specifically, the need to entertain children often results in increased levels of creativity, innovativeness and development of new products and services. Similarly, for those having limited resources, parents often need to bootstrap and engage in sharing or exchange to be able to arrive at the desired and/or required supplies. Again, as a result, mothers begin to think in a different, often entrepreneurial way about resources and access to them. This experience provides women with positive feedback about their role performance, and therefore strengthens their self-efficacy and self-confidence as a mother. While this may not necessarily transfer into entrepreneurship, it provides the needed evidence and increases the awareness of resources and competencies that the mother possesses. To sum up, motherhood potentially provides women with experiences that increase their self-efficacy as mothers.

Consequently, I argue that the reason why more and more women are engaging in entrepreneurship after becoming a mother stems from the increased level of self-efficacy and the positive feedback they receive on their capabilities and capacities as mothers (Suzuki, 2010). The direct experience and/or vicarious observation of managing a budget or time, of making others follow your leadership, provides the necessary social persuasion for women and gives them the required affirmation about the level and strength of their capability, concurrently strengthening their self-efficacy. Also, acquiring the identity of a mumpreneur – that is, combining the role identity of a mother with that of an entrepreneur – potentially changes how women think and feel about their own capabilities as entrepreneur. As argued above, the competencies of a mother show many similarities to those of entrepreneurs; therefore, it may be that once women realize this and start believing in their capabilities as mothers, they may begin to consider an entrepreneurial career as both possible and attractive for themselves.

## Discussion

The basic premise of this chapter is that motherhood is a resource and can act as a springboard for women's entrepreneurial action. While extant research focuses on and argues that motherhood often forces mothers to start ventures in order to balance their work with family life, or the need for a double income in the family (Duberley and Carrigan, 2013; Ekinsmyth, 2011; Jean and Forbes, 2012), this chapter highlights the positive effect that motherhood can have on women's self-efficacy, and consequently on their intention and willingness to engage in an entrepreneurship endeavor.

In answering the two research questions, the chapter has built on Albert Bandura's (1986) social cognitive theory to theorize that the nature of a mother's experience of child-rearing resembles in many ways the experience of starting and running a venture. More specifically, it has been argued that both 'projects' – child and venture – require the capability of arriving at new ideas and new opportunities, being innovative, taking risks, being a leader, and managing time, people and budgets. Women may acquire these capabilities as a direct experience of being a mother, and through feedback and encouragement on how well they perform in the mother's role (Bandura, 1977). The realization that competencies developed when raising a child can successfully be used in a context of entrepreneurship provides a boost to women's entrepreneurial self-efficacy. Consequently, this chapter argues that this insight is the reason why more and more women decide to enter into entrepreneurship after becoming mothers. These women have strengthened their self-efficacy and become convinced that they possess the required competencies to succeed in entrepreneurial endeavors.

### Motherhood as a resource, an identity and a practice

This chapter argues that motherhood is experienced by women as a resource, a practice and an identity, all of which are important for attracting more women into entrepreneurship. Their increased perception of their own self-efficacy stems from their experience as mothers. Such a view adds to the extant literature that focuses primarily on the possibility of drawing on a mother's gender role identity when creating the concept of the venture and implementing the idea (Leung, 2011). In that sense, this chapter argues that motherhood, with its child-rearing experience, can be transferred and made use of in other, not directly related, domains of life, such as entrepreneurship. Consequently, this chapter contributes to social cognitive theory by suggesting that a direct experience in one context can be translated into a direct experience in another if the content and nature of the experiences are similar. For example, managing a budget for a household is similar to managing a budget for a venture. Furthermore, learning to be a leader, and getting your child to participate in different activities and/or chores, is in some sense similar to getting stakeholders on board a new venture. In doing so, the chapter details that direct experience can be considered not only as domain-specific, but can be transferred when the nature and content of the experiences, skills and capabilities are similar.

## Self-efficacy comparisons between men and women

Extant research asserts that there are gender differences between men and women with regard to entrepreneurial self-efficacy and entrepreneurial intentions (Carter and Brush, 2004; Kourilsky and Walstad, 1998; Wilson et al., 2007). For example, when comparing male and female MBA students, it was found that women are more dependent on perceived self-belief than men, and female students are less inclined to consider an entrepreneurial career as an attractive option if they consider themselves as lacking sufficient skills and competencies (Betz and Hackett, 1981; Hackett and Betz, 1981; Kourilsky and Walstad, 1998; Lent and Hackett, 1987). However, no gender effects were found among active entrepreneurs (Wilson et al., 2007). This suggests that a substantial change in women's self-efficacy can be observed, such that women entrepreneurs have higher entrepreneurial self-efficacy than those women who are not entrepreneurs (Chen et al., 1998). Chen and colleagues suggest that the reason for the increased levels of entrepreneurial self-efficacy among the active women entrepreneurs might be a result of acquired experience over time. While extant research asserts that women are less likely to engage in an entrepreneurial action, this chapter suggests that motherhood could provide women with the experience relevant for entrepreneurship. As such, the increased entrepreneurial efficacy could stem from the direct experience of a similar content-wise task, although from a different domain; in this case, motherhood. Such an assumption concurs with Bandura (1992), who suggests that additional mastery experiences help to reduce gender differences.

Furthermore, authors have examined whether high self-efficacy levels in women precede or result from entrepreneurial experience. This chapter proposes that self-efficacy related to an entrepreneurial action among active mother entrepreneurs precedes actual entrepreneurial experience. The experience of motherhood can be transferable to the entrepreneurship context, leading to an increase in entrepreneurial self-efficacy. In other words, entrepreneurial self-efficacy will be built upon the experience of similar tasks learned in a different context (here, motherhood). Hence, this chapter helps to explain the variation within the differing levels of self-efficacy among young not-yet-entrepreneurs and active mother entrepreneurs by suggesting the particular role of the experience of raising a child in this process.

This proposition has important implications for women's entrepreneurship. As noticed by Wilson et al. (2007), self-efficacy is more important for female students than for male students, because women consider an entrepreneurial career as attractive and worth pursuing only when they perceive that their abilities to perform such activities successfully are sufficient (Betz and Hackett, 1981). It appears that many female students do not consider experiences gained throughout a course on entrepreneurship to be real. However, the experience of motherhood is very real. Hence, for those who are already mothers, building on their experience and the acquired skills appears to be a valid and effective way to help strengthen their self-efficacy levels. Shinnar et al. (2014) note that attempts to increase self-efficacy are important, in particular for producing innovation and staying creative throughout the cumbersome innovation process. This is why positively influencing self-efficacy through the use of adequate examples and tools, ones which women can relate to, is a key task for entrepreneurship education.

There are two other important implications for the argument developed in this chapter. First, motherhood is a source of rich experiences and skills, and educators – especially those in the vocational training centers – should build more on these experiences when educating women (mothers) about their potential entrepreneurship careers. On the one hand, making the mumpreneurs and/or potential mumpreneurs reflect on their competencies as mothers may help them to draw a parallel between raising a child and starting a venture. On the other hand, educators should help women entrepreneurs realize their full entrepreneurial potential by strengthening their self-efficacy and making them aware that building their venture on their identity can help them to increase their self-efficacy. The more salient the role of identity, the more the woman will be invested in performing the skills and competencies needed, and hence strengthen her belief in her capabilities. In other words, designing tools for women requires an additional focus on providing women with direct experience and strengthening their self-efficacy by awakening their awareness of the competencies they already possess. Furthermore, the specificity of the mumpreneurs requires that the educational offer is contextualized to their needs and their expectations. Second, while it is recognized that there are differences between men and women in their confidence levels and their motivation, this chapter suggests that neither women entrepreneurs nor mothers are a homogeneous group; their motivations, beliefs and needs differ, and require further clustering in order to provide effective policy tools for the respective clusters (for example, opportunity mumpreneurs, necessity mumpreneurs and childless women entrepreneurs). Simply said, taking into consideration the different needs and beliefs of the different subgroups of women entrepreneurs would help to create more effective policy tools.

## Conclusions

This chapter has dealt with two important questions related to the emerging phenomenon of mumpreneurship: why women who are mothers are more prone to becoming entrepreneurs, and whether motherhood can be considered a springboard for such entrepreneurial action. The argument developed in this chapter proposes that the experience of motherhood both helps mothers to acquire new competencies which are highly useful in the context of entrepreneurship, and provides a positive boost to their self-efficacy and self-confidence. Consequently, this chapter notes that motherhood is to be seen as a resource, an identity, a practice and a springboard for women's growing self-efficacy to engage in an entrepreneurial action. Further, the increased perception of self-efficacy is the reason for the growing number of mothers deciding to embark upon the entrepreneurship career path. Finally, this chapter highlights that women entrepreneurs are not a homogeneous group, which has implications for entrepreneurial education and policy-making alike.

## References

Ahl, H. (2007), 'Sex business in the toy store: a narrative analysis of a teaching case', *Journal of Business Venturing*, 22(5), 673–693.

Bandura, A. (1977), 'Self-efficacy: toward a unifying theory of behaviour change', *Psychological Review*, 84, 191–215.

Bandura, A. (1982), 'Self-efficacy mechanism in human agency', *American Psychologist*, 37, 122–147.

Bandura, A. (1986), *Social Foundations of Thought and Action*, Englewood Cliffs, NJ: Prentice Hall.

Bandura, A. (1989), 'Regulation of cognitive processes through perceived self-efficacy', *Developmental Psychology*, 25(5), 729–735.

Bandura, A. (1992), 'Exercise of personal agency through the self-efficacy mechanism', in R. Schwartzer (ed.), *Self-Efficacy: Thought Control of Action*, Washington, DC: Hemisphere, pp. 3–38.

Bandura, A. (1997), *Self-efficacy: The Exercise of Control*, New York: Freeman.

Bandura, A. (1999), 'A social cognitive theory of personality', in L. Pervin and O. John (eds), *Handbook of Personality*, 2nd edn, New York: Guilford Publications, pp. 154–196.

Benard, S. and S.J. Correll (2010), 'Normative discrimination and the motherhood penalty', *Gender and Society*, 24(5), 616–646.

Betz, N.E. and G. Hackett (1981), 'The relationship of career-related self-efficacy expectations to perceived career options in college women and men', *Journal of Counseling Psychology*, 28, 399–410.

Boyd, N. and G. Vozikis (1994), 'The influence of self-efficacy on the development of entrepreneurial intentions and actions', *Entrepreneurship Theory and Practice*, 14(4), 63–77.

Brush, C.G. (1992), 'Research on women business owners: past trends, a new perspective and future directions', *Entrepreneurship Theory and Practice*, 16(2), 6–30.

Brush, C., de Bruin, A. and F. Welter (2009), 'A gender-aware framework for women's entrepreneurship', *International Journal of Gender and Entrepreneurship*, 1(1), 8–24.

Carter, N.M. and C.G. Brush (2004), 'Gender', in W.B.S. Gartner, G. Kelly, Nancy M. Carter and Paul D. Reynolds (eds), *Handbook of Entrepreneurial Dynamics: The Process of Business Creation*, Thousand Oaks, CA: SAGE Publications, pp. 12–25.

Chen, C., P. Greene and A. Crick (1998), 'Does entrepreneurial self-efficacy distinguish entrepreneurs from managers?', *Journal of Business Venturing*, 13, 295–316.

Davidsson, P. (2004), *Researching Entrepreneurship*, New York: Springer.

Davidsson, P. and B. Honig (2003), 'The role of social and human capital among nascent entrepreneurs', *Journal of Business Venturing*, 18, 301–331.

De Bruin, A., C.G. Brush and F. Welter (2006), 'Introduction to the special issue: towards building cumulative knowledge on women's entrepreneurship', *Entrepreneurship Theory and Practice*, 30, 585–592.

Dempsey, D. and J. Jennings (2014), 'Gender and entrepreneurial self-efficacy: a learning perspective', *International Journal of Gender and Entrepreneurship*, 6(1), 28–49.

De Noble, A., D. Jung and S. Ehrlich (1999), 'Entrepreneurial self-efficacy: the development of a measure and its relationship to entrepreneurial action', Babson College Entrepreneurship Research Conference (BCERC) proceedings, Frontiers of Entrepreneurship Research. Wellesley, MA: Babson College, pp. 73–87.

DeTienne, D. and G. Chandler (2007), 'The role of human capital and gender in opportunity identification', *Entrepreneurship Theory and Practice*, 31(3), 365–386.

Douglas, S. and M. Michaels (2004), *The Mommy Myth: The Idealization of Motherhood and How It Has Undermined Women*, New York: Free Press.

Duberley, J. and M. Carrigan (2013), 'The career identities of "mumpreneurs": women's experiences of combining enterprise and motherhood', *International Small Business Journal*, 31(6), 629–651.

Eddleston, K. and G. Powell (2012), 'Nurturing entrepreneurs' work–family balance: a gendered perspective', *Entrepreneurship Theory and Practice*, 36(3), 513–541.

Eddleston, K., J. Veiga and G. Powell (2006), 'Explaining sex differences in managerial career satisfier preferences: the role of gender self-schema', *Journal of Applied Psychology*, 91(2), 437–445.

Ekinsmyth, C. (2011), 'Challenging the boundaries of entrepreneurship: the spatialities and practices of UK "mumpreneurs"', *Geoforum*, 42(1), 104–114.

Ekinsmyth, C. (2013), 'Managing the business of everyday life: the roles of space and place in "mumpreneurship"', *International Journal of Entrepreneurial Behavior and& Research*, 19(5), 525–546.

Ellison, K. (2005), *The Mommy Brain: How Motherhood Makes us Smarter*, New York: Basic Books.

Feldman, D. and M. Bolino (2000), 'Career patterns of the self-employed: career motivations and career outcomes', *Journal of Small Business Management*, July, 53–67.

Frese, M. and J. Sabini (1985), *Goal-directed Behavior: The Concept of Action in Psychology*, Hillsdale, NJ: Erlbaum.

García, M.-C.D. and F. Welter (2013), 'Gender identities and practices: interpreting women entrepreneurs' narratives', *International Small Business Journal*, 31(4), 384–404.

Gartner, W. (1988), '"Who is an entrepreneur?" is the wrong question', *American Journal of Small Business*, 12(4), 11–32.

Glauber, R. (2007), 'Marriage and the motherhood wage penalty among African Americans, Hispanics, and Whites', *Journal of Marriage and Family*, 69(4), 951–61.

Greene, F.J., L. Han and S. Marlow (2013), 'Like mother, like daughter? Analyzing maternal influences upon women's entrepreneurial propensity', *Entrepreneurship Theory and Practice*, 37(4), 687–711.

Grzelakowski, M. (2005), *Mother Leads Best: 50 Women who are Changing the Way Organizations Define Leadership*, Chicago, IL: Dearborn.

Gupta, V.K., D.B. Turban, S.A. Wasti and A. Sikdar (2009), 'The role of gender stereotypes in perceptions of entrepreneurs and intentions to become an entrepreneur', *Entrepreneurship Theory and Practice*, 33(2), 397–417.

Hackett, G. and N.E. Betz (1981), 'A self-efficacy approach to the career development of women', *Journal of Vocational Behavior*, 18(3), 326–339.

Heilman, M.E. (2012), 'Gender stereotypes and workplace bias', *Research in Organizational Behavior*, 32, 113–135.

Heilman, M.E. and T.G. Okimoto (2008), 'Motherhood: a potential source of bias in employment decisions', *Journal of Applied Psychology*, 93(1), 189–198.

Hughes, K.D. (2003), 'Pushed or pulled? Women's entry into self-employment and small business ownership', *Gender, Work and Organization*, 10(4), 433–454.

Innamorati, M., D. Sarracino, and N. Dazzi (2010), 'Motherhood constellation and representational change in pregnancy', *Infant Mental Health Journal*, 31(4), 379–396.

Jamison Griebenow, J. (2006), 'Healing the trauma: entering motherhood with posttraumatic stress disorder (PTSD)', *Midwifery Today*, 80, 28–31.

Jean, M. and C.S. Forbes (2012), 'An exploration of the motivations and expectation gaps of mompreneurs', *Journal of Business Diversity*, 12(2), 112–130.

Jones, K. and R. Tullous (2002), 'Behaviors of pre-venture entrepreneurs and perceptions of their financial needs', *Journal of Small Business Management*, 40(3), 233–248.

Kickul, J., F. Wilson and D. Marlino (2004, January), 'Are misalignments of perceptions and self-efficacy causing gender gaps in entrepreneurial intentions among our nations' teens?', presented at USASBE Annual Conference, Dallas, TX.

Kim, P., J. Leckman, L. Mayes, R. Feldman, X. Wang and J. Swain (2010), 'The plasticity of human maternal brain: longitudinal changes in brain anatomy during the early postpartum period', *Behavioral Neuroscience*, 124(5), 695–700.

Kourilsky, M.L. and W.B. Walstad (1998), 'Entrepreneurship and female youth: knowledge, attitudes, gender differences, and educational practices', *Journal of Business Venturing*, 13(1), 77–88.

Krueger, N. (1993), 'The impact of prior entrepreneurial exposure on perceptions of new venture feasibility and desirability', *Entrepreneurship: Theory and Practice*, 18(1), 5–21.

Krueger, N. (2007), 'What lies beneath? The experiential essence of entrepreneurial thinking', *Entrepreneurship Theory and Practice*, 31(1), 123–138.

Krueger, N. and D. Brazeal (1994), 'Entrepreneurial potential and potential entrepreneurs', *Entrepreneurship Theory and Practice*, 18(3), 91–104.

LaRossa, R. and M. LaRossa (1981), *Transition to Parenthood: How Infants Change Families*, Beverly Hills, CA: SAGE Publications.

Lent, R.W. and G. Hackett (1987), 'Career self-efficacy: empirical status and future directions', *Journal of Vocational Behavior*, 30(3), 347–382.

Leung, A. (2011), 'Motherhood and entrepreneurship: gender role identity as a resource', *International Journal of Gender and Entrepreneurship*, 3(3), 254–264.

Leung, A. and M. Uy (2010), 'Entrepreneurs' life-role values and work-family management strategies: the enactment of person–venture fit', Babson-Kauffman Entrepreneurship Research Conference, Lausanne, Switzerland.

Luckman, S. (2015), 'Women's micro-entrepreneurial homeworking', *Australian Feminist Studies*, 30(84), 146–160.

Mainiero, L. and S. Sullivan (2005), 'Kaleidoscope careers: an alternate explanation for the "opt-out" revolution', *Academy of Management Executive*, 19(1), 106–123.

Manolova, T., C. Brush and L. Edelman (2008), 'What do women entrepreneurs want?', *Strategic Change*, 17, 69–82.

Markowska, M. (forthcoming), 'An entrepreneurial career as a response to seeking a career challenge: the case of gourmet chefs', in S. Sullivan and S.G. Baugh (eds), *Seeking Challenge: Research in Careers*, Vol. 4, Charlotte, NC: Information Age Publishing.

Marlow, S. and M. McAdam (2013), 'Gender and entrepreneurship: advancing debate and challenging myths; exploring the mystery of the under-performing female entrepreneur', *International Journal of Entrepreneurial Behavior and Research*, 19(1), 114–124.

McGee, J.E., M. Peterson, S.L. Mueller and J.M. Sequeira (2009), 'Entrepreneurial self-efficacy: refining the measure', *Entrepreneurship Theory and Practice*, 33(4), 965–988.

McMullen, J.S. and D.A. Shepherd (2006), 'Entrepreneurial action and the role of uncertainty in the theory of the entrepreneur', *Academy of Management Review*, 31(1), 132–152.

Morrison, S. (2013), 'Mums do the business: the number of female entrepreneurs who juggle work and looking after their children is growing fast', *Independent*, September 29.

Muzik, M., H. Cameron, A. Fezzey and K. Rosenblum (2009), 'Motherhood in the face of trauma: PTSD in the childbearing year', *Zero to Three*, May, 28–33.

Parker, B. (2010), 'A conceptual framework for developing the female entrepreneurship literature', *Journal of Research on Women and Gender*, 1, 169–190.

Pitts-Taylor, V. (2010), 'The plastic brain: neoliberalism and the neuronal self', *Health*, 14(6), 635–652

Read, S. and S. Sarasvathy (2005), 'Knowing what to do and doing what you know: effectuation as a form of entrepreneurial expertise', *Journal of Private Equity*, 9(1), 45–62.

Richomme-Huet, K., V. Vial and A. d'Andria (2013), 'Mumpreneurship: a new concept for an old phenomenon?', *International Journal of Entrepreneurship and Small Business*, 19(2), 251–275.

Sandberg, S. (2013), *Lean In*, New York: Alfred A. Knopf.

Schindehutte, M., M. Morris and C. Brennan (2003), 'Entrepreneurs and motherhood: impacts on their children in South Africa and the United States', *Journal of Small Business Management*, 41(1), 94–107.

Schjoedt, L. and K. Shaver (2007), 'Deciding on an entrepreneurial career: a test of the pull and push hypotheses using the panel study of entrepreneurial dynamics data', *Entrepreneurship Theory and Practice*, 31(5), 733–752.

Shelton, L. (2006), 'Women entrepreneurs, work–family conflict and venture performance: new insights into the work family interface', *Journal of Small Business Management*, 44(2), 285–297.

Shinnar, R.S., D.K. Hsu and B.C. Powell (2014), 'Self-efficacy, entrepreneurial intentions, and gender: assessing the impact of entrepreneurship education longitudinally', *International Journal of Management Education*, 12(3), 561–570.

Skinner, E.A., M. Chapman and P. Baltes (1988), 'Control, means-ends, and agency beliefs: a new conceptualization and its measurement during childhood', *Journal of Personality and Social Psychology*, 54(1), 117–133.

Sullivan, S., M. Forret, L. Mainiero and S. Terjesen (2007), 'What motivates entrepreneurs? An exploratory study of the Kaleidoscope Career Model and Entrepreneurship', *Journal of Applied Management and Entrepreneurship*, 12(4), 4–19.

Suzuki, S. (2010), 'The effects of marital support, social network support, and parenting stress on parenting: self-efficacy among mothers of young children in Japan', *Journal of Early Childhood Research*, 8, 40–66.

Teti, D., and D. Gelfand (1991), 'Behavioral competence among mothers of infants in the first year: the mediational role of maternal self-efficacy', *Child Development*, 62, 918–929.

Thornton, D. (2014), 'Transformations of the ideal mother: the story of mommy economicus and her amazing brain', *Women's Studies in Communication*, 37(3), 271–291.

Walker, E. and B. Webster (2007), 'Gender, age and self-employment: some things change, some stay the same', *Women in Management Review*, 22(2), 122–135.

Wilson, F., J. Kickul and D. Marlino (2007), 'Gender, entrepreneurial self-efficacy, and entrepreneurial career intentions: implications for entrepreneurship education', *Entrepreneurship Theory and Practice*, 31(3), 387–406.

Wood, R.E. and A. Bandura (1989), 'Impact of conception of ability on self-regulatory mechanisms and complex decision making', *Journal of Personality and Social Psychology*, 56(3), 407–415.

Zellweger, T., P. Sieger and F. Halter (2011), 'Should I stay or should I go? Career choice intentions of students with family business background', *Journal of Business Venturing*, 26(5), 521–536.

Zhao, H., S.E. Seibert and G.E. Hills (2005), 'The mediating role of self-efficacy in the development of entrepreneurial intentions', *Journal of Applied Psychology*, 90(6), 1265–1272.

# 10 Kickstart or jumpstart? Understanding women entrepreneurs' crowdfunding performance

*Smita Srivastava, Pyayt P. Oo, Arvin Sahaym and Thomas H. Allison**

## Introduction

> *We have just about seven years of experience now in crowdfunding [in the United States], including equity and debt, and about four years in the United Kingdom. And we have, by some estimates, $33 billion worth of funding across equity, debt, and rewards crowdfunding.*

(Jason Best, Principal of Crowdfund Capital Advisors, CCA, 2016, quoted in Assenova et al., 2016)

Female-owned businesses and their survival prospects have been a topic of discussion for a considerable number of researchers (Jennings and Brush, 2013; Justo et al., 2015; Klapper and Parker, 2011). Prior research has identified several possibilities for the disproportionate failure of female-founded ventures: lack of access to financial resources (for example, funding) (Fairlie and Robb, 2009), prior managerial and employment experience (Boden and Nucci, 2000; DeTienne and Chandler, 2007), founding strategy (Carter et al., 1997) and entrepreneurial confidence (that is, self-efficacy) (Bandura, 1997; Wilson et al., 2007). While it is possible that lack of prior managerial and employment experience can be compensated by training, confidence and financial resources have fewer obvious solutions (Honig, 1998; Wilson et al., 2007). The recent revolution in funding new ventures embodied by crowdfunding is one potential remedy. In this chapter, we focus on how confidence plays a role in fundraising attempts by women entrepreneurs on a crowdfunding platform.

A broad consensus has emerged among researchers and practitioners that crowdfunding has already established itself as an important method for raising capital (Assenova et al., 2016; Oo and Allison, 2015). Crowdfunding involves nascent entrepreneurs making public calls for funding via the Internet, and potential capital providers evaluating those calls and making decisions for financing their projects (Belleflamme et al., 2014; Bruton et al., 2015). Crowdfunding entrepreneurs typically campaign for their projects and make 'an open call, mostly through the Internet, for providing financial resources either in the form of a donation or

207

in exchange for the future product or some form of reward' (Belleflamme et al., 2014).

Colombo et al. (2015) note that prior research has mostly discussed the nature, characteristics and success factors of crowdfunding. For example, scholars have tried to discern this phenomenon from other lending mechanisms such as online charity donations, peer-to-peer lending and microlending (Afuah and Tucci, 2012; Hildebrand et al., 2016; Zhang and Liu, 2012). As with microlending, a particular appeal of crowdfunding is the access to capital it provides women seeking to start or grow a venture (Bruton et al., 2011; Marom et al., 2014). As such, a growing set of research is examining how women-led crowdfunding projects perform (Greenberg and Mollick, 2017; Marom et al., 2014).

As with crowdfunding research in general, much of this early research on women-led crowdfunding projects has been descriptive. Thus, there is an opportunity to draw from theories previously applied to entrepreneurial resource acquisition research in order to close the gap between what we know about the determinants of women's crowdfunding outcomes, and what we need to know about this phenomenon. To do this, we explore how a project creator's gender, her entrepreneurial self-efficacy and prior experience influence her crowdfunding performance. This question is particularly deserving of a focused inquiry, since about 40 percent of firms in the United States are founded by women but only 6 percent of the women founders get funding from investors (Greenberg and Mollick, 2017). Interestingly, about 44 percent of the crowdfunders are women (Marom et al., 2014).

We address these issues through an examination of a sample of 197 woman-led projects on the Kickstarter platform. Kickstarter, a rewards-based crowdfunding platform, is the world's largest with more than 100,000 ventures successfully funded and more than US$2.2 billion in deal-flow. Our results support our theory (Figure 10.1) that the entrepreneurial self-efficacy, entrepreneurial passion and prior experience of women entrepreneurs are associated with their projects' crowdfunding performance. This chapter makes the following three key contributions to the theory and practice. First, we contribute to theory-building on crowdfunding by highlighting psychosocial factors that could influence women entrepreneurs' crowdfunding success. Second, this is one of the first studies to discuss the role of entrepreneurial self-efficacy in crowdfunding performance. Third, for practitioners, our results suggest that crowdfunding is a promising source of capital for women entrepreneurs as the likelihood of success is relatively higher, compared to seeking funds from traditional sources of funding, such as venture capitalists (VCs).

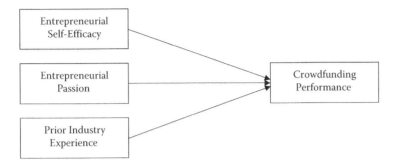

**Figure 10.1**    Theoretical model on performance of women entrepreneurs in crowdfunding platform

## Theoretical background and hypotheses

### Entrepreneurial self-efficacy and crowdfunding performance

McGee et al. (2009: 965) define entrepreneurial self-efficacy (ESE) as a construct 'that measures a person's belief in their ability to successfully launch an entrepreneurial venture'. In our context, entrepreneurial self-efficacy reflects a woman project creator's self-confidence in searching for product ideas, planning for market, motivating stakeholders, and managing human as well as financial resources. Entrepreneurial self-efficacy influences the level of interest in founding a venture which is a challenging goal in itself, persistence toward the achievement of this goal, and recovering quickly from failure over the course of venture (Bandura, 1997; Chen et al., 1998; McGee et al., 2009). Entrepreneurial self-efficacy also determines levels of commitment, in terms of time and resources, needed for the search of novel opportunities (Cassar and Friedman, 2009).

Prior research has shown that traditional financers – that is, angels, VCs and financial institutions – make their funding decisions based on a venture's ideas and opportunities, founder and team characteristics, market conditions, venture resource endowments, and their intuition (Chen et al., 2009; Robinson, 1988). Entrepreneurial self-efficacy not only reflects self-belief and confidence but also helps in the improvisation of ideas and strategies that influence venture performance (Hmieleski and Corbett, 2008). As such, there is ample reason to expect entrepreneurial self-efficacy to influence fundraising outcomes. Some research has reported that women have lower levels of self-efficacy (Gatewood et al., 1995). This makes examining women crowdfunders' entrepreneurial self-efficacy even more important since, though there is a theoretical basis for expecting an effect, it is unknown whether a women-only study context will yield results at variance with established theory.

Displays of higher levels of self-efficacy send positive signals of confidence, self-belief, persistence and potential for future performance (Gatewood et al., 1995; Hmieleski and Baron, 2008). Because the behavioral characteristics of belief, confidence and commitment have a bearing on the effective management of a project and ultimately the project's success (Gatewood et al., 1995; Hmieleski and Baron, 2008; Hmieleski and Corbett, 2008), we argue that higher levels of displayed entrepreneurial self-efficacy will lead potential funders to be more likely to provide capital. Formally:

*Hypothesis 1: Entrepreneurial self-efficacy of women entrepreneurs is positively associated with their crowdfunding performance.*

## Entrepreneurial passion and crowdfunding performance

Entrepreneurial passion reflects 'consciously accessible intense positive feelings experienced by engagement in entrepreneurial activities associated with roles that are meaningful and salient to the self-identity of the entrepreneur' (Cardon et al., 2009: 517). On a platform like Kickstarter, crowdfunding entrepreneurial narratives will be embedded with information about passion (Allison et al., 2013). Passion about the crowdfunding project is reflected through explicit and implicit cues including facial expressions, vocal intonation, gestures and animated body language (Cardon et al., 2009; Chen et al., 2009).

Prior research has shown that lenders such as venture capitalists often base a part of their funding decision on the technical, personal and interpersonal characteristics of the entrepreneur. Passion is one of key attributes they look for (Cardon et al., 2009; Chen et al., 2009). A key reason is that passionate entrepreneurs are more committed, better prepared and more knowledgeable about their projects (Chen et al., 2009). They are strongly inclined toward the activities they like and find important, and will invest their time and energy to make these activities successful (Vallerand et al., 2003). Entrepreneurs who are passionate about their project signal that they are intensely committed to their project; that they are motivated to build the venture (Chen et al., 2009). For these reasons, prior work has associated passion with overall performance (Cardon et al., 2009; Lerner et al., 1997). We extend this logic and propose that the same effects will also impact fundraising performance on crowdfunding platforms:

*Hypothesis 2: Entrepreneurial passion of women entrepreneurs is positively associated with their crowdfunding performance.*

## Prior industry experience and crowdfunding performance

Next, we discuss the role of women entrepreneurs' prior industry experience on crowdfunding performance. Prior industry experience provides entrepreneurs with a better understanding of the key constituents and stakeholders in the product market (for example, competitors, active investors, potential employees, suppliers, and so on) which helps them not only in their pitching for the projects but also in their project's long-term success (Dobrev and Barnett, 2005; Shane and Stuart, 2002). Indeed, prior industry experience is built on hands-on practical training and first-hand learning about the technology, stakeholders and product market (Davidsson and Honig, 2003). Delmar and Shane (2006) note that:

> much of the relevant knowledge about creating a new company is learned by doing . . . experience provides tacit knowledge of organizing routines and skills that have already been learned from their prior activities, and which can be transferred to the new venture . . . it provides tacit knowledge about how to run a new firm that has been learned from prior mistakes [and] previously encountered the problems. (ibid.: 222)

We believe that women entrepreneurs' prior industry experience will help them in identifying both core and peripheral needs of customers. This will lead to discovering associated opportunities (Kotha and George, 2012).

Although findings are robust about entrepreneurs' prior industry experience and investment from formal sources, research has yet to examine the role of prior industry experience in the context of women entrepreneurs' crowdfunding performance. Prior research has demonstrated that traditional investors such as VCs use prior industry experience as a key consideration in their funding decisions (Franke et al., 2008). We build on the findings that ventures founded by entrepreneurs with prior industry experience are more likely to secure VC funding as they show higher growth rate and overall performance (Rauch et al., 2005; Shane and Stuart, 2002). We believe that potential backers' decision-making behavior will parallel that of traditional investors. We expect that crowdfunding backers will also react positively to prior industry experience, as it is associated with knowledge, capabilities, legitimacy, access to social networks and higher venture quality. As such, we hypothesize the following:

*Hypothesis 3: Prior experience of women entrepreneurs in related industry is positively associated with their crowdfunding performance.*

## Method

### Sample and data collection

We drew our sample from Kickstarter, the largest crowdfunding site in the world. We selected a random sample of female-led projects from three categories: gaming, technology and product design. These industry categories were chosen because most projects in these categories are similar to traditional new ventures (Mollick and Kuppuswamy, 2014). There were two additional sampling criteria. First, we only included crowdfunding projects on behalf of individual entrepreneurs, rather than organizations. Second, we only included projects which had videos in which the entrepreneur was clearly shown. These criteria allow us to develop a sample of only woman-led crowdfunding projects, while also providing the data necessary to code entrepreneurial passion. The final sample consisted of 197 women-led crowdfunding projects.

Among the three product categories, 108 projects (54 percent) were from product design, 51 (20 percent) were from gaming, and 38 (26 percent) were from technology. The campaigns occurred during the period 2009–2013. The projects requested a mean funding amount of US$21,576. The overall success rate is 78 percent, which is relatively high compared to the Kickstarter average reported by Mollick (2014): 48 percent. This higher average success rate likely reflects the positive effect on crowdfunding performance of having a video (Mollick, 2014), and the higher chance of succeeding in crowdfunding that women have compared to men (Marom et al., 2015).

## Measures

Following prior studies (Colombo et al., 2015; Mollick, 2014), we measured crowdfunding performance dichotomously. If a campaign meets or exceeds its goal, it is coded 1, and 0 otherwise. Our study includes three independent variables: entrepreneurial self-efficacy, entrepreneurial passion and prior industry experience. We adapted McGee et al.'s (2009) established entrepreneurial self-efficacy scale. Each item was coded on a five-point Likert scale (ranging from 1 = 'low confidence' to 5 = 'high confidence'). Where necessary, scales were modified to fit the crowdfunding context (Chen et al., 1998; McGee et al., 2009). The last two items of the existing ten-item scale for entrepreneurial self-efficacy were not applicable in our crowdfunding context; as a result, we dropped these items. Given this change, we then checked construct validity. First, we conducted an exploratory factor analysis with 50 projects. The results supported a one-factor solution: all eight items (items are shown in Table 10A.1) had loadings greater than 0.60 on the factor. Internal consistency was also achieved with $\alpha = 0.85$. Second, once all data were collected, we performed confirmatory factor analysis. The analysis indicated that we have a sufficient overall fit for the one-factor model ($\chi^2 = 24.46$, $df = 14$, p = 0.04, CFI = 0.97, TLI = 0.95, RMSEA = 0.09, SRMR = 0.04).

For entrepreneurial passion, we adopted the established measure developed by Chen et al. (2009). Items are shown in Table 10A.2. High internal consistency was achieved ($\alpha = 0.88$). Consistent with Chen et al., we used a five-point Likert scale (ranging from 1 = 'never' to 5 = 'very frequently'). Prior industry experience was dummy coded as 1 if an entrepreneur mentioned that she had prior related industry experience, and 0 otherwise. Coding was performed by two independent coders for the first 50 projects. After 50 projects were coded, interrater agreement was evaluated. Reliabilities were high (that is, r > 0.8). Due to the high interrater reliability, the remaining 147 projects were rated by a single coder (Cuddy et al., 2015).

To minimize alternative explanations, we included a broad set of controls. First, prior crowdfunding experience on Kickstarter was controlled for (dummy coded), under the assumption that experience may lead to a better campaign. Second, because a team of entrepreneurs may have more resources than a sole entrepreneur (Mosakowski, 1998), we controlled for whether the venture was launched by an individual or a team (dummy coded, team = 1, 0 otherwise). Third, consistent with prior findings showing that internal social capital has an effect on the outcome of the campaign (Colombo et al., 2015), we controlled for internal social capital. Fourth, because some projects were featured as 'staff picks', which might give such projects greater exposure, we controlled for whether a given project had this designation (dummy coded, featured on Kickstarter = 1, 0 otherwise). Fifth, since media coverage can be a signal of quality, can bring more attention and can provide legitimacy (Deephouse, 2000), we controlled for this by examining whether a campaign had such coverage, as reflected on their crowdfunding page (dummy coded, media coverage = 1, 0 otherwise). Sixth and finally, consistent with prior studies (Mollick, 2014), we controlled for the duration and funding goal (log transformation) of each campaign.

## Results

Table 10.1 shows means, standard deviations and a correlation matrix for the variables included in the statistical models. We checked for multicollinearity with variance inflation factors (VIFs). The results indicated that the maximum value is 1.46 and the mean value is 1.18. Both are within accepted limits. Table 10.2 presents our logistic regression models. Model 1 is limited to controls, Model 2 adds all predictors. In Hypothesis 1, we predicted that entrepreneurial self-efficacy is positively related to crowdfunding performance. Consistent with our theory, we found that the coefficient estimate is positive and statistically significant ($\beta = 1.029$; $p = 0.004$). Thus, Hypothesis 1 is supported. Hypothesis 2 predicted that high entrepreneurial passion is positively related to crowdfunding performance. We also find support for this hypothesis ($\beta = 0.853$; $p = 0.027$). Finally, Hypothesis 3 predicted that prior industry experience helps women entrepreneurs in succeeding with their campaigns. This, too, was supported ($\beta = 1.123$; $p = 0.046$).

## Discussion

This chapter builds a theoretical framework for predicting women entrepreneurs' crowdfunding performance. Given that women entrepreneurs are playing an important role in the economy, and 40 percent of entrepreneurial firms are founded by women, this issue also has immense practical implications. Our analysis with 197 female-led projects on Kickstarter from three industry categories (product design, gaming and technology) reveal that entrepreneurial self-efficacy, entrepreneurial passion and prior industry experience of women entrepreneurs are positively related to crowdfunding performance. Our results are consistent with our developed hypotheses. Our study provides support for the idea that women entrepreneurs with high entrepreneurial self-efficacy engender more support from potential backers through their strong self-belief and ability to tackle difficult tasks, resulting in a successful crowdfunding performance. Their entrepreneurial passion appears to serve as an indicator of greater preparedness and commitment, which in turn will lead the backers to believe in their venture ideas.

**Table 10.1** Descriptive statistics and correlations[a]

| Variables | Mean | s.d. | 1 | 2 | 3 | 4 | 5 | 6 | 7 | 8 | 9 | 10 |
|---|---|---|---|---|---|---|---|---|---|---|---|---|
| Dependent variable | | | | | | | | | | | | |
| 1. Crowdfunding Performance | 0.78 | 0.41 | | | | | | | | | | |
| Control variables | | | | | | | | | | | | |
| 2. Prior Crowdfunding Experience | 0.12 | 0.43 | 0.12 | | | | | | | | | |
| 3. Individual/Team | 0.36 | 0.49 | 0.13 | -0.05 | | | | | | | | |
| 4. Internal Social Capital | 2.93 | 4.54 | 0.21 | 0.12 | -0.08 | | | | | | | |
| 5. Featured on Kickstarter | 0.23 | 0.42 | 0.26 | 0.02 | 0.02 | 0.18 | | | | | | |
| 6. Media Coverage | 0.07 | 0.26 | 0.10 | -0.03 | 0.08 | 0.15 | 0.08 | | | | | |
| 7. Duration of Campaign | 36.40 | 13.84 | -0.19 | -0.09 | -0.05 | -0.08 | -0.04 | -0.01 | | | | |
| 8. Goal of Campaign (Logged) | 8.90 | 1.38 | -0.35 | -0.09 | 0.09 | -0.02 | -0.05 | 0.24 | 0.17 | | | |
| Independent variables | | | | | | | | | | | | |
| 9. Entrepreneurial Self-Efficacy | 3.38 | 0.88 | 0.23 | 0.02 | 0.24 | 0.05 | 0.18 | 0.19 | -0.08 | 0.31 | | |
| 10. Entrepreneurial Passion | 3.34 | 0.74 | 0.28 | 0.11 | 0.15 | 0.16 | 0.13 | 0.08 | -0.05 | 0.08 | 0.42 | |
| 11. Prior Industry Experience | 2.67 | 30.96 | 0.04 | -0.02 | 0.10 | -0.01 | 0.13 | -0.02 | -0.03 | 0.04 | 0.07 | -0.02 |

**Note:** [a] $N = 197$. Correlations with absolute greater than 0.16 are significant at $p < 0.05$.

**Table 10.2**   Regression analysis for campaign result

| Variables | Model 1 | Model 2 |
|---|---|---|
| Control Variables | | |
| *Prior Crowdfunding Experience* | 1.334 | 0.640 |
| *Individual/Team* | 1.452*** | 1.012* |
| *Internal Social Capital* | 0.307*** | 0.332*** |
| *Featured on Kickstarter* | 3.875*** | 3.350** |
| *Media Coverage* | 2.523** | 2.488* |
| *Duration of Campaign* | −0.025 | −0.024 |
| *Goal of Campaign (Logged)* | −1.005*** | −1.453*** |
| *Industry Dummies* | | |
| Independent Variables | | |
| *Entrepreneurial Self-Efficacy* | | 1.029*** |
| *Entrepreneurial Passion* | | 0.853** |
| *Prior Industry Experience* | | 1.123** |
| N | 197 | 197 |
| Chi-square | 82.909 | 105.688 |

**Notes:**
*** $p < 0.01$, ** $p < 0.05$, * $p < 0.1$
Industry controls (dummy variables) included in analysis but not reported.

While our study makes some important contributions, it is also important to be mindful of the trade-offs we made in order to achieve these findings. In order to maximize the similarity of crowdfunding projects to traditional ventures, we limited our sampling frame to those categories previously established to be most reflective of such ventures. However, future research might take a broader view of crowdfunding projects in order to better understand the crowdfunding phenomenon overall. Further, we measured entrepreneurial passion manifested through facial expressions, body movement, tone of voice and other non-verbal cues which may overlap with impression management cues (Baron, 1989). While there is good evidence for this type of espoused passion measure, psychometric measures of passion might provide further confidence in our findings.

Given the nearly equal representation of women entrepreneurs on crowdfunding platforms, this study suggests some directions for future research. For example, future studies can develop a deeper understanding of factors that may moderate the relationship between entrepreneurial self-efficacy, passion and crowdfunding performance of women entrepreneurs. On the other hand, it would be interesting to explore whether female backers are more prone to fund women entrepreneurs due to their social identification with 'women' (Brown, 2000), or whether male backers are coming forward to back women entrepreneurs. Since crowdfunding could be women entrepreneurs' most promising source of early-stage funding, it is important to better understand the overall role of narratives in helping entrepreneurs to establish a relationship with backers. Future research could do this by conducting a content analysis of the narratives used on crowdfunding platforms. For example, it would be interesting to examine the extent to which social identity espoused by crowdfunders impacts crowdfunding performance.

## Conclusion

We began this study motivated by a belief in the importance of women entrepreneurs, and with the desire to better understand the interaction between confidence and passion in influencing fundraising performance. Given that crowdfunding is a promising avenue for many women entrepreneurs to access needed financial resources, our results contribute to both the theory and practice by showing that high levels of self-efficacy (confidence) and passion among women entrepreneurs result in better fundraising outcomes through crowdfunding. In this chapter, we begin to connect the dots between women entrepreneurs and access to resources via crowdfunding. We provide an initial look at factors influencing the crowdfunding performance of women entrepreneurs. We provide a broader understanding of entrepreneurial passion and entrepreneurial self-efficacy by examining their effect in the novel resource acquisition context of crowdfunding. Overall, this work is another step towards understanding how to increase the survival rate of the women-led ventures through innovative venture funding.

Note
* All authors contributed equally.

## References

Afuah, A. and C.L. Tucci (2012), 'Crowdsourcing as a solution to distant search', *Academy of Management Review*, 37(3), 355–375.

Allison, T.H., A.F. McKenny and J.C. Short (2013), 'The effect of entrepreneurial rhetoric on microlending investment: an examination of the warm-glow effect', *Journal of Business Venturing*, 28(6), 690–707.

Assenova, V., J. Best, M. Cagney, et al. (2016), 'The present and future of crowdfunding', *California Management Review*, 58(2), 125–135.

Bandura, A. (1997), *Self-Efficacy: The Exercise of Control*, New York: Freeman.

Baron, R.A. (1989), 'Impression management by applicants during employment interviews: the "too much of a good thing" effect' in R.W. Eder and G.R. Ferris (eds), *The Employment Interview: Theory, research, and practice*, Newbury Park, CA: SAGE Publications: pp. 204–215.

Belleflamme, P., T. Lambert and A. Schwienbacher (2014), 'Crowdfunding: tapping the right crowd', *Journal of Business Venturing*, 29(5), 585–609.

Boden, R.J. and A.R. Nucci (2000), 'On the survival prospects of men's and women's new business ventures', *Journal of Business Venturing*, 15(4), 347–362.

Brown, R. (2000), 'Social identity theory: past achievements, current problems and future challenges', *European Journal of Social Psychology*, 30(6), 745–778.

Bruton, G., S. Khavul, D. Siegel and M.Wright (2015), 'New financial alternatives in seeding entrepreneurship: microfinance, crowdfunding, and peer-to-peer innovations', *Entrepreneurship Theory and Practice*, 39(1), 9–26.

Bruton, G.D., S. Khavul and H. Chavez (2011), 'Microlending in emerging economies: building a new line of inquiry from the ground up', *Journal of International Business Studies*, 42(5), 718–739.

Cardon, M.S., J. Wincent, J. Singh and M. Drnovsek (2009), 'The nature and experience of entrepreneurial passion', *Academy of Management Review*, 34(3), 511–532.

Carter, N.M., M. Williams and P.D. Reynolds (1997), 'Discontinuance among new firms in retail: the influence of initial resources, strategy, and gender', *Journal of Business Venturing*, 12(2), 125–145.

Cassar, G. and H. Friedman (2009), 'Does self-efficacy affect entrepreneurial investment?', *Strategic Entrepreneurship Journal*, 3(3), 241–260.

Chen, C.C., P.G. Greene and A. Crick (1998), 'Does entrepreneurial self-efficacy distinguish entrepreneurs from managers?', *Journal of Business Venturing*, 13(4), 295–316.

Chen, X.-P., X. Yao and S. Kotha (2009), 'Entrepreneur passion and preparedness in business plan presentations: a persuasion analysis of venture capitalists' funding decisions', *Academy of Management Journal*, 52(1), 199–214.

Colombo, M.G., C. Franzoni and C. Rossi-Lamastra (2015), 'Internal social capital and the attraction of early contributions in crowdfunding', *Entrepreneurship Theory and Practice*, 39(1), 75–100.

Cuddy, A.J., C.A. Wilmuth, A.J. Yap and D.R. Carney (2015), 'Preparatory power posing affects nonverbal presence and job interview performance', *Journal of Applied Psychology*, 100(4), 1286.

Davidsson, P. and B. Honig (2003), 'The role of social and human capital among nascent entrepreneurs', *Journal of Business Venturing*, 18(3), 301–331.

Deephouse, D.L. (2000), 'Media reputation as a strategic resource: an integration of mass communication and resource-based theories', *Journal of Management*, 26(6), 1091–1112.

Delmar, F. and S. Shane (2006), 'Does experience matter? The effect of founding team experience on the survival and sales of newly founded ventures', *Strategic Organization*, 4(3), 215–247.

DeTienne, D.R. and G.N. Chandler (2007), 'The role of gender in opportunity identification', *Entrepreneurship Theory and Practice*, 31(3), 365–386.

Dobrev, S.D. and W.P. Barnett (2005), 'Organizational roles and transition to entrepreneurship', *Academy of Management Journal*, 48(3), 433–449.

Fairlie, R.W. and A.M. Robb (2009), 'Gender differences in business performance: evidence from the Characteristics of Business Owners survey', *Small Business Economics*, 33(4), 375–395.

Franke, N., M. Gruber, D. Harhoff and J. Henkel (2008), 'Venture capitalists' evaluations of start-up teams: trade-offs, knock-out criteria, and the impact of VC experience', *Entrepreneurship Theory and Practice*, 32(3), 459–483.

Gatewood, E.J., K.G. Shaver and W.B. Gartner (1995), 'A longitudinal study of cognitive factors influencing start-up behaviors and success at venture creation', *Journal of Business Venturing*, 10(5), 371–391.

Greenberg, J. and E.R. Mollick (2017), 'Activist choice homophily and the crowdfunding of female founders', *Administrative Science Quarterly*, 62(2), 341–374.

Hildebrand, T., M. Puri and J. Rocholl (2016), 'Adverse incentives in crowdfunding', *Management Science*, 63(3), 587–608.

Hmieleski, K.M. and R.A. Baron (2008), 'When does entrepreneurial self-efficacy enhance versus reduce firm performance?', *Strategic Entrepreneurship Journal*, 2(1), 57–72.

Hmieleski, K.M. and A.C. Corbett (2008), 'The contrasting interaction effects of improvisational behavior with entrepreneurial self-efficacy on new venture performance and entrepreneur work satisfaction', *Journal of Business Venturing*, 23(4), 482–496.

Honig, B. (1998), 'What determines success? Examining the human, financial, and social capital of Jamaican microentrepreneurs', *Journal of Business Venturing*, 13(5), 371–394.

Jennings, J.E. and C.G. Brush (2013), 'Research on women entrepreneurs: challenges to (and from) the broader entrepreneurship literature?', *Academy of Management Annals*, 7(1), 663–715.

Justo, R., D.R. DeTienne and P. Sieger (2015), 'Failure or voluntary exit? Reassessing the female under-performance hypothesis', *Journal of Business Venturing*, 30(6), 775–792.

Klapper, L.F. and S.C. Parker (2011), 'Gender and the business environment for new firm creation', *World Bank Research Observer*, 26(2), 237–257.

Kotha, R. and G. George (2012), 'Friends, family, or fools: entrepreneur experience and its implications for equity distribution and resource mobilization', *Journal of Business Venturing*, 27(5), 525–543.

Lerner, M., C. Brush and R. Hisrich (1997), 'Israeli women entrepreneurs: an examination of factors affecting performance', *Journal of Business Venturing*, 12(4), 315–339.

Marom, D., A. Robb and O. Sade (2014), 'Gender dynamics in crowdfunding (Kickstarter): evidence on entrepreneurs, investors, deals and taste based discrimination', *Investors, Deals and Taste Based Discrimination* (October 10).

Marom, D., A. Robb, and O. Sade (2015), 'Gender dynamics in crowdfunding (Kickstarter): evidence on entrepreneurs, investors, deals and taste-based discrimination', *Investors, Deals and Taste-Based Discrimination* (December 6).

McGee, J.E., M. Peterson, S.L. Mueller and J.M. Sequeira (2009), 'Entrepreneurial self-efficacy: refining the measure', *Entrepreneurship Theory and Practice*, 33(4), 965–988.

Mollick, E. (2014), 'The dynamics of crowdfunding: an exploratory study', *Journal of Business Venturing*, 29(1), 1–16.

Mollick, E. and V. Kuppuswamy (2014), 'After the campaign: outcomes of crowdfunding', UNC Kenan-Flagler Research Paper No. 2376997, accessed January 9, 2014 at https://ssrn.com/abstract=2376997.

Mosakowski, E. (1998), 'Entrepreneurial resources, organizational choices, and competitive outcomes', *Organization Science*, 9(6), 625–643.

Oo, P.P. and T.H. Allison (2015), 'Crowdfunding an entrepreneurial career: the role of prior paid employment in crowdfunding', paper presented at the Academy of Management Proceedings, August 7–11, Vancouver.

Rauch, A., M. Frese and A. Utsch (2005), 'Effects of human capital and long-term human resources development and utilization on employment growth of small-scale businesses: a causal analysis', *Entrepreneurship Theory and Practice*, 29(6), 681–698.

Robinson, R.B. (1988). 'Emerging strategies in the venture capital industry', *Journal of Business Venturing*, 2(1), 53–77.

Shane, S. and T. Stuart (2002), 'Organizational endowments and the performance of university start-ups', *Management Science*, 48(1), 154–170.

Vallerand, R.J., C. Blanchard, G.A. Mageau, et al. (2003), 'Les passions de l'âme: on obsessive and harmonious passion', *Journal of Personality and Social Psychology*, 85(4), 756–767.

Wilson, F., J. Kickul and D. Marlino (2007), 'Gender, entrepreneurial self-efficacy, and entrepreneurial career intentions: implications for entrepreneurship education1', *Entrepreneurship Theory and Practice*, 31(3), 387–406.

Zhang, J. and P. Liu (2012), 'Rational herding in microloan markets', *Management Science*, 58(5), 892–912.

# Appendix

**Table 10A.1**   Entrepreneurial self-efficacy rating scale

| Items | Scale* |
|---|---|
| *Searching* | |
| How much confidence does the speaker have in her ability to come up with a new idea for a product or service? | 1 2 3 4 5 |
| How much confidence does the speaker have in her ability to design a product or service that will satisfy customer needs and wants? | 1 2 3 4 5 |
| *Planning* | |
| How much confidence does the speaker have in her ability to estimate customer demand for a new product or service? | 1 2 3 4 5 |
| How much confidence does the speaker have in her ability to determine a competitive price for a new product or service? | 1 2 3 4 5 |
| How much confidence does the speaker have in her ability to estimate the amount of start-up funds and working capital necessary to start the business? | 1 2 3 4 5 |
| How much confidence does the speaker have in her ability to design an effective marketing/advertising campaign for a new product or service | 1 2 3 4 5 |
| *Marshaling* | |
| How much confidence does the speaker have in her ability to get others to identify with and believe in the vision and plans for a new business? | 1 2 3 4 5 |
| How much confidence does the speaker have in her ability to clearly and concisely explain verbally/in writing the business idea in everyday terms? | 1 2 3 4 5 |

**Note:**   * 1 = low confidence, 2 = moderate confidence, 3 = uncertain, 4 = much confidence, 5 = high confidence.

**Table 10A.2**   Entrepreneurial passion rating scale

| Items | Scale* |
|---|---|
| The presenter(s) had energetic body movements. | 1 2 3 4 5 |
| The presenter(s) had rich body language | 1 2 3 4 5 |
| The presenter(s) showed animated facial expression | 1 2 3 4 5 |
| The presenter(s) used a lot of gestures | 1 2 3 4 5 |
| The presenter's face lit up when he/she talked | 1 2 3 4 5 |
| The presenter(s) talked with varied tone and pitch | 1 2 3 4 5 |

**Note:**    * 1 = never, 2 = rarely, 3 = occasionally, 4 = frequently, 5 = very frequently.

# Index

Printed and bound by CPI Group (UK) Ltd, Croydon, CR0 4YY

23/04/2025

14660962-0004